Candlestick Charting

FOR

DUMMIES®

by Russell Rhoads

WILEY

Wiley Publishing, Inc.

Candlestick Charting For Dummies®

Published by
Wiley Publishing, Inc.
111 River St.
Hoboken, NJ 07030-5774
www.wiley.com

Copyright © 2008 by Wiley Publishing, Inc., Indianapolis, Indiana

Published simultaneously in Canada

For general information on our other products and services, please contact our Customer Care Department within the U.S. at 877-762-2974, outside the U.S. at 317-572-3993, or fax 317-572-4002.

For technical support, please visit www.wiley.com/techsupport.

Wiley also publishes its books in a variety of electronic formats. Some content that appears in print may not be available in electronic books.

Library of Congress Control Number: 2008923126

ISBN: 978-0-470-17808-9

Manufactured in the United States of America

10 9 8 7 6 5 4 3

About the Author

Russell Rhoads is a trader and analyst for Peak Trading Group in Chicago. His career in trading and market analysis covers over 17 years. He has a BBA and MS in Finance from the University of Memphis and has done graduate level work in Financial Engineering at the Illinois Institute of Technology. Russell also holds the Chartered Financial Analyst designation.

Dedication

To Bobbie, Dusty, Maggie, Emmy, and especially Merribeth.

Author's Acknowledgments

The most thanks must go to my wife Merribeth who through a very difficult year, that included producing this book, always was willing to yield to the time I needed to complete this project. Maggie, my daughter, was also always a helpful participant by working quietly alongside of Daddy when he needed to work. To Emmy, who discovered how to push buttons while this book was being written, thanks for not turning the computer off when Daddy hasn't saved his work.

Thank you to a few current professional associates who've been very helpful recently: Mike Wilkins, Bill Annis, and Patrick Guinee. Also, there are some people that I professionally lost touch with that helped guide my career, and I feel I've never properly thanked them: R. Patrick Jones, Mickey Hoffman, and Michael Orkin. These people stand out the most in my mind, so I'm taking this opportunity.

As far as the mechanics of putting the book together, Stacy Kennedy, Acquisitions Editor, Chrissy Guthrie, Senior Project Editor, and Carrie Burchfield, Copy Editor, were extremely helpful for this non-writer. Tim Brennan, the technical editor, did an excellent job pointing out areas that needed some improvement. Brittain Phillips gets a special thank you for taking what I'm trying to say and making it readable. Also, I can't go without acknowledging Michelle Hacker, Editorial Manager, who introduced me to the people at Wiley Publishing, Inc. Without her I never would've had the chance to produce a book.

Publisher's Acknowledgments

We're proud of this book; please send us your comments through our Dummies online registration form located at www.dummies.com/register/.

Some of the people who helped bring this book to market include the following:

Acquisitions, Editorial, and Media Development

Senior Project Editor: Christina Guthrie

Acquisitions Editor: Stacy Kennedy

Copy Editor: Carrie A. Burchfield

Editorial Program Coordinator: Erin Calligan Mooney

Technical Editor: Tim Brennan

Editorial Manager: Christine Meloy Beck

Editorial Assistants: Joe Niesen, David Lutton, Leeann Harney

Cartoons: Rich Tennant (www.the5thwave.com)

Composition Services

Project Coordinator: Katie Key

Layout and Graphics: Carl Byers, Reuben W. Davis, Alissa D. Ellet, Stephanie D. Jumper

Proofreaders: John Greenough, Penny Stuart

Indexer: Potomac Indexing, LLC.

Special Help: Tim Gallan, Natalie Faye Harris, Megan Knoll

Publishing and Editorial for Consumer Dummies

Diane Graves Steele, Vice President and Publisher, Consumer Dummies

Joyce Pepple, Acquisitions Director, Consumer Dummies

Kristin A. Cocks, Product Development Director, Consumer Dummies

Michael Spring, Vice President and Publisher, Travel

Kelly Regan, Editorial Director, Travel

Publishing for Technology Dummies

Andy Cummings, Vice President and Publisher, Dummies Technology/General User

Composition Services

Gerry Fahey, Vice President of Production Services

Debbie Stailey, Director of Composition Services

Contents at a Glance

Table of Contents

Introduction

*Y*ears ago, when I was playing around with my first quote machine on the floor of one of the Chicago exchanges, I came across the candlestick charting function. My personal charting software, which I ran on a DOS-based PC with no hard drive (yikes!), had no such function. When the candlestick chart popped up on the screen, I was fascinated by what came up, and my curiosity was piqued. The charting system looked useful and promising, but I didn't know much about it. It wasn't like I could just run an Internet search on candlestick charts to find out more, so I proceeded to the exchange library to find out about candlesticks.

The exchange library was stocked with just about every investment and trading related book in and out of print, but I was surprised to find very little information on my newly discovered method of charting prices. I could find only one book about candlestick charting, along with a couple of articles. And the articles were about the book! Not exactly what I'd call a wealth of information.

Fast forward to today. Candlestick charting is now far more of a mainstream trading tool than it was when I first saw it flash up on the screen of that primitive exchange floor computer. In fact, I recently noticed that the charts used in the *Wall Street Journal* are now candlestick charts. But although candlestick charts are more common in the financial world, not very many traders take full advantage of the vast potential of candlesticks.

I'm hoping to do my part to change that with this book. Candlestick charts can be hugely helpful in nearly every aspect of trading, and savvy traders should take the time to understand candlesticks and how they can enhance and enrich any trading strategy.

About This Book

This book isn't intended to be an end-all-be-all guide to profitable trading. It's meant to provide readers with some insight into how candlesticks are created and how they can be used to analyze the psychology behind what happens over the course of trading days. (When I say "psychology," I'm not trying to conjure up images of Freud and Rorschach tests; I'm talking about the motivating factors that help to determine how the market behaves.)

I hope that the candlestick methods described in this book help readers to make trading and investment decisions that lead to solid profits, but unfortunately, there's no guaranteeing that. What I can guarantee is that after reading this book (or even parts of this book), you can gain a useful understanding of what candlesticks are, what they represent, and how they can be used in trading.

Conventions Used in This Book

To help you navigate this book, I use the following conventions throughout:

- ✔ *Italics* are used for emphasis and to highlight new words that are presented with easy-to-understand definitions.
- ✔ **Boldfaced** text is used to indicate key words in lists.
- ✔ `Monofont` is used for Web addresses.

I make an effort to use as many examples as possible in the text, and each and every example I present is one that I found while searching through actual charts. I did that to show you not only how common it is to come across these candlestick patterns in everyday trading, but also how eminently possible it is to use them in live trades. They're out there, and they're waiting for you to harness their power!

Also, with each new candlestick pattern that I introduce, I present at least one case where it succeeds in producing a useful signal and one where it produces a dud. Candlesticks are terrific, but they're not perfect, and recognizing the failure of a signal is just as important as picking up on a valid signal.

What You're Not to Read

When you come across the Technical Stuff icon, you may skip ahead because this icon indicates information that's additive to trading knowledge, but not essential to gaining knowledge about candlestick charting.

You can also skip the sidebars that are placed throughout the text if you're pressed for time or you want only the essential information. Sidebars contain nonessential material, and you can tell them apart from the rest of the text because they're placed in gray shaded boxes.

Foolish Assumptions

Because knowledge of candlesticks varies widely from trader to trader — even traders with the same amount of trading experience can differ quite a bit in their candlestick know-how — I've made the assumption that you have at best a very basic understanding of what comprises a candlestick chart. My apologies if you already know a little about candlesticks, but hey, it never hurts to review and hone those essential candlestick skills. I build understanding from the ground up, beginning with how to create individual candlesticks and finishing with how complex candlestick patterns can be combined with other forms of technical analysis. Also, I'm operating under the assumption that you've had some sort of experience trading a stock or at least a mutual fund. I assume that you've spent some time looking over stock charts in the past too.

How This Book Is Organized

I've organized *Candlestick Charting For Dummies* into five parts. Each part offers a different set of information and skills that you can take away to incorporate in your personal trading strategy. You get a feel for candlestick basics or understand some simple candlestick patterns and how to trade based on them. You tackle some more complicated patterns and figure out how it's possible to use candlesticks in tandem with other popular technical indicators. The possibilities for candlestick charts are many and varied, and I do my best to touch on a wide range of their uses and benefits.

Part 1: Getting Familiar with Candlestick Charting and Technical Analysis

In the first part of this book, I introduce candlestick charting and some other basic charting concepts. You may be wondering what advantages candlesticks have over other types of charts. Believe me, the rewards are plenty, and you can read all about them in Chapter 2. Want to know what price data elements are combined to generate a candlestick? That's all contained in Chapter 3, along with some information on how to embrace the other types of data that you may run into when reviewing candlestick charts. And in the last chapter of Part I, I also let you know how to tap into a variety of free and for-purchase electronic resources for charting, which are critical in today's high-tech trading environment. I even include a low-tech alternative: how to draw charts yourself.

Part II: Working with Simple Candlestick Patterns

Part II features descriptions and explanations of some of the most basic and common candlestick patterns. The simplest candlestick patterns involve just one day or one period of price data, and you can find information on those patterns in Chapters 5 and 6.

Two-stick candlestick patterns are one step up from those basic patterns, but just a single step up in complexity can provide quite a bit of additional information and versatility. Some extremely helpful two-stick candlestick patterns pop up frequently on candlestick charts, and if you want to really capitalize on candlesticks in your trading strategy, you need to know how to identify and trade them. Don't worry; I've got you covered in Chapters 7 and 8, which wrap up Part II.

Part III: Making the Most of Complex Patterns

Three-stick patterns are the most complex patterns that I deal with in this book, and their nuts and bolts are explained in this part. (Three-stick patterns in Part III — convenient, right?) Like their one- and two-stick counterparts, three-stick patterns tell you what a market or security is about to do next, and the added stick means that these patterns are a bit more rare but that much more exciting. You can get your three-stick candlestick pattern bearings in Chapters 9 and 10.

Part IV: Combining Patterns and Indicators

I begin Part IV with Chapter 11, which offers a more in-depth discussion of several other technical indicators. It's useful for any trader to understand a variety of indicators because you can use them alone, to confirm your candlestick signals, and in combination with candlestick patterns.

Although candlestick patterns alone have proven to be reliable trading tools, using them in combination with other indicators can greatly enhance their ability to predict the future direction of a market or a stock. In the rest of Part IV, I take some simple and complex patterns and combine them with pure technical indicators to show you how coupling the two techniques can lead to profitable trading. The chapters in this part are chock-full of fascinating real-world examples from a variety of markets and industries.

Part V: The Part of Tens

You can't have a *For Dummies* book without a Part of Tens, and this book is certainly no exception. The final part includes a few helpful lists, including myths about trading, a few things to keep in the back of your mind about charting, and some resources that you can consult to further your candlestick understanding.

Icons Used in This Book

I used the following icons throughout the book to point out various types of information:

When you see this icon, you know you want to store the accompanying nugget of candlestick or trading wisdom somewhere safe in your brain.

This icon offers hands-on advice that you can put into practice as you trade. In many cases, the information found next to this icon tells you directly how to conduct a trade on a pattern or technical analysis method.

If you ignore this information, you can wake up one day in a den full of writhing, angry pit vipers. Okay, so it's not *that* bad, but this icon really helps you avoid making costly trading mistakes.

This icon flags places where I get really technical about charting. Although it's great information, you can safely skip it and not miss out on the discussion at hand.

Where to Go from Here

To figure out which area of this book to dive into first, think hard about what facet of candlestick charting you want to understand. Want to get grounded in the basics, or polish up on a few candlestick fundamentals that you may have forgotten since you read that online article about candlestick charting months ago? Check out the next page, on which Part I begins.

If you want to get cracking and find out about a few real candlestick patterns and how they can tell you what a market or security is going to do next, I suggest that you flip to one of the chapters in Parts II or III. I cover many candlestick pattern examples in those chapters — more than enough to give you plenty to look for as you pore over charts on the Web or on a charting software package.

You may have been recently exposed to some other technical indicators and it's possible that reading about candlesticks alongside some of that familiar material may help you get your feet wet. If so, make a beeline for Part IV, and enjoy!

The water's fine no matter where you choose to dive in, and you're just a few page-turns away from adding a powerful weapon to your trading arsenal.

Part I
Getting Familiar with Candlestick Charting and Technical Analysis

The 5th Wave — By Rich Tennant

"Trendlines? Channels? Breakouts? I say we stick the money in the ground like always, and then feed this guy to the sharks."

In this part . . .

I don't know of any traders or investors who've taken the time to fully understand candlestick charting and then not used the techniques in their trades. After you've taken the time to grasp candlestick basics, it's tough to deny their advantages over other types of charts, and the profits can certainly speak for themselves. But the basics must come first, and that's what Part I is all about.

I begin this part by setting candlesticks in context with several other types of charts, so you can get a feel for candlestick benefits. After that, I explain the price action and signals that candlestick charts generate, and I show you how a candlestick is constructed and what its variations can mean. To close Part I, you look at the range of electronic resources available for candlestick charting, which you can exploit with just a few clicks of your mouse.

Chapter 1

Understanding Charting and Where Candlesticks Fit In

. . . .

In This Chapter

▶ Taking a look at options for charting and why candlesticks are superior

▶ Making sense of candlestick construction

▶ Exploring the wide variety of candlestick patterns

▶ Using technical analysis alongside your candlestick charts

▶ Understanding a few trading and investing basics

. . . .

*T*he advent of the Internet has leveled the playing field for securities traders. Access to markets once meant placing orders through a broker, and now it's little more than a couple of mouse clicks away. Commission rates are dramatically lower, and access to market information is now in many cases free. Getting into securities trading is now easier than it ever has been, and the result is a whole generation of investors and traders that handle their finances without professional help. Technology allows these people to enjoy many new types of market information, and one of the best tools available is candlestick charting.

Candlestick charting methods have been around for hundreds of years, but candlesticks have caught on over the past decade or so as a charting standard in the United States. I've been working with candlestick charts for quite a few years, and I've seen many traders — novice to professional — develop a fierce loyalty to candlesticks after taking the time to understand their uses and potential. I think you'll feel the same way, and this book is the first step on the path to conquering candlesticks.

The material contained in this chapter exposes you to many of the facets of candlestick charting that continue to fuel its rise as one of the most popular charting techniques. I begin with the overall role of candlesticks within the context of charting. I cover the advantages of candlestick charting, and the basics of candlestick construction. I also take the opportunity at the end of this chapter to discuss how to get started as well as give some insight into the characteristics and habits that successful traders employ in their pursuit of profits. Enjoy, and happy charting!

Considering Charting Methods and the Role of Candlesticks

With advancements in technology and the growing availability of trading and investing resources available to traders, many options exist for the charting of securities. There are several different types of charts and dozens of variations and features to be configured on each type. It's important that you're clear on the options and, perhaps more importantly, why candlestick charting is at the top of the heap. This section explains.

Getting a feel for your options for charting

When it comes to alternatives to candlestick charting, the three main charting contenders are as follows:

- **Line charts:** These charts are simple and helpful for short-term decisions, but they're quite limited in the amount of data presented.

- **Bar charts:** These are much more useful than line charts and are the most common, but they're not as versatile as candlestick charts.

- **Point and figure charts:** These are tried-and-true charting methods, and they're great for recognizing support and resistance levels, but they're far less dynamic than candlestick charts.

Each one of these charting methods can be used effectively to ratchet up the effectiveness of your trading strategy, but they pale in comparison to candlestick charts for a number of reasons, a few of which I describe in the next section.

Realizing the advantages of candlestick charting

You'd be hard pressed to find someone who's more enthusiastic about candlestick charting than yours truly. I can go on and on about the advantages that candlesticks afford. If you want to read more of my gushing about the many great advantages of candlestick charting, turn to Chapter 2, but here are my top reasons:

✔ One of the best features of candlestick charting in general is the visual appeal and readability. You can glance at a candlestick chart and quickly gain an understanding of what's going on with the price of a security. You can also tell whether sellers or buyers have dominated a given day, and get a sense of how the price is trending.

✔ Also, even after reading up on the most rudimentary of candlestick basics, you can easily spot the opening and closing price for a security on a candlestick chart. These price levels can be very important areas of support and resistance from day to day, and knowing where they are can be extremely helpful, especially for short-term traders.

✔ Candlesticks aren't just a pretty face. Candlestick charts also feature specific patterns that you can identify and use to decide when it's time to buy, sell, or wait on a trade or investment. These patterns can be a real boon to your work with securities, and you can combine them with other technical indicators for even more reliable results.

Understanding Candlestick Components

You can't trade and invest effectively by using candlestick charts unless you understand candlestick patterns, and you may have a very hard time understanding those patterns if you aren't familiar with basic candlestick construction. Candlestick charting starts with the knowledge of what it takes to make a candlestick and how changes in that basic information impact a candlestick's appearance and what it means. For starters, you need to know what goes into creating a candlestick's wick (the thin vertical line) and its candle (the thick part in the middle).

The following four pieces of information are combined to create a candlestick:

✔ **Price on the open:** The price at which a security opens on a given period is the first piece of information used in creating a candlestick. Depending on whether the security's performance is bullish or bearish, the opening price corresponds to either the bottom edge of a candlestick's candle or the top edge.

Candlesticks that represent *bullish* price action appear *white* on a chart, and candlesticks that represent *bearish* price action appear *black*.

✔ **High price:** The highest price that a security reaches during a given period corresponds to the top of a candlestick's wick. If a security opens at a certain price and then trades consistently lower than that price throughout the period, there won't be any wick at all above the candle.

✔ **Low price:** The lowest price that a security reaches during a period corresponds to the bottom of a candlestick's wick. If the price action for that period is extremely bullish and prices trade higher than the open, there won't be any wick below the candle.

    ✔ **Price on the close:** After a security finishes trading during a given period, its closing price is the last piece of information used to create a candlestick. Depending on the security's performance during that period, the closing price can correspond to either the top edge of a candlestick's candle (if the period was bullish) or the bottom edge (if the period was bearish).

As a true candlestick devotee, I believe that you can gain far more insight into a period's trading by looking at a candlestick than you can by looking at another type of charting tool. Want proof? Take a look at Figure 1-1.

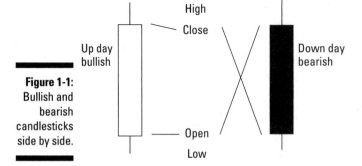

Figure 1-1:
Bullish and bearish candlesticks side by side.

You can tell right away that the up day has a white candle and the down day has a black candle. That simple difference alone clearly reveals the nature of the price action that took place during that period. In the case of the candlestick with the black candle, there was more selling pressure than desire to buy. And the candlestick with the white candle indicates that there was more buying pressure than desire to sell.

Why is this so important? Candlestick charts quickly clue you in on the type of buying and selling that's been going on during a given period and where it may occur again. In many cases, the buyers continue to buy and the sellers continue to sell during subsequent periods or if the price reaches a level that has spurred them to action in the past.

For more information on candlestick construction, refer to Chapter 3.

Working with Candlestick Patterns

The components of a candlestick may be the bones of candlestick charting, but candlestick patterns are the heart and soul. Patterns appear on candlestick charts as simple, single-stick occurrences or complex, multi-stick formations, and many different types of patterns can tell you what may be in store for a security that you've had your eye on for trading or investing. And knowing what may lie ahead can be the difference between a profitable trade and a flop.

Candlestick patterns indicate when prevailing trends reverse or when they continue. Both types of patterns are very useful because they tell you when to get into a trade, when to get out of a trade, when a trade you're in may make no sense, and even when to hang onto a trade you're already in. Check out Chapters 5 through 10 for more info on identifying and trading on a wide variety of candlestick patterns.

Simple patterns

Some candlestick patterns are very simple: A single candlestick on a chart can serve as a candlestick pattern. A single candlestick that signifies time to buy or sell is very appealing to traders who are just starting to work with candlestick charts because after you understand the basics of candlestick construction, you can immediately start identifying simple patterns and using them to make more informed trading decisions. Flip to Chapters 5 and 6 for several great examples of how just one candlestick can tell you what a security's price is going to do in the immediate future.

I also consider double-stick candlestick patterns as simple patterns, and you can explore several varieties in Chapters 7 and 8.

Complex patterns

When a candlestick pattern includes three periods' worth of price action (three candlesticks), I consider it a complex pattern. Many complex candlestick patterns require specific price activity over the course of three days for the pattern to be considered valid, and I discuss a range of them in Chapters 9 and 10.

Complex candlestick patterns can be frustrating at times because you may watch with anticipation as a pattern develops nicely for the first two days only to fizzle out on the third.

Complex candlestick patterns are more rare than their simple counterparts, but they can be worth the wait. Because the conditions and criteria for a complex pattern are so specific, it's more likely that the signals they offer will be good ones.

Making Technical Analysis Part of Your Candlestick Charting Strategy

A stunning amount of mathematical ingenuity is applied to security trading analysis. The options for technical analysis can be as simple as the average of a few days of closing prices and as complex as applying calculus to price action to indicate the momentum of prices. The possibilities are endless, and you shouldn't be shy about including some of them in your trading strategy alongside candlestick charts.

Take the time to get familiar with an array of technical indicators to make you a more versatile trader and enrich your work with candlestick charts. For example, it's great when you spot a candlestick pattern indicating that it's time to buy, and at the same time, your favorite technical indicator is also flashing a buy signal. Combining trading tools helps build your confidence and can help you quickly determine when a trade isn't going to work out, allowing you to exit with minimal losses.

I explore several different types of technical indicators in Chapter 11 and clue you in on a few ways that you can combine these indicators with candlestick patterns in Part IV (Chapters 11 through 15). Find a few technical indicators that match up to the type of trading you want to pursue and add them to your candlestick charts. Read up on the choices, and if Chapter 11 isn't enough, you can always turn to *Technical Analysis For Dummies* (Wiley) by Barbara Rockefeller. The added understanding of technical indicators can really aid you in your candlestick charting efforts.

Trading Wisely: What You Must Understand Before Working the Markets

Security trading and investing can be a financially rewarding and fulfilling experience, but it's far from a risk- and stress-free undertaking. I want to make clear to you a few key points and concerns before diving into my candlestick charting discussion, so that you're fully aware of what you're up against and what you can do to maximize rewards and minimize risks.

Trading can be an expensive endeavor

There's money to be made on the security markets, but don't be fooled into thinking that earning profits is easy or effortless. Many smart people have taken on trading as a hobby or profession and been quickly humbled by poor trades and losses. Do your homework and practice wise money management, or you could end up joining their ranks!

By doing homework, I mean look at charts and develop a trading plan. The more you prepare, much like for a test, the better your trading results should be. I've seen a direct correlation between the level of trading success I've achieved and how much time I've put into preparing for trading situations. As far as wise money management, the key here is making sure to take a loss when it becomes apparent a trade isn't going to work. Take the loss and move on. Take this loss early and quickly before it becomes a much bigger loss.

The most important rule for managing your trading and investing funds is to not risk money that you can't afford to lose. There are many obvious and unforeseen risks in the financial markets. If your lifestyle changed dramatically because a trade or investment wiped out your account, then you're probably putting too much of your personal net worth on the line.

Paper trading costs you nothing but time

Paper trading refers to the practice of tracking trades on paper that haven't been traded in an account. Professional traders tell you that paper trading isn't the same as putting real money at risk on the markets. As a professional trader, I totally agree. The emotional rollercoaster involved with making and losing money can't be matched in a dry run. But if you're a novice who's just starting to understand the ways of the market, I think paper trading is a great idea. The risks are nil, and the educational benefits are outstanding. Even after 15 years of trading experience, I still tend to paper trade new ideas or systems for a while before putting real money to work.

If you're new to trading, test out your trading ideas and refine your trading strategy by signing up for a trial account online with an electronic broker. (You can read all about electronic trading resources in Chapter 4.) All you stand to lose is a little time and some pride. But that's better than jumping right into a live trading scenario and getting taken to the cleaners!

Developing rules and sticking to them

Throughout this book, I stress the importance of setting rules for yourself and sticking to those rules. I just can't stress enough what a good practice that is for any trader. Making and losing money on the market is a very emotional experience, and one of the main reasons some traders lose big when they should lose just a little (or even win) is that they let their emotions take control of their trading. You can help take emotions out of the equation if you develop trading rules and adhere to them no matter what happens.

Create a set of trading rules for yourself, and stick to those rules. Include rules such as the following:

- ✔ When to get into trades
- ✔ Where to place stops in various trading situations
- ✔ What amount of money to risk on trades and investments
- ✔ When to get out of trades, either with a loss or profit

Write down your rules and keep them handy for a quick review when you're in the midst of a trade, and you're having second thoughts about what action to take.

I've been trading for a long time, and I can say without reservation that creating and adhering to a set of trading rules is the best way to reward yourself both personally and financially for the effort you put into the markets. I always follow the rules that I've set for myself, and although it may sound crazy, at this point I'm more proud of my rules than I am of my profits. All traders have to come up with their own sets of rules that talk to their trading style and comfort with risk, and you should keep that in mind and jot down potential rules as you explore the contents of this book.

Chapter 2

Getting to Know Candlestick Charts

*E*ver wonder why a trader or investor would choose candlestick charts over other types of charts when analyzing price action of investments or markets? Well, this chapter provides some answers.

Trading and investing aren't easy undertakings, and they're certainly not easy professions. Most traders — professional and amateur alike — and investors struggle just to keep up with the market's performance as measured by the Standard & Poor's 500 Index (S&P 500). The S&P 500 is an index comprised of 500 of the largest stocks traded in the United States (U.S.) and is considered representative of the stock market as a whole.

In order to be one of the successful few who beats the market and other market participants, you should strive to develop a competitive advantage or some unique insight, commonly referred to as your "edge," that you believe most market participants aren't using or considering. I can't say that using candlestick charting provides an edge by itself — and it does come with a couple of potential problems. But when combined with recurring patterns and other technical indicators, you can find your edge!

In this chapter, I cover candlestick charts — the good and the bad — and I review a handful of alternative charting methods. But in the end, you understand why candlestick charting is the way to go!

Brief history of candlestick charting

The history of candlestick charting stretches back to Japanese rice traders in the 17th or 18th century. This fact is why candlestick charts are frequently referred to as Japanese candlestick charts. A very smart man named Munehisa Homma developed the methodology of monitoring the price of daily rice trading, and his methods eventually evolved into what traders and other market watchers call candlestick charting.

Homma found that having a visual representation of daily rice trading allowed him to make more informed buy-and-sell decisions during the hectic trading day. It's said that Homma once had a streak of over 100 winning trades!

Fast forward to the early 1990s, when Steve Nison published a book and magazine article on candlestick charting. Until then, candlestick charting wasn't widely used. Nison's first book, *Japanese Candlestick Charting Techniques* (Prentice Hall Press), served as an introduction to candlestick charting methods for many traders and investors in the United States. Over the next 15 years, the acceptance and use of candlestick charting became widespread, and the use of computer software for analyzing recurring patterns proved profitable for many traders.

Recognizing the Many Benefits of Candlestick Charting

Trading, investing, and charting styles are plentiful. You can spend hours debating what type of approach to the markets is the best. For me, and for a growing number of other traders, the benefits of a candlestick chart versus other types of charts aren't really debatable. Let me tell you why.

Changes and developments in the way stocks and other securities are traded (and *when* they're traded) have made trading an increasingly complex undertaking. (For more info, see the nearby sidebar, "What makes up a day?") Because trading is becoming more and more complex, the need for a consistent, dynamic charting method is more important than ever. Traders need easy-to-read charts that allow them to make quick decisions and efficiently analyze patterns. Candlesticks offer those benefits and many more, all covered in this section.

Seeing is believing: Candlesticks are easy to read

It sounds pretty simplistic, but one noteworthy advantage candlesticks have over other charts is their readability. For many people who strain to read the fine print and also for the younger traders who don't want to deal with the headaches that can come from staring at bar charts all morning, candlesticks are an attractive option. Consider Figure 2-1, which displays a bar and a candlestick in a side-by-side comparison.

Figure 2-1 gives you a basic idea of why candlesticks are easier to read, but it doesn't really provide a full picture of why they're also much better at helping traders to visually interpret price action (how the stock or market traded during the day relative to the opening price), which is an essential skill for successful trading. Take a look at Figure 2-1, which takes a couple of weeks' worth of trading data and displays it using traditional bar charts and candlestick charts, respectively.

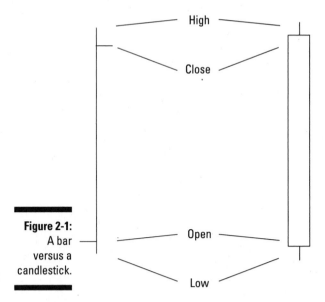

Figure 2-1:
A bar versus a candlestick.

What makes up a day?

The definition of a trading "day" used to be very simple. Trading was done on a central exchange with specific opening and closing times. For example, trading on stocks listed on the New York Stock Exchange (NYSE) began at 9:30 a.m. and ceased at 4:00 p.m. Now trading in these stocks commences on some electronic communication networks (ECNs) hours before the NYSE opens and hours after it closes. (An ECN is a network of brokerage firms and traders, which allows for trading directly between the brokerage firms and traders.) A "day," therefore, is much different than it was in the past. Throw in futures exchanges and currency markets that trade almost 24 hours a day, and this issue becomes even more confusing. With all that trading outside of exchange hours, what constitutes an actual day, for data purposes?

Currently, in the case of stocks, the official open and close are based on the primary exchange they trade on, but in this world of expanding electronic trading, the actual open and close are becoming more blurred. With respect to futures markets that trade almost 24 hours a day, it's almost impossible to pin down a day. For daily testing, I use data between 7 a.m. eastern standard time (EST) and the close at 3 p.m. to constitute a day.

Notice the dramatic difference between the bar chart and the candlestick chart. By comparing them, you can clearly interpret what's occurred from day to day, including the openings, closings, and how they change from day to day. The candlestick chart is a superior way to interpret the price action from day to day when compared to a bar chart. Don't worry — I cover how to read candlestick charts extensively in several other chapters, but even in this simplistic example you can see that knowing where a stock closed relative to its open on a given day is a powerful piece of information that you can glean quickly from a candlestick chart.

You can spot bears and bulls quickly

Knowing a security's closing price relative to its opening price during a certain period is vital information. Candlestick charts allow you to quickly identify the days when a closing price is above an opening price and vice versa.

I like to think of the daily price action as a battle between bears and bulls. Bears win when the price of a security closes lower than its open, and bulls win on the days when the close settles higher than the open.

Figure 2-2 is a great example of bearish and bullish days on a candlestick chart. Although the two candlesticks are the same size and shape, you can tell the difference between a bear and a bull:

- ✔ **The bear:** The black filled-in candlestick indicates a bearish performance by the security because the close is much lower than the opening price.

- ✔ **The bull:** The hollow (white) candlestick indicates a bullish performance, meaning that the opening is lower than the close.

Chapter 1 covers hollow candlesticks that show a higher close than open and a filled-in candlestick that shows a lower close than open.

Understanding the ways that prices are trending is very useful information when making buy-or-sell decisions. The old saying "The trend is your friend" is a constant reminder that you always want to be on the more dominant side of price action. By recognizing whether the bulls or bears are the more dominant group, you can be conscious of the trend and better prepared to stay on the right side of the market.

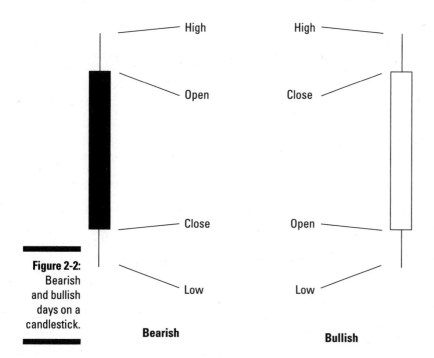

Figure 2-2:
Bearish
and bullish
days on a
candlestick.

Bulls and bears

The terms *bull* and *bear* have been in the trading lexicon for many years. Both terms apply to people and market trends. A *bull* is a market participant that expects or wants the market to move higher, but it is also an expression to explain when the market goes up: bullish market. A *bear*, on the other hand, expects the market to decline (person) and indicates a declining market. But where did these terms come from?

Although there's some debate over the origins of the two terms, they may be attributed to a man named Thomas Mortimer, who wrote about the precursor to the London stock exchange in the late 1700s. He wrote that a bull bought stocks without putting any money down with the hope of selling at a higher price before having to settle up. And according to Mortimer, a bear sold stock he didn't own without putting up any money also hoping to exit the position at a profit before he was forced to settle up.

Seeing into the future (sort of)

The goal of charting and technical analysis isn't to see what's happened in the past, but to attempt to predict the future. Basically, if you can predict the future for a majority of the time, you should be able to profit nicely through wise investing and trading. Because candlestick charts are chock-full of info, they aid a trader as she works to predict and profit from future price moves.

For example, a trader may study old candlestick charts and notice that when a security's closing price is much higher than its opening price, it seems to open higher the next day — a situation commonly referred to as a *gap opening*. That trader can buy the security on the close of the day and place an order to sell the next day, thus making a profit. Figure 2-3 provides a clear visual example of a gap opening.

Just by studying past price action on old candlestick charts, the trader in this section's example is able to predict a small piece of the future and use it to turn a profit. History does repeat itself in markets and trading, and you can use this repetition to your advantage by considering past candlestick charts, which can be a cinch to read. But always keep in mind that as with all aspects of technical analysis and investing, past results do not ensure future returns.

At the very least, be sure to pay attention to price gaps, because they indicate an increase in volatility in the price of a security. When there's an increase in volatility, there's an increase in trading opportunity. Many other types of patterns, including those that incorporate candlesticks, reappear and may be profited from.

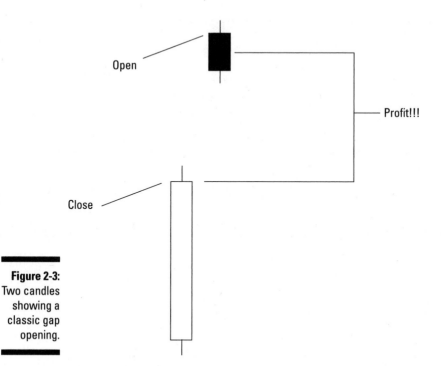

Open

Profit!!!

Close

Figure 2-3:
Two candles
showing a
classic gap
opening.

Showing price patterns

Recognizing patterns on candlestick charts is easy, and you can combine two or more candlestick charts to flesh out a reliable pattern that can lead you to profitable trading. For example, a common price pattern that serves as a good sell signal is depicted in Figure 2-4.

The pattern is a two-day pattern, and the third day is a common reaction to the first two days. Here's the typical progression:

1. **The first day is a strong open-to-close day.**

   The closing price is considerably higher than the opening price. The first day is a victory for the bulls.

2. **The second day reveals very little price action because the close is very near the open.**

   The second day is a wash because higher prices entice more bears to be sellers.

Understanding price gaps

Price gaps are very common in the financial markets, and occur on charts when no overlap exists between consecutive period highs and lows. For instance, if XYZ stock's high is 81 and its low is 80 on a given day, and then the next day it opens higher than 81 — let's say 83 — and trades in a range between 82 and 84, a gap with no trading exists between 81 and 82. That stock *gapped higher* and never closed the gap. If the stock had opened much lower — 77 or 78, for example — and never reached the previous day's low, it would've *gapped lower*.

So what causes price gaps? These gaps are usually the result of news about a certain security being released outside of market hours. It's not uncommon: Most companies release their quarterly earnings or other big news either after the market closes or before it opens. The market adjustment to that news causes price gaps.

Also, a gap may occur on specific stocks just because they're moving up or down due to a gap in the overall market. This may occur due to a release of some economic news before the market opens or possibly due to a macro event such as a terrorist attack.

You should remember that gaps always get filled when the high to low price action of a future day covers the price range where no trades occurred. But you can't always tell when gaps will be filled. When the dot.com bubble was building, some Internet stocks had several price gaps on their way up to stratospheric valuations. These gaps were eventually filled, but anyone trying to short these stocks for the gap being filled would've ended up in the poorhouse before any gap filling took place. (Take a look at the "Selling short, in short" sidebar for more information on shorting.)

3. **After this shift from bullish to neutral price action, the following day is a down day.**

   The third day is a winning day for the bears!

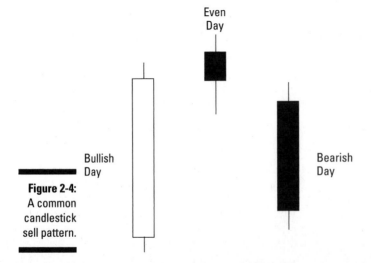

Even
Day

Bullish
Day

Bearish
Day

Figure 2-4:
A common
candlestick
sell pattern.

Once again, a trader who studies candlestick charts and patterns can easily spot this change. Such a momentum shift is useful to someone who owns a security and is considering selling or a trader who has the ability to sell short. (See the sidebar "Selling short, in short" in this chapter for more information.)

Admitting the Potential Candlestick Charting Risks

After more than 15 years of using candlestick charts to inform my trading decisions, I can honestly say that I have a difficult time coming up with any substantial arguments for using other common types of charts over candlestick.

In the interest of fairness, however, and to help you realize the truly versatile and useful nature of candlesticks, I offer a couple of minor potential chinks in the candlestick chart's armor:

- ✔ **They don't work in the *very* short term.** Candlestick charts are an excellent display of price action, but for some extremely short-term trading strategies, the patterns that reveal themselves on a daily candlestick chart may not develop on the much shorter time frame — five minutes or less, for example.

  I like to think of candlestick charts as a visual representation of the battle between the bulls and bears, which is played out in the price action of a stock. That battle takes some time to play out, so patterns on a very short-term chart may not produce signals that can be properly interpreted and traded.

  Candlesticks aren't as useful to intraday "scalping" or day trading strategies where hold periods are generally shorter. This speaks more to the utility of the chart and the intended behavior of the trader.

- ✔ **They don't reflect trade volume outside of regular market hours.** The advent of increased electronic trading means that there can sometimes be significant volume traded outside of regular market hours. This trading can cause patterns that don't reflect the full picture to appear on a candlestick chart.

  For example, if a stock officially opens at 9:30 a.m. at a price of $50, but traded as low as $49 during the pre-market hours (on an electronic trading network), the open may not be a true reflection of where the stock initially traded on the day. That means that the open recorded on the candlestick is somewhat inaccurate. Also, if the stock never trades down to $49 during the day, the low on the chart may not be an accurate depiction of the day's price action.

Selling short, in short

One of the most well-known trading adages is "Buy low, sell high" — the simplest way to turn a profit in a market. But other ways exist, including *short selling* or *shorting* a security. This somewhat counterintuitive process involves selling a security first and then buying it back later. Traders who practice this strategy are known as *shorts*.

The mechanics of selling short can be fairly complex, but I'll try to sum them up:

1. **A short borrows a stock from a bank that holds it for the owners, expecting the price of the stock to go down.**

2. **He then sells the borrowed stock to a buyer.**

3. **When the stock price drops, he buys the stock back and returns it to the bank at the original (higher) price, and pockets the difference.**

Shorts get a bum rap and are often accused of being responsible when a stock trades lower. Companies have even sued shorts on claims that they spread negative rumors to drive down the company's stock price. But short sellers are really just a part of the overall market mechanism, and they can actually help keep companies honest, because they're constantly on the lookout for companies with deteriorating fundaments or evidence of suspicious accounting.

Comparing Candlestick Charts with Alternative Charting Methods

Knowing a bit about the options that exist outside of candlestick charts serves as a point of reference and makes clear the benefits of using candlestick charts when analyzing price data.

Although they're not as versatile and useful as candlesticks, each of these alternative charts has its benefits:

- ✔ *Line charts* are simple and straightforward.

- ✔ *Bar charts* are important to understand because they're still relatively prevalent.

- ✔ *Point and figure charts* are great for revealing support and resistance levels.

I'm confident that you'll be a believer in candlesticks when it's all said and done, but understanding the alternatives is certainly worth your time.

Line charts

A line chart is a line on a chart that displays security prices over time. A line chart represents the price — usually the closing price — of a security from one period to the next.

On a very short-term basis, a line chart is definitely a proper choice for decision making. However, since no other information is displayed, attempting to formulate any sort of trading strategy from a line chart of price action wouldn't be a worthwhile venture.

Figure 2-5 is a line chart of three months of daily closing prices for a stock.

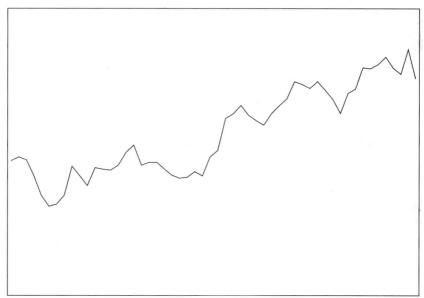

Figure 2-5:
A line chart.

Bar charts

A traditional bar chart contains bars that represent price action from period to period. Each bar is basically a vertical line that shows the difference between the high and the low of the period. The top of the bar is the high and the bottom is the low. The distance between the two is similar to the wick of a candle on a candlestick chart. (The wick is discussed more in Chapter 1.) The finishing touch on a bar chart is a little notch on the left of the bar that's made to mark where the security closed. Figure 2-6 is a single bar that normally appears on a bar chart.

Figure 2-7 is a chart of the same data that appeared in the line chart in the previous section (Figure 2-5).

Bar charts have been the industry standard for some time, but are quickly being replaced by candlestick charts. When the *Wall Street Journal* starts using a new charting convention (as it has with candlestick charts), the convention is considered to be the industry standard.

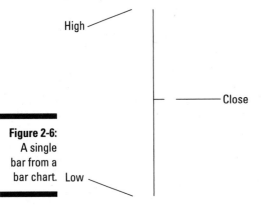

Figure 2-6:
A single
bar from a
bar chart.

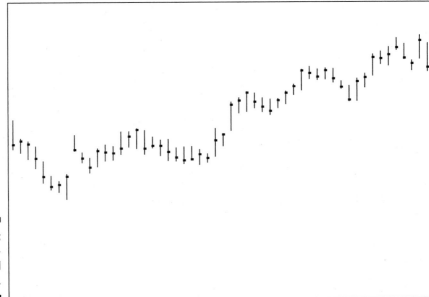

Figure 2-7:
A run-of-
the-mill
bar chart.

Point and figure charts

Point and figure charting is another type of stock charting that's been around so long it deserves a mention when covering methods of charting. A point and figure chart is composed of x's and o's drawn on a sheet of graph paper. This chart isn't constructed using a set time frame but is instead based on reversals of price. The x's make up a series of up moves without a certain price reversal, while the o's represent a series of down moves without a price reversal.

Figure 2-8 is a point and figure depiction of the same data that composes the line and bar charts in the two previous sections. The figure values each square with one point and adds a new column with a change of direction of at least two points, based on the close. For example, if day one has a closing price of 75 and day two has a closing price of 78, you draw x's from 75 to 78. If on day three the closing price is 76 — a 2-point reversal — a new column is added, and o's are placed in the 77 and 76 squares. If the price stays in the 76 to 77 range for a few days, no changes are made to the chart.

Point and figure charts are unique because they purely reflect price moves. Because time isn't factored in, you don't need to update the chart if a stock stays at a certain price for some time. On the other hand, when a price trades between two prices several times — bouncing between 50 and 55, for example — a point and figure chart offers a very clear display of those levels, which are called support levels and resistance levels. In this case, 50 is the support level and 55 is the resistance level.

If you can properly recognize support and resistance levels, you can potentially use that knowledge to make a tidy profit. Using the example in the preceding graph, if you can buy at 50 and sell at 55 several times over, the returns can be astounding. So why aren't point and figure charts right up there with candlesticks in terms of usefulness? It's simple: Support and resistance levels show up well on candlestick charts too, and candlesticks also contain a variety of other information.

Although interesting and unique, point and figure charting is really a throwback to a time when stock prices were charted based on the closing prices found daily in the financial press and were meticulously kept by hand. Its use has fallen by the wayside with the advent of technology.

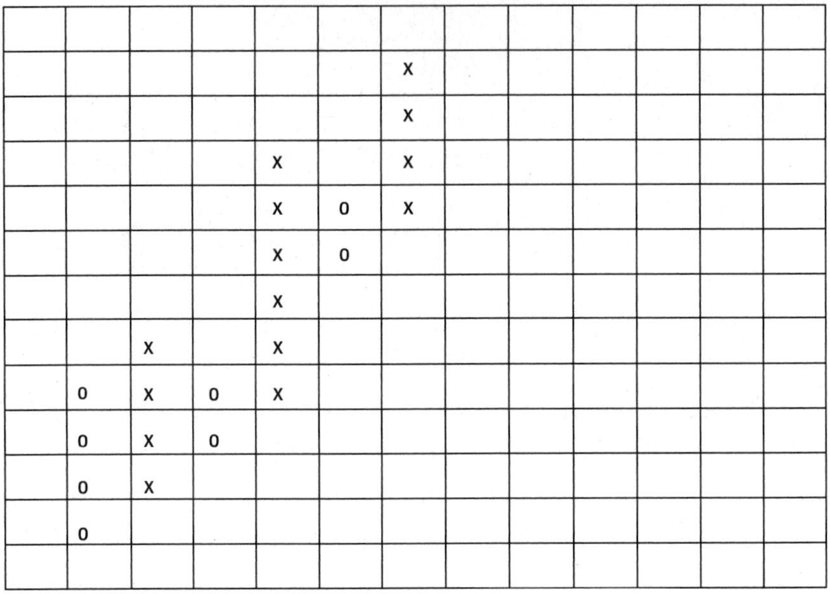

							X					
							X					
					X		X					
					X	O	X					
					X	O						
					X							
		X			X							
	O	X	O		X							
	O	X	O									
	O	X										
	O											

Figure 2-8:
A point and
figure chart.

Chapter 3

Building a Base of Candlestick Chart Knowledge

In This Chapter
▶ Understanding the basic components of candlestick charts
▶ Working with additional information on candlestick charts

*T*o take full advantage of candlestick charts, you must understand how they're constructed. From the basic pieces of information used to generate a candlestick to the various additions and extra pieces of data that can be tacked onto a chart, you need to know just what you're looking at before you can make wise trading decisions. You need to be familiar with candlestick nuts and bolts before delving into their interpretations and uses.

In this chapter, I offer a solid foundation of candlestick know-how. I start with the data that goes into constructing individual candlesticks. Although candlesticks can represent the action of a security over a wide variety of time periods, the basic information used to build them is the same. I also cover the other pieces of data that are commonly included on a candlestick chart — added features that enhance the usefulness and readability of the chart.

Constructing a Candlestick: A Core of Four

For any security, each day of trading includes four key components in terms of data: opening price, closing price, highest price traded on the day, and lowest price traded on the day. These four pieces of data are needed to construct the individual bars that make up candlestick charts. Several bars, created by using the data from several days or periods, are generated in succession to produce a full candlestick chart.

Candlestick charts may be applied to the performance of securities over a variety of time periods. I use them on charts from as short-term as five minutes per bar to as long-term as a week per bar. A five-minute chart may be applied to a day or two of activity, while the weekly chart would be applied to a period of several years. Although those are two vastly different time frames, a candlestick chart is appropriate for both, and candlesticks would work for many different time periods in between.

Price on the open

The first piece of data used to construct a candlestick is the opening price for the day. For stocks, in most cases, it's the official opening price on a specified primary exchange.

Recording an opening price on a candlestick

On a single candlestick, the thin vertical line is the wick, and the thick part in the middle is the candle. The opening price on a single candlestick will always be either the top or bottom of the candle, and it's created on the chart using the price scale on the chart's vertical axis. A hollow (white) candle is bullish, meaning that the opening price is lower than the closing price. (See Chapter 2.) If you see a hollow candle, the bottom of the candle is the opening price. Conversely, a filled-in (black) candle is bearish, meaning that the opening price is higher than the closing price. In that case, the top of the candle is the opening price.

Dealing with the challenges of pinning down an opening price

Because many securities are now trading on multiple exchanges or electronic trading networks, pinning down an exact opening price can be difficult, which makes constructing a candle a difficult endeavor.

For example, I was recently trying to trade a stock on which very significant — and misinterpreted — news came out before the opening of the trading day. The stock had closed the day before at $48 per share, but was trading on one of the electronic communication networks (ECNs) two hours before it was to open on the New York Stock Exchange at $45 per share. Over the next two hours, the breaking news was better understood, and the stock started to trade higher. It actually opened at about $51 per share. Although several thousand shares traded between $45 and $51 in the two hours leading up to the opening price, the official open for the day was $51.

For futures contracts on commodities — agreements between two parties to buy or sell a certain product on a predefined date (see the nearby sidebar, "Focus on futures" for more details) — attempting to determine the opening price for a day can be even more difficult. Many futures markets now trade both electronically and on a trading floor. A perfect example is Japanese Yen.

What's the stock market?

When most people think of the stock market, they picture stock traders in brightly colored jackets shouting and hand signaling orders in a giant room. This is actually how the commodity markets function. The stock market, or at least the floor of the New York Stock Exchange (NYSE), is more like a giant bank lobby with each stock having a particular place or post where transactions for that stock take place. The person in charge of manning this post is known as the specialist, and his job is to facilitate trading of a particular stock between the multitudes of buyers and sellers in an orderly manner.

A specialist takes all the buy-and-sell orders and attempts to match them up. In some cases, when an abundance of sellers exists but not enough buyers, the specialist may help with orderly trading by buying shares from the sellers. When there are several buyers and not enough sellers, the specialist may act as a seller to keep the market orderly. Specialists also assimilate buy-and-sell orders before the official market opening to determine an opening price, and they do the same thing on the close.

When I began my career 15 years ago, virtually all stock trading in the United States was done either on the floors of the NYSE or the American Stock Exchange (AMEX), or through a network of brokers known as the National Association of Securities Dealers Automated Quotation System (NASDAQ). If I wanted to buy shares of IBM, which traded on the NYSE, I called a broker and gave him an order. He forwarded my order to someone working on the exchange floor, or in some cases directly to the specialist. If I were to purchase shares of Microsoft, (symbol MSFT), which traded on the NASDAQ, I called a broker who either traded directly with me, matched me with a seller, or traded with another broker through the NASDAQ market.

Today there are multiple venues for those stocks traded on the listed exchanges and those on the NASDAQ. The broker I use for my personal stock trades has an automated feature that automatically selects the best market for the order I enter. I never know anymore if my orders go to the exchange floor, and as time goes on, fewer and fewer of my orders make it there. Instead, the orders are traded over an electronic communication network set up for trading stocks without using the primary exchange or the specialist. Brokers and large institutions use these networks to trade stocks without sending the orders to the floor of the primary exchange.

Yen futures trade on the Chicago Mercantile Exchange (CME) and on their corresponding electronic platform, called Globex. The pit for the CME opens at 7:20 a.m. central time and closes at 2:00 p.m Monday through Friday. But the Globex trading hours run from Sunday at 5 p.m. central until 4:00 p.m. on Friday, with only an hour break each afternoon. So how do you determine the open? *Note:* These hours are accurate as of December 2007 and subject to change.

For such a convoluted situation, I use the pit data for analysis purposes, but since the most volume is traded during the hours that the pit is closed, I always have to reevaluate what I consider to be the open. For some other examples of futures contracts that have both pit trading hours and electronic hours, see Figure 3-1.

Chicago Board of Trade - ECBOT

Agricultural	Ele. Open	Ele. Close	Pit Open	Pit Close
Corn	18:30 c 9:30 c	6:00 c 13:15c	9:30 c	13:15c
Soybeans	18:31 c 9:30 c	6:00 c 13:15c	9:30 c	13:15c
Wheat	18:32 c 9:30 c	6:00 c 13:15c	9:30 c	13:15c

Interest Rate				
2 Year	18:00 c	16:00 c	7:20 c	14:00 c
5 Year	18:00 c	16:00 c	7:20 c	14:00 c
10 Year	18:00 c	16:00 c	7:20 c	14:00 c
30 Year	18:00 c	16:00 c	7:20 c	14:00 c

Index				
DJIA	18:15 c	16:00 c	7:20 c	15:15 c

CME - Globex

Index	Ele. Open	Ele. Close	Pit Open	Pit Close
S&P 500 Index	17:00 c	16:00 c	8:30 c	15:15 c
NASDAQ 100 Index	17:00 c	16:00 c	8:30 c	15:15 c
Nikkei 225 Index	2:00 c	16:30 c	8:00 c	15:15 c
Russell 2000 Index	17:00 c	16:00 c	8:30 c	15:15 c
S&P MidCap 400	17:00 c	16:00 c	8:30 c	15:15 c

Currency				
Australian Dollar	17:00 c	16:00 c	7:20 c	14:00 c
British Pound	17:00 c	16:00 c	7:20 c	14:00 c
Canadian Dollar	17:00 c	16:00 c	7:20 c	14:00 c
Euro FX	17:00 c	16:00 c	7:20 c	14:00 c
Japanese Yen	17:00 c	16:00 c	7:20 c	14:00 c
Mexican Peso	17:00 c	16:00 c	7:20 c	14:00 c
Swiss Fran	17:00 c	16:00 c	7:20 c	14:00 c

Interest Rate				
Eurodollar	17:00 c	16:00 c	7:20 c	14:00 c
Libor	17:00 c	16:00 c	7:20 c	14:00 c

Commodities				
Feeder Cattle	9:05 c	13:00 c	9:05 c	13:00 c
Pork Bellies	9:10 c	13:00 c	9:10 c	13:00 c
Lean Hogs	9:10 c	13:00 c	9:10 c	13:00 c
Live Cattle	9:05 c	13:00 c	9:05 c	13:00 c

NYMEX - Globex

Energy	Ele. Open	Ele. Close	Pit Open	Pit Close
Crude Oil	18:00 e	17:15 e	9:00 e	14:30 e
Gasoline Futures	18:00 e	17:15 e	9:00 e	14:30 e
Natural Gas	18:00 e	17:15 e	9:00 e	14:30 e
Heating Oil	18:00 e	17:15 e	9:00 e	14:30 e

Metals				
Gold	18:00 e	17:15 e	8:20 e	13:30 e
Silver	18:00 e	17:15 e	8:25 e	13:25 e
Copper	18:00 e	17:15 e	8:10 e	13:00 e
Aluminum	18:00 e	17:15 e	7:50 e	13:15 e

Figure 3-1:
Futures contracts that have both pit trading and electronic hours.

In Figure 3-1 you see that, for futures contracts, the actual opening price for a session can be hard to determine. One good solution is to use the opening price for the first trade during the pit session.

High and low price for the session

The second and third pieces of data that are essential for constructing a candlestick are the high and low prices for a session. No tricks here — the high price is the highest point the security's price reaches during the session, and the low is the lowest point reached during the same session. Because there may be some flexibility in what you consider a trading session, it may be the high and low that have traded between 6:30 a.m. and 2:00 p.m. Your session would be 6:30 a.m. to 2:00 p.m.

Focus on futures

When explaining how futures contracts work, I always love to use my example about buying a lawn mower at the home improvement superstore.

Imagine that it's December 15, and you know that when spring rolls around in May, your old rusty lawnmower just isn't going to cut it, so to speak. You need a new mower. The mower you want is expected to cost $500 on May 1, which will be the first day you really need to cut the grass. You don't want to pay that much for a mower, and you're in luck, because your home improvement superstore is the only one in the world that offers lawnmower futures. And May 1 just so happens to be the day that May lawnmower futures (if they existed) expire. The price of a May lawnmower futures contract is $400, so you make a small deposit — maybe 10 percent of the mower contract size of $400 — and buy one futures contract through your mower futures broker. When May 1 rolls around, you'll have the ability to pay $400 for your new lawnmower, even though the market price is $500. But who would offer such an attractive deal?

The seller of the futures contract can be a lawnmower dealer who's more than happy to lock in a price of $400 to sell a lawnmower on May 1. After all, it would help that dealer to plan production accordingly by locking in a guaranteed number of mower sales at a set price. It can also be a speculator who thinks mowers will be on sale at the home improvement superstore for $300 at some point before May 1, which would allow him to buy the mower at a discount and then sell it to you for $400 on May 1, generating a $100 profit.

The futures markets were created to allow farmers a mechanism for locking in the price of their crops and eliminating the risk that when their crops were ready to be sold, the selling price would not be enough to cover their costs and provide a profit. For farmers, whose livelihood is so dependent on factors out of their control, this method was extremely helpful to eliminate selling price as one of the major risks.

Incorporating high and low prices into a candlestick

The high and low prices for a session or day are used to make the thin vertical line or wick of the candlestick (see Chapter 1 for a visual of the basic candlestick). The top of the wick represents the high price for the session, and the bottom of the wick represents the session's low price.

You need to define what your trading session is, and the wick represents the range from the high down to the low. This can be for the formal exchange floor or pit trading times, or, as discussed earlier, for a period you decide to represent a trading session.

If a security opens at a certain price and then drops in price steadily throughout the course of the session, you won't see any wick at all extending above the candle. If, on the other hand, the security opens at a certain price and increases in price during the session without ever dropping below the open, you won't see any wick extending below the candle.

How low (or high) can you go? Deciding on a high and low price

As with opening prices, high and low prices can be tough to nail down because of the various electronic trading venues operating today. If big news on a particular security breaks before the official open or after the close, it may very well trade higher or lower on an electronic trading venue than it does on its primary exchange.

It's even more likely that the futures contracts will trade at prices above the exchange session high or below the exchange session low, due to the fact that the electronic futures markets are active 24 hours a day. Nowhere is this more evident than futures on currencies. The currency market is a true 24-hour market, and news across the globe is constantly impacting currency movements. Because of that volatility, it's very possible that there will be a lot of price action outside of normal exchange pit trading hours.

For more insight into the dramatic difference between 24-hour activity and exchange hour activity, see Figure 3-2. Both are charts of futures contracts on the Swiss Franc price versus the U.S. dollar. These contracts trade from 7:20 a.m. to 2:00 p.m. central time on the floor of the CME, and trade up to 23 hours a day between Sunday evening and Friday afternoon on the CME's Globex system. Figure 3-2a is a chart of the price action over the course of a couple of months using *only* data from pit trading hours. Figure 3-2b uses the same time period but takes into account all trading hours.

Frankly (ahem), the Franc chart has so many gaps that it's basically not even worth trying to analyze. It's highly unlikely that you'd work out a profitable method of trading based on this chart. There's very little opportunity to catch the many dramatic price moves that occur in the hours outside of normal or exchange trading hours. You just don't have enough information to make smart (and profitable) moves. Figure 3-2b, on the other hand, gives you a fuller picture of the price moves of the futures, and allows you to make well-informed decisions about buying and selling.

Currencies aren't the only futures contracts that experience these types of overnight moves. Bond futures and stock index futures such as Chicago Board of Trade's ten-year government bond futures contract or the S&P 500 Index futures that trade at the CME also see price action in the overnight session, while the underlying bond and stock markets are closed. Traders are even starting to see price moves for true commodity futures trading overnight that aren't properly caught on charts.

When it comes down to it, the choice of what to use for a day is up to the individual trader. For instance, if you're looking to put on longer term trades, the prices that trade outside of normal trading hours may not mean as much to you as it would to a trader trying to catch very short-term moves as short as a few minutes. Also, what you use for a day may just depend on how much time you can devote to watching the markets. I think most casual traders may just want to focus on the primary exchange's trading hours or the price action that occurs over the course of a normal work day.

Figure 3-2:
Daily chart of Swiss Franc futures using only pit trading data (a) and using data from all trading hours (b).

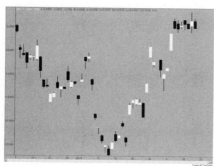 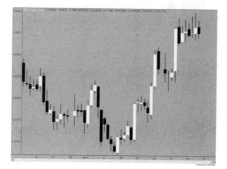

Price on the close

The fourth and final piece of data used to build a candlestick is a security's closing price. The *closing price* is the final price that's traded on a security during the day. These are the closing numbers that appear in the stock tables in newspapers, and the prices that investment professionals use to monitor their day-to-day performance. As with the other data used in creating a candlestick, closing prices are getting tougher and tougher to pin down.

Recording a closing price on a candlestick

Depending on the performance of a security, its closing price may appear in one of two places on a candlestick:

- If the security had a bullish performance on a given day, the candle part of the candlestick is hollow (white). In that case, the closing price is represented by the top of the candle.
- If the security performed bearishly, the candle is filled in (black), and its bottom marks the closing price for the day.

Trying to pin down a closing price

Just like the opening, high, and low prices (see previous sections), the closing price can be a real challenge to pin down because of the presence of electronic trading networks. Also, stocks and futures stay open for some time after their official exchanges close, so pinpointing what the market believes the true value for a stock or futures contract is at the end of the day is actually really difficult.

Although trading continues beyond the primary market's hours, stocks do generally trade for an hour or so after the exchanges close. Usually the trading in stocks after 4 p.m. EST on the electronic trading networks is pretty light in volume, but on days with significant earnings announcements or other news, several million shares of a stock may trade after the close.

One example of this after-close trade is what's referred to as *earnings season*. This time period is when many companies report their quarterly financial results to the financial and investing community. During a recent earnings season, both Microsoft (MSFT) and Google (GOOG) reported their earnings. Both stocks traded many millions of shares after the 4 p.m. official close of the NASDAQ, the primary trading market for both. With such a high volume of trading, this price action is significant enough to be included in charts.

For the earnings season in question, the investment community ("the street") wasn't terribly impressed with either company's results, and the stocks traded off pretty significantly as a result. Microsoft's official closing share price at 4 p.m. EST was 31.51, but in the "after hours" the stock traded down to 30.90, which is a nearly 2 percent drop from the closing price at 4 p.m. and 0.02 percent below the official low for the day of 30.93 per share.

The difference in Google's stock was even greater. The official 4 p.m. close was 548.59 a share, but after checking, the post market trading revealed a final price of 508.70 a share. That's more than 7 percent lower than the 4 p.m. close! It was also quite a bit lower than even the official low of the day, which was 542.24 a share.

Considering Additional Information Included on Candlestick Charts

In addition to the basic information (described in the earlier sections of this chapter), most candlestick charts automatically include many other pieces of data. This added data allows you to quickly digest how the stock has traded in the past and gives you some fundamental activity, such as dates of earnings releases or dividend payments, which may also appear on charts.

In this section, I clue you in on a few pieces of information that may be included on your candlestick charts.

Volume

In trading lingo, *volume* is the number of shares traded during a certain period of time. A volume measurement usually appears in the bottom quarter to bottom third of a chart. Figure 3-3 is a chart of Google showing roughly 60 days leading up to July 19, 2007.

In the bottom of the chart in Figure 3-3, daily volume for Google's stock has been between 1 and about 11 million shares per day during this period. Notice the second trading day in July, which was July 3, just before a mid-week Independence Day holiday. That was a half day for the market, and the volume measurement is barely a blip. On the other end of the spectrum, have a look at the high volume on the last day of the chart. That high volume came in anticipation of the earnings that were to be released after the market closed. And the volume measurement on the last day of the chart doesn't even include the 4.5 million shares traded after the 4 p.m. close!

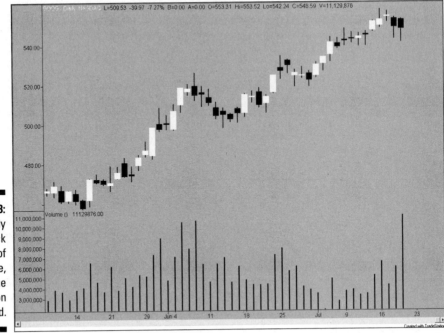

Figure 3-3:
Daily
candlestick
chart of
Google,
with volume
information
included.

Many technical analysts put quite a bit of emphasis on volume as it relates to certain chart patterns. For instance, if a stock trades down to what's considered a support level (flip back to Chapter 2 for more info on support levels) on a day with significant volume, many traders may give this support level more credence and consider buying. The reason is that the increase in volume indicates a high level of buy interest emerging at this level. If support is tested on a low volume day, such as July 3, a trader may wait for more volume to trade to confirm this support level. Low volume days sometimes contain unreliable price action where the price has whipped around due to a lack of liquidity.

Open interest

In the case of futures charts, *open interest* takes the place of volume. Before discussing open interest on a chart, an explanation of exactly how it's determined and what it means is in order.

Put simply, open interest is the number of outstanding futures contracts. When a buyer and a seller involved in a futures contract initiate new positions, the open interest increases by one contract.

When you trade a futures contract, whether you're buying or selling, you're also either opening or closing a position. If you have no position, and you buy a futures contract, that's an opening position. When you sell that contract, you're closing the position. This can work for selling, too. If you have no position to begin with, and you sell a contract, you've opened a short position. When you buy this contract back or cover the short position, you're closing a position. For more information on shorting, see Chapter 2.

When both the buyer and seller in a trade are opening positions, the open interest of contracts increases. If only one of the participants in a trade is opening a new position, then the open interest doesn't change. Finally, if both participants in a trade are closing positions, the open interest decreases.

Figure 3-4 is a very simple example of how open interest increases and decreases. Here's how the days break down:

- ✔ **Day 1:** Assuming that Day 1 on the chart is the first day the futures contract displayed trades, the beginning open interest is zero. For display purposes, two contracts trade, and both the buyer and seller are initiating new positions. These new positions create two new contracts.

- ✔ **Day 2:** On Day 2, there are four more contracts initiated by both the buyer and seller, and the open interest increases to six contracts.

- ✔ **Day 3:** On Day 3, things get a little trickier. Mr. A decides to sell his two contracts, and Ms. D decides to buy back (cover) two of the contracts she'd previously sold short. This reduced the open interest by two contracts.

- ✔ **Day 4:** Finally, on Day 4, Mr. C sells his four contracts, but Mr. A buys them, so these open contracts are transferred, and no new contracts are created. The open interest doesn't change.

Figure 3-5 is a chart of soybean futures, which expire in November 2007. I actively trade the soybean futures market, so this chart is near and dear to my heart. The open interest appears in the same area on the chart as the volume did on the chart of Google in Figure 3-3. Notice the increase in open interest during the life of this contract moving from left to right on the chart. This increase is due to the time approaching expiration, but also due to the fact that the summer of 2007 was a volatile market (although basically all summers are volatile in the wild world of beans).

Figure 3-4:
A simple example of how open interest is created.

Open Interest

Day	Action	Open Interest
Day 1	A buys 2 contracts and B sell 2 contracts	2
Day 2	C buys 4 contracts and D sells 4 contracts	6
Day 3	A sells his 2 contracts and D covers 2 contracts	4
Day 4	C sells 4 contracts and A buys 4 contracts	4

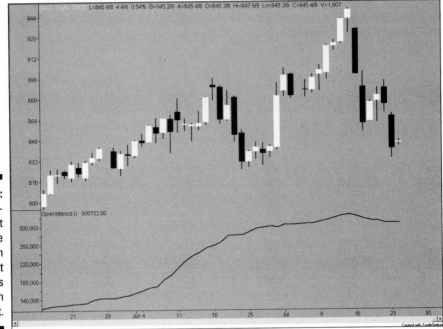

Figure 3-5:
A candle-
stick chart
of the
soybean
market
futures
with open
interest.

As beans topped out, so did open interest. That would've sparked some traders to sell beans, because there were fewer new participants coming into the market at higher prices. The same would be true if beans had been dropping dramatically. Either way, a reversal of open interest along with a reversal of certain candlestick patterns (more on those in Parts II and III of this book) are two items worth looking out for when considering a trade.

Technical indicators

Numerous technical indicators may automatically appear on the charts you generate. Technical indicators are ways of analyzing current trends in the market in hopes of being able to predict future trends. You can usually expect to see some sort of average of closing prices (a moving average), and possibly another basic technical indicator, on a chart. Don't let them rattle you, because you can remove them if you want, or — even better — alter them to your personal preferences. (I discuss a variety of technical indicators in detail in Part IV.) Take a look at Figure 3-6 — a chart that includes a moving average, one common type of technical indicator.

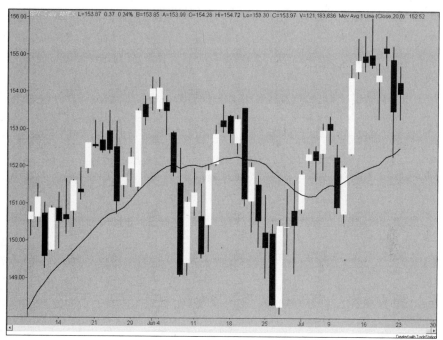

Figure 3-6:
A chart that
includes a
moving
average.

Among the different types of technical indicators are those that need their own space on a chart, much like volume or open interest. Figure 3-7 is a chart with a technical indicator known as the relative strength index (RSI) on the bottom. The RSI indicates the trend of price movements. (RSI is covered in depth in Chapter 13.) The crooked line is the calculated RSI; the lines at 30 and 70 are permanent and signify where a market is considered overbought or oversold (more on that in Chapter 13, as well).

As you can see, the RSI takes nothing away from the rest of the chart and actually provides some useful additional information that you can take into consideration when making chart-based decisions.

Fundamental information

Charts containing fundamental information aren't particularly common, but the addition of that information can be extremely useful. Fundamental information can include dividend dates, earnings release dates, stock splits, and the number of days people with inside information (*legal* inside information) may have bought or sold stock. This info relates almost exclusively to charts of stocks, so I stick to stocks in this section's discussion.

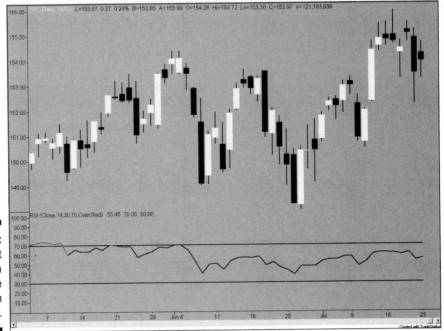

Figure 3-7:
A chart that
includes a
relative
strength
index (RSI).

Needless to say, monitoring how a stock performs around the time dividends are paid or earnings are reported is helpful. If some patterns tend to repeat themselves, trying to trade around these dates may be a profitable strategy. Also, keep an eye on how stocks are bought and sold by company officials who have an intimate knowledge of their company's business activities.

Dividend dates

The usefulness of dividends as a way of making a profit on the market comes and goes. Sometimes investors are focused on buying stocks for their dividend yields, and other times price appreciation is a much more lucrative endeavor. Like all market cycles, dividend paying stocks fall in and out of favor, and the focus on dividends waxes and wanes. For now, though, it's very possible that some stocks that pay higher than average dividend yields trade in a certain pattern around their dividend dates. If the dates on which dividends are paid are noted on your charts, you may very well be able to recognize a pattern that surrounds these dates and buy or sell to profit from it.

Deciphering dividend dates

When it comes to dividends, consider four important dates:

✔ The date the dividend is declared by a company

✔ The date the stock trades with an adjustment for the dividend, or the ex-dividend date

If you own a stock the day before the ex-dividend date, then you receive the dividend. If you buy it on the ex-dividend date, you don't receive the dividend. For trading purposes, focus on the day before the ex-dividend date, because that's when you want to own the stock to receive the dividend.

✔ The record date, two trading days after the ex-dividend date, which is the date on which the owners of a stock are identified as eligible to receive a dividend

✔ The payable date, which is when you get your dividend check

For an example, look at the following dates for the second dividend paid by IBM in 2007:

- Declared   4/24/2007
- Ex-Date   5/8/2007
- Record Date   5/10/2007
- Payable   6/9/2007

Earnings dates

During each quarter of the year, companies are required to release a summary of their earnings for the previous quarter. These numbers are usually distributed via press releases, which are quickly picked up by news wires and the financial press. Traders react to the resulting news. The press releases are usually followed an hour or two later by conference calls that feature members of the companies' management teams answering questions from industry analysts regarding the recently released earnings. These calls are important, because the outlook for the company is typically discussed in detail.

These earnings release dates are by far the most important four days of the year for many companies, and their stocks are usually at their most volatile just before and after the subsequent conference calls. At the very least, if you're interested in trading a particular stock, be aware of when the company is scheduled to release its next earnings report.

In a charting capacity, seeing how the stock trades before and after earnings dates can be useful for trading decisions. For example, if a company generally trades higher going into its earnings release, buying a week before the earnings date and selling the day before may be a profitable strategy. Also, if a company usually reacts strongly to its earnings announcements (either good or bad), but seems to reverse this move a few days later, this can lead to a good short-term trading strategy. Either way, it should be clear that having earnings date info on the charts you use isn't a bad thing, and it can set you on the path to making a nice profit, if you can spot a usable pattern.

You can find numerous sources for earnings dates or earnings calendars on the Internet. The following are links to a few of the better (and free) ones:

- Earnings calendar at Yahoo! Finance:

  `http://biz.yahoo.com/research/earncal/today.html`

- Marketwatch.com's earnings calendar:

  `www.marketwatch.com/tools/calendars/earnings.asp`

- Briefing.com's earnings calendar:

  `www.briefing.com/Investor/Private/Calendars/Earnings Calendar.htm`

- Earnings.com's calendar:

  `www.earnings.com`

Stock splits

Sometimes when the price for a stock reaches a high level, a company announces that it's paying a stock dividend or splitting the shares in two. The timeline for a stock split is very similar to that of a dividend, and split information is sometimes included on charts. A company will announce a split, which is usually considered a positive event for the stock. The announcement indicates what type of split it is (2 for 1, 3 for 1, and so on) and the date that the split will be effective.

That date is the day that shareholders own more shares at a lower price, and it's the date that's noted on a chart, typically with a big letter *S* or a note about the type of split.

So how does splitting work for you? If you own 10 shares of that stock, you own 20 on the split date. The price of the stock is usually adjusted accordingly. For example, if a stock is trading at $100, and the stock splits so each share held becomes two shares, that's considered a 2 for 1 split, and the price of each new share is then $50. The dollar amount is the same, but the number of shares is increased.

Splitting shares allows for more broad ownership of a stock. Many people can afford to buy 100 shares of a stock that trades for $15 a share ($1,500); few people can afford 100 shares of a stock that trades for $200 a share ($20,000). The idea is that the more broad the ownership, the better the performance of shares.

Stock split information on a chart is useful when a company's stock has had recurring reactions to stock splits. Generally, a stock rallies after the news of a split, although whether this fact is logical is debatable, because a stock split doesn't necessarily mean that something has fundamentally changed within the company. Unfortunately, the announcement of a split isn't common on a chart. But since the date the split is effective is generally available, you can easily focus on how the stock trades leading up to the split and afterward, and make appropriate trading decisions.

Insider trading: the legal kind

Legal insider trading — not the kind of insider trading that results in executives wearing handcuffs on the evening news — is the trading activity of company executives in their company's stock. In this context, an *insider* is anyone officially associated with a company, or even an owner of 10 percent or more of a company's stock.

The option to buy stock can be a major part of the compensation package for employees of public companies. From the company's standpoint, it makes sense to offer employees another incentive to work hard for the financial well-being of the company and the strength of its stock. Employees of a company may also buy stock in the open market when they believe the company's prospects are bright.

Owners of 10 percent or more of stock may have access to some information that you may not have. You can't blame them if they make decisions on buying or selling that stock based on their insider information. However, by law they must report this trading activity within a few days of making such transactions, and the resultant data is public and sometimes ends up on charts!

On the flip side, at times, employees who own shares may choose to sell. It's a bit tricky, as the stock may be sold for personal reasons — a major purchase like a home or child's college education, for example — or it can be a signal that an employee believes a stock's price has reached a level where it's prudent to sell shares. In this case, following an insider's lead and selling that stock may prove profitable or help you avoid a loss.

To see what insider trading information looks like on a chart, take a gander at Figure 3-8.

When insider trading information is included on candlestick charts, the indications of insider activity are usually very easy to read. In Figure 3-8, the *B* indicates insider buying, and the *S* indicates insider selling. (Splits also use the *S*. But splits normally have a 2 for 1 or some numbers along with the split. It really varies from chart service to chart service.) Some other charts use up arrows to indicate buying and down arrows to indicate selling. This chart includes buying in September and selling in October. It appears the insiders in this company do a very good job of trading their own stock!

Trying to trade along with insiders has such a following that not only does insider trading information appear on some charts, but also services and newsletters are devoted to disseminating the information. One service, InsiderScore, even ranks individual insiders by how well they have bought and sold shares in the past!

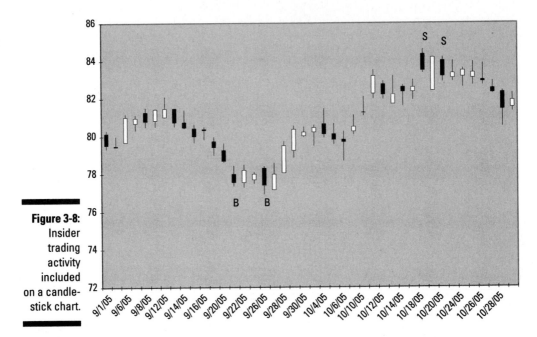

Figure 3-8:
Insider
trading
activity
included
on a candle-
stick chart.

Do an Internet search for *Insider Trading Newsletter,* and you'll get more results than you'd know what to do with.

Chapter 4

Using Electronic Resources to Create Full Charts

*A*fter you're armed with an understanding of why candlestick charts are so useful and what it takes to create a candlestick, you're ready to spread your wings and do some charting. You can take the appropriate data and build a chart in many different ways, and in this chapter I provide you with some insight on the easiest and least expensive ways to do just that. I begin the chapter with the easiest method, which is to let a candlestick-friendly Web site do the heavy lifting. And the sites I describe will do it all for free, if you're willing to put up with a few banner ads (a small price to pay for some very handy services).

After taking a look at some free online options for candlestick charting, I present the basics of creating candlesticks using Microsoft Excel. Candlestick charting has caught on so quickly that it's now a standard feature in Excel's charting section. Finally, at the end of the chapter, I cover a few of the best low-cost charting packages that are widely available and make sense for individual traders and, to a lesser extent, investors.

One quick note for those of you who are left-handed. I use right-click versus left-click in some of the instructions in this chapter. Please keep in mind that I'm right-handed, so I'm referring to the way I would be clicking a mouse. If you happen to be left-handed and have the mouse set up specifically for a left-handed user, remember that when I say to right-click, readers with adjusted mouse settings need to left-click.

Turning to the Web for Candlestick Charting Resources

Like so many other areas of life, trading and technical analysis have been greatly impacted by the Internet over the past few years. You can visit multiple Web sites where you can get low-cost or even free financial information, and, of course, candlestick charts are included. A quick Internet search on candlestick charts produces more results than you'll know what to do with.

In this section, I cover a handful of the best Web sites you can use to view candlestick charts, showing you how to create charts on these sites and pointing out other various features you can find there. Each of the sites mentioned are excellent for obtaining free charts but also have a plethora of other information you can use to help you make better trading and investing decisions.

Using Yahoo! Finance for charting, trading, and investing

If you're looking for a free, user-friendly Web site that's packed with useful information, steer your Internet browser to the finance section of Yahoo! This dynamic site offers many features that greatly enhance your charting experience, including the ability to download free data that you can manipulate however you want. And just like all good charting packages, Yahoo! makes candlestick charting available to all users.

In addition to charts, Yahoo! Finance offers a variety of information on stocks and markets that can provide you with enormous amounts of data, company fundamentals, and even message boards full of both rumors and facts. It's all just a few clicks away.

Creating a candlestick chart on Yahoo! Finance

Using Yahoo! Finance to build a candlestick chart is a breeze. All you need is a computer with an Internet connection. To generate a chart, work your way through the following steps:

1. **Get to Yahoo! Finance from the main Yahoo! page by clicking Finance or by using the URL** `www.finance.yahoo.com`.

2. **Enter the symbol of the stock or index you want to chart in the bar to the left of the Get Quotes button, and then click that button.**

   That click takes you to an information page for the stock or index you've chosen.

If you don't know the symbol of the stock or index, simply click Finance Search to the right of the Get Quotes button.

3. **After you're on the information page, click Basic Chart in the blue box on the left of the page (Technical Analysis is another possible choice that you can visit later to explore more of Yahoo!'s charting features).**

A basic line chart appears, with clickable options for making changes to the chart. The categories are for Range (time), Type, Size, and Scale.

The scale of a candlestick chart can be either linear or logarithmic in the way its pricing data is displayed. A linear chart displays prices without any adjustments. A logarithmic chart adjusts data in order to better depict performance in an investment (long-term) scenario. Logarithmic charts make sense for long-term investing, but aren't very useful on, say, a daily chart of stock prices that's used for trading.

4. **Select the Range (from one day to five years) you prefer, and then click Cdl, for candlestick, as the Type.**

It's as simple as that! After you've completed these easy steps, you should see a beautiful candlestick chart that looks very similar to Figure 4-1.

Figure 4-1: A candle-stick chart created on Yahoo! Finance.

If on Step 3 you opted to click Technical Analysis instead of Basic Chart, you'd have a number of other choices, including

- ✔ Moving Avg (various moving averages)
- ✔ EMA (various exponential moving averages)
- ✔ Indicators (various indicators)
- ✔ Overlays (indicators that show up on top of the price chart)

I encourage you to play around with these until your hand is cramped. There's no better way to master the ins and outs of charts than manipulating them and looking at as many as you can. You can also flip to Chapter 11 of this book for more info on technical analysis and the ways you can combine those methods with your candlestick charts.

I like the Yahoo! Finance site for many things, but the flexibility of its charting is somewhat limited. For example, my favorite time period is a three-month daily chart, and Yahoo! currently doesn't offer a three-month option. However, a beta charting package is being tested, and I'm confident that the functionality of Yahoo!'s charts will be expanded in the near future.

Checking out Yahoo! Finance's other useful features

If you want to take advantage of Yahoo! Finance's other resources, spend some time examining the information page for a specific stock:

1. **Get to Yahoo! Finance from the main Yahoo! page by clicking Finance or by using the URL www.finance.yahoo.com.**

2. **Enter the symbol of the stock or index you want to chart in the bar next to the Get Quotes button, and then click that button.**

   That click takes you to an information page for the stock or index you've chosen.

In the blue box on the left of the page, you can find many sources of data and other handy functions. Among them is a unique feature that Yahoo! provides for accessing historical daily opening, high, low, and closing price data, with volume information that you can download into Microsoft Excel using the Historical Price choice. (Skip ahead to "Creating Candlestick Charts Using Microsoft Excel" later in this chapter for more info on how to work with candlesticks in Excel.)

For another informative and sometimes fun area of Yahoo! Finance, check out the Message Board section. This area includes discussions that focus on specific stocks. In the case of some controversial companies, the discussions can be pretty heated, to the point of being amusing. But the boards aren't just good for lively conversation. They're also a good place to turn for information and rumors if a stock's price is moving without any apparent reason.

To top it all off, Yahoo! allows you to build your own portfolio, which you can use to monitor news and prices for any stocks you specify. You can also access real-time quotes — most quotes available on the Internet are delayed — for a small fee, and take advantage of excellent financial calendars for upcoming earnings and economic statistics.

Working with BigCharts.com

BigCharts.com is a charting site affiliated with MarketWatch.com, an excellent financial site that offers a ton of free information. For charting purposes, I suggest going directly to www.bigcharts.com.

Creating candlestick charts on BigCharts.com

BigCharts.com is easy to navigate, and with just a few clicks you can generate terrific charts. To create a candlestick chart, take the following steps:

1. **Go to www.bigcharts.com.**

2. **Enter a stock symbol in the bar at the top of the page and click Advanced Chart.**

   That click takes you to a page that features a one-year bar chart for the stock you entered.

3. **Click Chart Style on the left side of the page.**

   A few drop-down menus appear.

4. **Select Candlestick from the Price Display drop-down menu.**

5. **Select your preferred range from the Time drop-down menu.**

6. **Click the orange Draw Chart button, and a candlestick chart should appear in seconds.**

   If you follow these steps, you should end up with a candlestick chart similar to the one shown in Figure 4-2.

After you've mastered setting up a basic candlestick chart on BigCharts.com, I suggest playing around with the various buttons and drop-down menus that appear on the left side of the page. You can choose from several technical indicators and a wide range of time frames, and you can increase or decrease the size of your chart.

Figure 4-2:
A candle-
stick chart
created on
BigCharts.
com.

BigCharts.com offers interactive charts that can be fascinating and useful. Interactive charts are a Java-based feature allowing you to scroll over your chart to display additional data. You can also use them to draw your own trendlines, which many traders find very useful.

Using a couple of other great (and free) features of BigCharts.com

In addition to its free services, BigCharts.com boasts a number of functions and areas that require payment for access. Plenty of information about those options is available on its site, but I want to highlight two more of its free features, which won't cost you any of your hard-earned trading profits.

On the page where you can view the candlestick charts you generate, look just above the chart to find several choices for more information. One click gives you access to news, other industry members or competitors, market advisor commentary, analysts' opinions, SEC filings, insider activity, as well as recent annual reports and company profiles.

Also, if you're willing to register (registration is free) then you can set up your own portfolio, view message boards geared specifically toward your favorite companies, and sign up for alerts, which e-mail you automatically to let you know about price changes and news.

Charting on CNBC.com

In recent years, CNBC has become a primary source for market information on television. The folks at CNBC have also put a lot of effort into their Web site, which offers charting functionality in addition to the content that relates to their TV programs.

The charting function on CNBC.com is easy to use, and the professional functions allow you to do things like compare securities and overlay technical indicators. One downside is a lack of flexibility, but the site is being constantly updated, and more flexibility can emerge in the future.

Generating candlestick charts on CNBC.com

Here's how to take advantage of CNBC.com's free candlestick charting offerings:

1. **Direct your Internet browser to www.cnbc.com.**

   Near the top of the page, you'll see a box for entering a symbol, with the links Quote and Chart directly above it.

2. **Click Chart, enter your symbol, and click the Go button to the right of the box.**

   You should see a line chart for the stock you entered.

3. On the Chart Style drop-down menu, select Candle.

The chart is refreshed, and a candlestick chart appears in place of the line chart. After taking all these steps, you should end up with a candlestick chart like the one shown in Figure 4-3.

Figure 4-3: A candlestick chart created on CNBC.com.

CNBC.com gets an A+ for its chart-making simplicity. You can also choose from many time frames and indicators, and you can even add flags to the chart for events like earnings releases, stock splits, and dividend pay dates.

Another attractive feature is the ability to add notes to your charts, such as, "I should have bought this stock right here" before a big up day. Of course, notes aren't any good if you can't save your charts, but CNBC.com has that covered, too. Register at their site (basic registration is free), and you can save your charts *and* your chart settings, so you don't have to select every last option each time you return to the site.

CNBC.com also offers additional information on the companies you select, including news, profiles, earnings, recommendations, and competitors' stats. You can also click the Peers tab to see a graphical representation of some peer companies. The Financials tab provides a quick overview of the company's financials on both an annual and quarterly basis, and the Ownership tab gives an overview of the company's owners, some insider holding information, and a graphical breakdown of insider activity.

Tapping into CNBC.com's other useful features

Since the Web site's revamping in 2007, many CNBC anchors have blogs that feature entries on their specific areas of expertise. You can also use the Investing Tools link, which includes the ability to create a portfolio watch list and perform some stock or mutual fund screening, all at no cost to you.

Because CNBC is a successful financial television franchise, CNBC.com is loaded with video highlights and other ways to review the issues discussed on CNBC during the trading day. Unless you're a professional trader and you have CNBC on all day, it may be of interest to you to catch up on their Web site to see what professionals are focusing on.

Using Reuters.com for candlestick charting

Reuters is a world renowned source of financial information. Its Web site is very much geared toward professionals, but that doesn't mean that it can't be useful for newcomers to the candlestick charting game. Also, Reuters is truly a global organization, so its site is great for looking up information on foreign stock markets and currencies.

How to candlestick chart with Reuters.com

Take the following steps to create a candlestick chart of your own on Reuters.com:

1. **Go to www.reuters.com/investing.**

   You'll see several choices on the left side of the page.

2. **Click Stocks, and the Stocks Information page opens.**

3. **Type your stock symbol in the box next to the blue Go button.**

   Make sure that the button next to the word Symbol is checked, and choose Chart from the drop-down menu.

4. **Click the Go button.**

   That gives you a one-year line chart, under which are a few buttons that indicate the types of charts that you can draw.

5. **Click the third button from the left — the one with the familiar candlesticks.**

6. **Choose your preferred date range from the button choices or the drop-down box on top of the chart.**

   You should be looking at a candlestick chart that closely resembles the example in Figure 4-4.

Figure 4-4:
A candle-stick chart created on Reuters.com.

Although at first glance there appears to be nothing significantly different about Reuters.com compared to the other sites I've mentioned in this chapter, there are some nice features on the site that I like:

- ✔ You can easily overlay the price action of key competitors or a market index.
- ✔ You can also overlay several customizable technical indicators.

Play around with the options on the site to find what looks promising and what works best for you.

Checking out Reuters.com's other useful features

Reuters's global scope means that the company's Web site presents a large amount of international information, including data on foreign markets, currencies, bonds, and commodities. When I'm traveling and need a quick update of global markets, I almost always turn to Reuters.com.

As a financial news source, the Business page on Reuters.com rivals many of the top financial newspapers. The site has a wonderful stock screener, which allows you to search for trading or investment ideas by searching on certain fundamental or technical criteria, and contains in-depth profiles of companies.

Creating Candlestick Charts Using Microsoft Excel

Microsoft Excel is an excellent tool for running all sorts of financial analyses. One of the great features of Excel is its charting tool, and, of course, that tool includes candlestick charts as one of its choices.

In this section, I explain the process for creating a candlestick chart with Excel, from finding and entering the data to building the chart. I even clue you in on a few ways to add some additional information to your Excel candlestick charts, including moving averages, trendlines, and volume data.

Finding the data for your chart

Before you can create an Excel candlestick chart, you need to compile the right data. There are multiple sources for data, and a quick Internet search can turn up dozens of options, some of which I explore earlier in this chapter. (See "Turning to the Web for Candlestick Charting Resources".) Of those options, I typically use Yahoo! Finance for its ease of use, and that's the source I proceed with in this section. (See the section "Using Yahoo! Finance for charting, trading, and investing".)

To get the data into Microsoft Excel, follow these steps:

1. **Go to www.finance.yahoo.com.**

2. **Enter a stock symbol in the box at the top of the page and click the Get Quotes button.**

   For this example, I use IBM.

3. **In the blue box at the left of the page, click Historical Prices.**

4. **Above the data is a box labeled Set Date Range; use that to set the range of dates for which you want to obtain data, and to specify whether you want daily, weekly, or monthly data.**

   I chose June 1, 2006, to July 31, 2006, and daily data.

5. **After making your choices, click the Get Prices button just below the date choice boxes.**

6. **Scroll down below the data table and right-click your mouse on the Download To Spreadsheet link and select Save Target As.**

   A save box opens; save your file under My Documents, and use your symbol (I'll use IBM) for a file name. Make sure that you're saving as a Microsoft Excel Comma Separated Values file, and click the Save button.

7. **After the download is complete, click Close.**

   Congratulations! You now have the data needed to create a candlestick chart using Microsoft Excel! Now you just need to make a couple of minor modifications to the data and then create a chart. You're almost there!

Making sure the data is in the correct format

Unfortunately, Microsoft Excel needs your data to be in a very specific format, and, of course, it doesn't come directly from Yahoo! Finance in that format. You need to make some quick adjustments to make sure that your numbers are in order.

Basically Yahoo! gives you the right data but in the wrong order. Follow the steps below to reverse the data and get you ready for the fun part: building a chart! Follow these steps:

1. **In your saved Excel data file from Yahoo!, start by deleting the Adj. Close column.**

   To delete this data, click the column letter in the gray box above the word Volume (most likely column F) and drag your cursor to the next column (most likely column G). Both columns will be highlighted.

2. **While the columns are still highlighted, choose Edit and then Delete.**

   You're left with five columns of data: Date, Open, High, Low, and Close.

3. **Highlight all your data, and choose Data and then choose Sort.**

4. **Under Sort By, select Date.**

   Make sure the button next to Ascending is selected, and then click OK. The data is now ready for creating a chart.

Building an Excel candlestick chart

Excel is a great way to get your feet wet building a chart. It also gives you some experience as to what's behind the chart. Commercial packages that do all the work for you don't give you that type of experience.

At the time of this writing, I used Excel 2003, but I was just starting to work with the 2007 version. The 2007 version is quite a change from the 2003 version and is a little different to use. However, there are added features in the 2007 version that make it worth your while. Also, eventually, this new version will be the standard, and you won't have a choice. For now, as most people still seem to have the 2003 version, the examples use that version.

Now it's time to build a candlestick chart:

1. **Highlight all the data in your spreadsheet, without highlighting the headers.**

2. **Click Insert, and from the available choices select Chart.**

   Step 1 of 4 of the Chart Wizard appears.

3. **Under Chart Type, scroll down and highlight Stock.**

   To the right of this box appear four chart choices; click the top right one, which looks like a little candlestick chart.

4. **Click Next at the bottom of the dialog box, and then click Next at Step 2 of 4.**

   That brings you to Step 3.

5. **Click the Axes tab, and under Category (X) axis, click Category.**

   Also, make sure the Category (Y) axis button is checked. This step eliminates missing days (such as weekends and holidays) from your chart.

6. **Click the Gridlines tab.**

   Make sure there are no check marks in any of the boxes.

7. **Click the Legend tab and make sure that the box next to Show Legend is deselected.**

8. **Click Next to open Step 4 of 4.**

9. **Click the button next to As new sheet.**

10. **Click Finish.**

    A new sheet with a candlestick chart has been added to your spreadsheet!

Congratulations! You're now the proud owner of an Excel candlestick chart. Feel free to right-click the chart to view all the options available for your tinkering pleasure. For example, when you right-click one of the black candles, a Format Down Bars box opens, and you can change the color of all down bars (bars for days when the close was lower than the open). The opportunities for modification on Excel candlestick charts are many and varied.

For a point of reference, Figure 4-5 is a chart I created in Excel following the above instructions. If you made all the correct clicks, your chart should look very much like this example.

Although Excel's candlestick charting is a very nice feature, it doesn't allow for much flexibility. If you want to change time frames, for instance, you may need to completely rebuild your chart. But you can add in some additional information to make your charts more functional. How? Read on through the rest of this section to find out.

Adding a moving average to an Excel candlestick chart

If you're interested in dressing up your Excel candlestick charts with some added information, *moving averages* are a good place to start. A moving average is the average of the closing prices for today and looking back a certain number of days. For instance, a five-day moving average would be the closing today added up along with all the closing prices of the previous four days with that total divided by 5. The process is easy, and the result gives you that much more room to analyze and interpret. (Flip to Chapter 11 for more on moving averages.)

Follow these instructions to add a moving average to your Excel chart:

1. **With your candlestick chart sheet open in Excel (see preceding section), select Chart on the menu bar, and a drop-down menu box opens.**

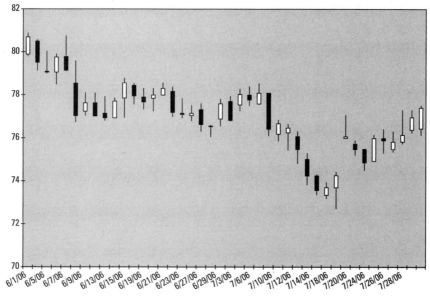

 2. **Select Add Trendline.**

    The Add Trendline box should open. There are six types of trendlines from which to choose. Highlight Moving Average at the bottom right.

 3. **In the Period box to the right of the Moving Average box, scroll the number up to 5.**

    This step provides you with a five-period moving average.

 4. **In the Based on series box at the bottom, highlight Close to ensure that your moving average is based on closing prices.**

 5. **Click OK at the bottom of the box.**

    Your chart should now contain a moving average. If you're using the same IBM data that I'm using, your chart should look like Figure 4-6.

Notice that the moving average doesn't start until the fifth time period. This is not usually the case in charting-specific software, just a quirk that appears on Excel. The problem with this quirk is that if you try to add a moving average with a large number of data points, it may end up looking like Figure 4-7.

You have to search a bit for this moving average. See it? It's the small line on the right side of the chart. The line is pretty short because this is a 30-period moving average, and as you can see, it's not very useful because it only appears on a tiny portion of the chart.

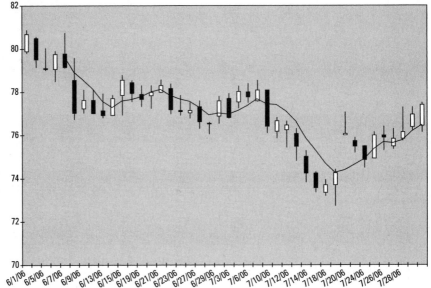

Figure 4-6:
A basic candlestick chart with a five-period moving average created in Excel.

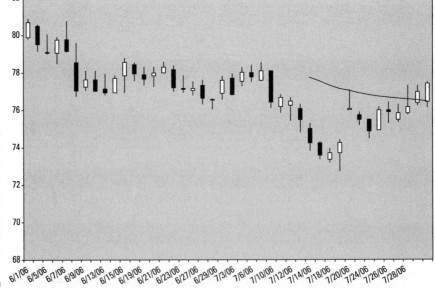

Figure 4-7:
A basic candlestick chart with a 30-period moving average created in Excel.

Adding a trendline to an Excel candlestick chart

Another function you can enjoy when using Microsoft Excel for charting is the *trendline* function. It's found in the same area as moving averages (see the preceding section), so if you can add a moving average, you can easily add a trendline. A *trendline* is a line that indicates the direction of a trend either higher or lower. The line is usually drawn based on the lows (in the case of an uptrend) or the highs (based on a downtrend) of the price action in the trend. For more information on trendlines and how to interpret them with candlestick charts, turn to Chapter 11.

But for now, get going on adding a trendline to your chart:

1. **With your chart sheet open in Excel, select Chart on the menu bar.**

   A menu box will open.

2. **Select Add Trendline to open the Add Trendline box.**

3. **Highlight the top left box, which is Linear.**

   This choice is the default, so it may already be highlighted.

4. **Click OK.**

   If you've continued using the data from the previous examples in this chapter, your Excel chart with an added trendline should resemble Figure 4-8.

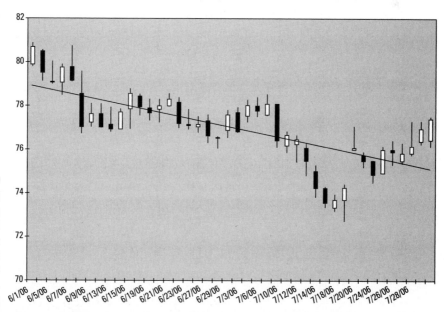

Figure 4-8: A basic Excel candlestick chart with a trendline added.

Adding volume data to an Excel candlestick chart

The most difficult type of add-on for Excel candlestick charts is a *volume chart*. There are a lot of additional steps involved with this operation, and if it gets to be too taxing, you may want to leave the volume charts to the free online charting services described earlier in this chapter or the charting packages discussed at the end of the chapter.

Formatting the data for your chart

In order to create a chart with candlesticks on top and volume on the bottom (the standard presentation), download the data from Yahoo! Finance in its raw form and then continue with the following:

1. **To begin formatting the data in the correct order (Date, Volume, Open, High, Low, Close), start by deleting column G (Adj. close).**

2. **Highlight column B, click Insert, and select Columns.**

   All columns except column A (Date) will move to the right, and column B will be empty.

3. **Highlight column G, click Edit, and select Copy.**

4. **Highlight column B, click Edit, and select Paste.**

   Column B should now contain your Volume data.

5. **Highlight column G again, click Edit, and select Delete.**

   Column G will be empty.

6. **Highlight columns A through F, click Data, and select Sort.**

   Make sure that the Sort By choice is Date and the button next to Ascending is checked, and then click OK.

Creating the actual chart

Now you can make a chart with volume! The steps are very similar to creating the basic Excel candlestick chart:

1. **Highlight all the data in your spreadsheet.**

2. **Click Insert, and from the available choices, select Chart.**

   Step 1 of 4 of the Chart Wizard appears.

3. **Under Chart Type, scroll down and highlight Stock.**

   In the Chart sub-type, select the bottom right choice.

4. **Click Next, which takes you to Step 2 of 4.**

5. **Click Next to open Step 3 of 4.**

6. **Select the Axes tab and make sure that under Primary Axis then Category (X) axis the button next to Category is selected.**

7. **Select the Gridlines tab and make sure that all boxes are deselected.**

8. **Click the Legend tab and make sure that the box next to Show legend is deselected.**

9. **Click Next at the bottom of the box to advance to Step 4 of 4.**

10. **Click the button next to As new sheet and click Finish.**

The result should be a chart similar to Figure 4-9. Notice the overlap of the volume and the pricing data. You're almost finished, but to correct that overlap and make the chart more readable, you need to make some small adjustments.

Making the chart presentable

To make your chart fully readable, you need to adjust the range of the data on the left side of the chart by doing the following:

1. **Right-click one of the gray row number cells on the left side of your chart and click Format Axis.**

   The Format Axis box will open.

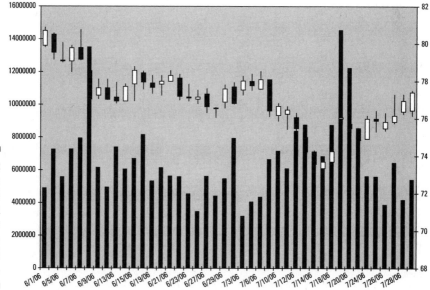

Figure 4-9:
A basic Excel candlestick chart with volume before final adjustments.

2. **Click the first two boxes under Auto to deselect Minimum and Maximum.**

   Make sure the Minimum is set at 0. For Maximum, take the default number and multiply it by 3. In my IBM example, the maximum is 16,000,000, so I would replace that with 48,000,000.

3. **Click OK.**

Your chart should now have the volume data clearly visible on the bottom and the pricing action set nicely at the top. Your final result should look like Figure 4-10.

Exploring Your Charting Package Software Options

I've spent my career working on institutional or professional trading desks, and I can confidently say that the tools available to individual traders have come to rival what the professionals use. You may want to consider making the relatively small investment to tap into an attractive array of charting and analysis options.

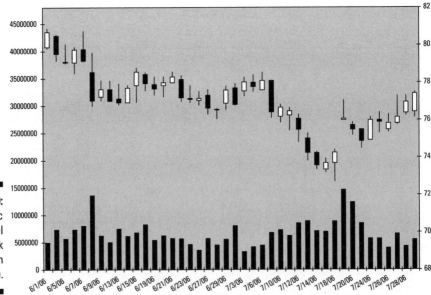

Figure 4-10: A basic Excel candlestick chart with volume.

Many low-cost charting software packages are available for download for your candlestick charting endeavors, and I could probably write a whole book about them, but for this chapter, I've chosen three of the most popular offerings. All three of these have a core group of users that argue the merits of their chosen software, but it's best for you to consider what each package offers and choose the one that best suits your needs.

Remembering a few key points when selecting charting software

When deliberating on which charting package may be right for you, you need to consider several key factors. First and foremost, make sure the software has the ability to display candlestick charts. This book is full of reasons why candlestick charting is a superior way to display price data, and there's really no reason to waste time or money with a package that isn't candlestick friendly. Some of the other factors you'll want to consider are price, data (where it comes from, what it costs, and so on), and applicability to the type of security you're trading. All are covered in this section.

Considering price

Price should be a primary concern when choosing charting packages. Any money you lay down for the software has to be recouped through trading. Although trading or investing may likely be more of a hobby than a business for you, you should approach the profit and loss aspect in a very businesslike manner. Suppose you're making an average of $2,000 a month trading, but you're spending $3,000 on systems and equipment. You may be having fun, but is it worth $1,000 a month?

Some charting packages can be downloaded at no cost, and then the providers charge you each month to use the service. Others charge you for the one-time download *and* for monthly service. Pricing for trading software ranges from around $50 to $1,000 per month, depending on the level of functionality you need. I pay about $200 per month for various services, and when tracking my trading profits, I deduct these expenses at the beginning of each month.

If you're planning to execute only a handful of trades per month, you may be happy with an offering on the low end of this range. On the other end of the spectrum, a trader sitting in front of a screen all day trying to make a living wants all the bells and whistles that come with a high-end system.

Determining data demands

Different charting packages offer various options in terms of the data you need to get the most from the software. For example, you can have access to data that displays price moves in periods as short as a minute or as long as a month. But if you're trading over the course of a few days, you don't need access to minute-by-minute data, and a chart made up of monthly data wouldn't be of much use. You would most likely want to use a chart that displays data in a daily format.

You also need to consider how "fresh" you need your data to be, and make sure that the charting package you're considering is adept at dealing with the right type of data. (By fresh, I mean data that's being updated as the trades occur, or "real-time" quotes.) If you're looking to work with trading time frames of less than a day, you may need real-time quotes, which can be costly. (Most of the free quotes you get online are delayed by 15 or 20 minutes.) And if you're going to be paying for real-time data, you want to make certain that your charting software is built to work with that kind of data.

The exchanges charge for real-time data, and some of the fees are much higher for professionals than for nonprofessional traders. There isn't much difference between the fees for pros and nonpros in the commodity exchanges, but the stock and option exchange fees for real-time data are based heavily on your professional status. Table 4-1 shows examples of the fees charged by TradeStation for access to various exchanges (see the section "TradeStation" later in this chapter). It provides a useful illustration of why you should be sure to sign up as a nonprofessional.

Table 4-1	Monthly Professional versus Nonprofessional Fees		
Exchange	*Professional*	*Nonprofessional*	*Difference*
American Stock Exchange	$30.20	$1.00	$29.20
NASDAQ (Level II)	$56.00	$10.00	$46.00
New York Stock Exchange	$127.25	$1.00	$126.25
Option Price Authority	$32.25	$3.00	$29.25

Factoring in what you'll be trading

Another consideration for your choice of charting software is what you'll be trading. Some packages are better equipped for handling stocks, and others are more compatible with futures or commodities. There's an 80-percent rule that you can use here. Get the software that's appropriate for 80 percent of the trading you'll actually be doing, not the trading that you hope to get into in the future.

You may want to see if international markets are available if you think you may expand in that direction in the future. Also, if you're considering trading options, the differences can be pretty dramatic. Make sure your focus is on how the software works with your markets of choice.

Considering a few charting package options

To give you an idea of the charting packages available for individual traders and investors, in this section, I highlight three of the most popular package options. By no means are these the only options available, but they've been around for quite some time, enjoy a wide user base, and offer conferences or classes where you can discover more about using the packages.

Each of the charting packages discussed in this section offer some sort of free trial. Take advantage of these risk-free test runs and don't limit yourself to just these three.

eSignal

I'm not sure if it's a positive or a negative, but the variety of offerings from eSignal can be a bit overwhelming. The company has several products that run the gamut of sophistication from programs for amateurs to intricate software made for the pros. The best way to illustrate the breadth of its product line is to examine its products' price range: Basic eSignal is as low as $95 a month, while the most expensive product — Advanced GET — can run more than $1,500 a month.

For novice purposes, focus on eSignal, the flagship product. It's more than adequate if you're just getting started with charting and trading. It also covers all domestic markets and allows you the choice of real-time or delayed data. And eSignal also offers free seminars all over the country where you can find out more about the product and charting in general, even if you don't use eSignal.

As a positive, the eSignal brand offers a full suite of very professional products, and as you work your way up to being a very successful full-time trader, you can also move your way up its product line. More information on eSignal's products can be found at www.esignal.com.

MetaStock

MetaStock is actually a product of Reuters, which I discussed earlier in this chapter. MetaStock offers what it calls real-time or end-of-day data, but it actually charges for its software platform, which starts at around $499. It also adds a monthly fee starting at $59.

The software is very expensive but very powerful and may be the most professional offering out there for individuals. MetaStock certainly has versatility going for it — the program covers virtually every market you would even consider trading in the world.

Check out MetaStock at www.equis.com.

TradeStation

One of the nice features that TradeStation has is the ability to back test trading strategies. One of the best methods for determining a trading plan is to back test your trading ideas. This process involves taking historical data and seeing what would've happened if you had applied and traded a set of rules to this data — sort of an "If I would've known then what I know now" approach.

TradeStation's back testing feature uses a programming language called EasyLanguage. It takes some time to master, but it has a wide user base, and classes are frequently offered online and at various sites across the country to teach this programming language.

After you find the strategies that allow you to retire young, you can use TradeStation's automated trading feature to implement these strategies. This function allows you to set up some trading systems in advance of when you want them to become active, and TradeStation takes care of the rest. It's a great option if you work during the day but still want to get in on some short term trading.

Go online to www.tradestation.com for info on TradeStation's charting package.

In addition to offering a very solid, easy-to-use charting software package, TradeStation is also a brokerage firm. It's actually a publicly traded brokerage firm, so you can trade with it or trade its stock, which has the symbol TRAD. You may be thinking, "Why do I care if it's also a brokerage firm?" Well, this is useful to know because if you use its brokerage arm for trading, you actually get to use their charting package free of charge (as long as you conduct a minimum number of trades each month; otherwise, the base price is $249 per month).

Part II
Working with Simple Candlestick Patterns

The 5th Wave   By Rich Tennant

"Sell."

In this part . . .

Many traders get interested in candlestick charting because of the usefulness of candlestick patterns for figuring out what a market or security is going to do next. In fact, there's a good chance that you picked up this book with hopes of tapping into the potential of candlestick patterns. If that's the case, you're going to love Part II.

This part is loaded with explanations of simple — one- or two-stick — candlestick patterns. I explain how to identify the patterns on a candlestick chart and how you can use them to make wiser trading decisions. All the discussions center on real world examples, so you can quickly see how these patterns play out in a variety of markets.

Chapter 5

Working with Straightforward Single-Stick Patterns

In This Chapter

▶ Taking advantage of purely bullish single-stick patterns

▶ Understanding bearish single-stick patterns and their uses

*I*t's time to begin diving into individual- and multi-period candlestick patterns. Many patterns give buy and sell signals, and some serve as a heads-up that a big move is on the horizon (although it's not always clear just what that big move will be!)

Most candlestick patterns are valid based only on the market activity of the previous few days. For instance, some patterns indicate a change in trend. Using one of these without knowing about the previous trend wouldn't be very useful. Usually, the context in which you find a pattern tells you a great deal about what you should do based on that pattern. There are, however, some single-stick patterns that are considered either bullish or bearish regardless of the context, and those patterns are what I focus on in this chapter.

This chapter explores the signals that may be given off from single-stick candlestick patterns, some bearish and some bullish. (The constructions of these patterns are covered back in Chapter 3 if you need to have a quick look at what's behind these patterns.) I demonstrate what may have happened during a particular day trading-wise to result in the formation of a significant single candlestick on your chart. (I say significant, because candlestick patterns are often used to forecast future price action.) I give examples of a candlestick signal working well and also cases where the pattern may not give such a positive signal. If you know how to recognize and trade on these examples, they should provide some reliable tools that you can add to your trading toolbox.

The Bullish White Marubozu

The most bullish of patterns is the long white candle. It represents a day during which the bulls controll trading and push prices higher from the opening to the closing. As the price moves up, sellers come in, but not enough to keep the price from continuing its rise. Any time sellers show up during this day, the buyers buy from them, and prices move higher. With the long white candle closing near the high, odds are the bulls aren't done with their buying and will be back for more on the following day. There just wasn't enough supply of stock by sellers to keep the buyers from pushing the price up.

The Japanese term for a long white candle is the *white marubozu.* There's a slight difference between a marubozu and a long white candle: The long white candle may have some wick exposed on both ends. A true white marubozu has either the opening price equal to the low for the day, the closing price equal to the high, or both. A long white candle may not have the open equal to the low or the close equal to the high, but its open should be near the low and the close near the high. A true white marubozu has either the opening price equal to the low for the day, the closing price equal to the high, or both leaving no wick.

The Japanese names given to certain candlestick patterns or individual candlesticks can reveal important characteristics. Loosely translated, marubozu means bald or little hair. These single-stick patterns earned their name because they don't have much of a wick on either end of the candlestick. The sticks are bald!

Due to the baldness, the marubozu is a unique type of white candle. There are several specific types of long white candles. Although they all depict bullishness during the day, there are some unique characteristics to keep an eye out for, which are covered in this section.

Understanding long white candles

One common feature of the long white candle (see Figure 5-1) is an open near the low of the day and a close near the high of the day. This indicates that buying has taken place throughout the day.

Figure 5-2 is an instraday chart of the price action that results in a long white candle on a daily chart. An *instraday chart* is a chart that depicts the price action during a time period that is less than a day, such as on a 5-minute or 30-minute basis. Each candlestick represents the price action for this subperiod of a day. The day that corresponds to Figure 5-2, which is the price action of a single day made up of 30-minute pricing periods, features an opening price near the low of the day and a closing price near the high of the day. A textbook long white candlestick has a long candle with no wick, but that doesn't happen very often, and long candles that have a little wick on either or both ends are still considered long white candles.

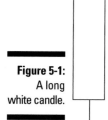

Figure 5-1:
A long
white candle.

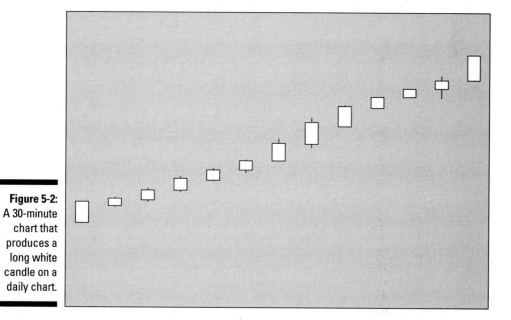

Figure 5-2:
A 30-minute
chart that
produces a
long white
candle on a
daily chart.

To figure out if you're looking at a long white candle, determine the area covered by the difference between the close and the open. If it's at least 90 percent of the area covered by the difference between the high and low, you have a long white candle.

For the day in Figure 5-2, the bulls were in charge from the beginning of the day to the end. There's just no disputing this, because the price does nothing but go higher over the course of the day, and the close is near the high of the day; the bulls will probably stay in charge for the near future. It's just that bullish. You usually have the chance to act on such a case because there may be some trading below the closing price of the long white candle in the next couple of days, and you can place a buy order lower than the closing price but within the range of the long white candle to try to get an attractive entry point.

On a long white candle day, a lot of price action is covered in a very short amount of time. Stocks — and markets for that matter — don't move in one direction without some sort of move in the opposite direction. This normal retracing of prices gives you a chance to act on this bullish signal.

The long white candle signaling an uptrend

Check out Figure 5-3, where you can see a few days where the price action is lower than the high of the long white candle. After seeing this bullish signal, you have several days to buy.

Sometimes signals don't work, and it's critical that you recognize this. With long white candlesticks, the low price on the candlestick is a good support level.

Support is a level where if market conditions are consistent, buyers are expected to support the price of a security. If this support doesn't hold, whatever buy signal you're dealing with has changed, and the signal shouldn't be acted on. In that case, you should exit your position fairly quickly. You may take a small loss, but getting out before prices fall even lower prevents you from taking a much larger loss later on.

Look again at Figure 5-3, where I point out the low of the day on the long white candle and also note that the price doesn't trade below that support level over the next few days. If you watch that stock and see that the support level is broken, you should consider that the bullish signal failed and no longer valid.

I can't stress enough that when a signal is no longer valid, any trades based on that signal should be exited, and no new positions based on it should be undertaken. Many small losers turn into big losers when the small loss isn't quickly realized and corrected.

The long white candle failing as a long signal

What happens when the support level revealed by a long white candle is broken? Take a look at Figure 5-4. This chart shows a nice long white candle and then a quick violation of its support level. The failure of this stock to hold support means that the long white candle on the chart doesn't mean bullish action is going to continue!

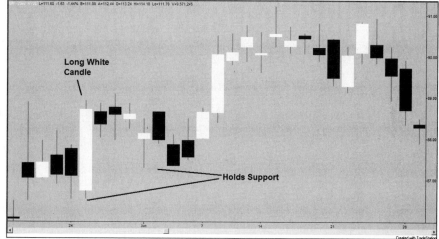

Figure 5-3:
A long white candle followed by a nice buying opportunity.

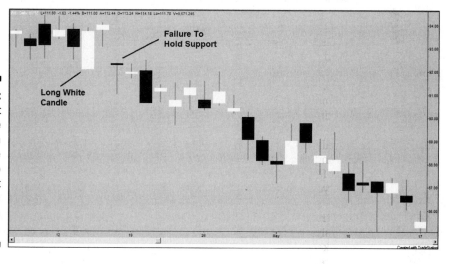

Figure 5-4:
A chart showing the failure of a long white candle to hold support and the resulting price action.

How do you cope with a failed signal? Take preemptive action. Place an order that triggers when a signal fails. This process is known as a *stop order*. When you're trading long, stop orders are known as *sell stop orders* or *sell stops*. A sell stop is placed below the current market price of a stock and triggered when the price reaches this level. For example, if a stock is trading at 51, you can place your sell stop order at 50. As long as trading stays over 50, nothing will happen. However, once the price hits 50, a sell order is executed, protecting you against further drops in price. Use stops when initiating positions to minimize the damage caused when a signal turns bad.

Identifying the three variations of the long white candle

There are three versions of the long white candle. Although slightly different in appearance, the three variations of the long white candle or marubozu single-day pattern all represent a day during which the bulls were in control from the open to the close.

The white marubozu

The first is the most bullish of them all: a long white candle with no wick. The day begins on the low and finishes on the high. This results in a white marubozu, or as my three-year-old would call it, a white rectangle. Check out Figure 5-5 for the result.

Figure 5-5:
A white
marubozu.

The closing white marubozu

The second version of the long white candle is another white marubozu, which is known as the closing white marubozu. On this single-stick pattern, the close is equal to the high, so there is no wick on top of the stick. Figure 5-6 is a closing white marubozu.

The opening white marubozu

The third variation of the long white candle is the opening white marubozu. This pattern's opening price is equal to the low of the day, and as a result, there's no wick on the bottom. Figure 5-7 is an opening white marubozu.

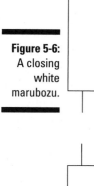

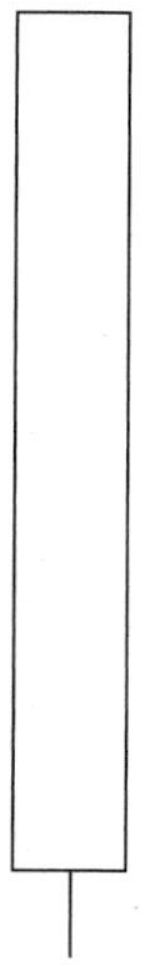

Figure 5-6:
A closing white marubozu.

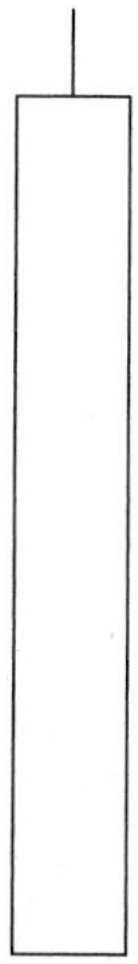

Figure 5-7:
An opening white marubozu.

The Bullish Dragonfly Doji

The *doji* is a type of candlestick pattern with variations and is created when the open and close are equal, so there's essentially no stick on the candlestick. Dojis are almost all wick. Take a look at Figure 5-8, which includes a few different types of dojis. As you can see, a doji looks more like a cross or a *t* than a pattern on a candlestick chart.

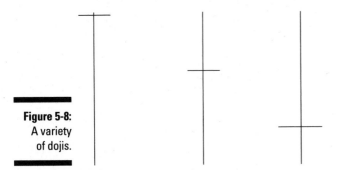

Figure 5-8:
A variety
of dojis.

Loosely translated, doji means *blunder* or *mistake*. It's said that the pattern got its name because a whole day's worth of trading just to end up back at the starting point seems like a goof, but price action isn't ever a mistake, so I'm not crazy about that explanation.

Although there are several varieties of dojis, you can count on them all to be fairly frustrating for traders. For a doji to be created, a day must begin and end with the same price, so a whole lot of trading takes place, but when it's all said and done, the price is right back where it started. Dojis are differentiated by the location of the open and close on the wick — where trading begins and ends on a given day.

At first glance, dojis may not seem very exciting, but don't be fooled. Doji patterns are usually associated with a market turn, even though they depict a day where the battle between bulls and bears is fairly equal. Even though the battle for the day is a draw, one side soon overpowers the other. It's like a prolonged tug of war that ends when one team is violently yanked into the mud. For the tug of war that's a doji pattern, that yank in price action usually occurs sometime in the next few days or even on the following day.

Although dojis do indicate some indecision, in some instances, a doji may be more bullish or bearish depending on the price action. A dragonfly doji is one of those cases. It is fairly bullish in nature due to the price action that is behind this pattern.

Recognizing a dragonfly doji

The dragonfly doji is unique in that three of the four candlestick components — the open, high, and close — are equal. A dragonfly doji comes from a day when a stock opens, trades down during the first part the day, and then at some point starts to trade back up, eventually closing on the high (which is also the open). In terms of bears and bulls, on a dragonfly doji day, the bears initially decide they're going to rule the day, and the resulting lower prices lead the bulls to decide it's time to buy. The bulls then take over and push the price up as they dominate the rest of the day, until the price is right back where it started. Refer to Figure 5-9 for a classic example of a dragonfly doji.

For an illustration of the inner workings of a day that results in a dragonfly doji, check out Figure 5-10. This figure features a 30-minute chart of the price action that occurs over the course of a day to cause a dragonfly doji. The bears dominate the first half of the day, but the bulls take over in the afternoon, and the result is a close equal to the open — all that struggling during the day for nothing.

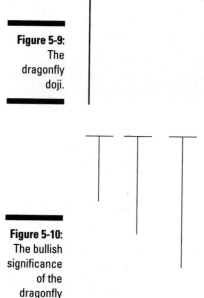

Figure 5-9:
The dragonfly doji.

Figure 5-10:
The bullish significance of the dragonfly doji.

Bullishness ⟶

The price action behind a dragonfly doji bodes very well for those hoping that prices go higher, because a price at which people buy aggressively has been set at the low end of the wick. The low of a dragonfly doji day is considered a near-term support level, because it's clear that buyers came in at that level and turned the trend from down to up.

The length of a wick from the high to low doesn't have to be any specific distance to qualify as a dragonfly. However, the wick length can signify the amount of bullish significance a dragonfly doji has for future price action. Put simply, the longer the wick, the more bullish the pattern. Figure 5-11 illustrates this point.

Figure 5-11 displays price action that creates a dragonfly doji on a daily chart. Dragonfly dojis appear when the open and close are very near or equal to the high, so the beginning and ending of this chart are equal. The price action during this day is very interesting. The bears take over from the open and push the price down. Eventually, though, lower prices entice buyers and they get aggressive, pushing the price back up to the open and settling on the high of the day.

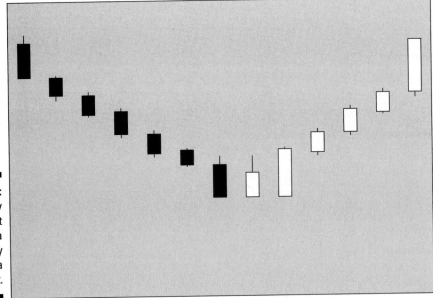

Figure 5-11: Intraday action that results in a dragonfly doji on a daily chart.

Trading based on a dragonfly doji

You can make smart trades based on the dragonfly dojis you see in your charts. Two charts can help:

✔ One in which a dragonfly doji indicates a nice buying opportunity

✔ One in which a dragonfly doji fails pretty badly

First the good one. Much like the long white candle I discuss earlier in this chapter, the dragonfly doji helps you establish a solid support level to buy with confidence. In Figure 5-12, notice how the bottom end of the dragonfly doji wick works as a support level, which is held as the security remains bullish for several days. The dragonfly doji appears after some range trading, and it's followed by a quick breakout of prices that reach new highs. Although the first day following the dragonfly doji shows an opening price lower than the previous close, the dragonfly's low price isn't violated, and the signal remains valid. Sticking with this valid signal leads to some nice profits!

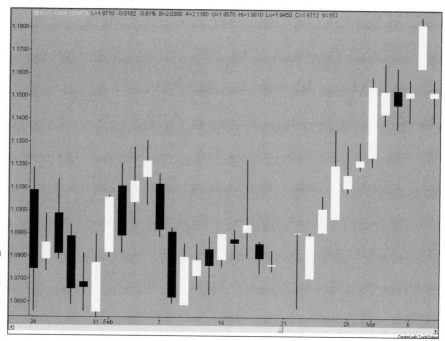

Figure 5-12: A dragonfly doji that pays off.

Now for a dragonfly doji that doesn't work out too well. The dragonfly that appears in Figure 5-13 looks promising, but it's followed the next day with a low that's lower than the bottom of the dragonfly's wick. And as you can see, the next moves are even lower.

The low of the dragonfly doji is a significant support level, but when that level is violated, it negates the dragonfly's buy signal. When a level is violated, get out as soon as possible.

The Bearish Long Black Candle

The long black candle is a direct counterpart of the long white candle discussed earlier in this chapter. It's a long candlestick compared to other candlesticks on the same chart, and most or all of it is made up by a solid candle.

The long black candle is as bearish as it gets. To see one of these candles means that sellers take over at the beginning of the day and push prices lower and lower until the end of the day. Typically, these sellers are just selling to get out, and their price sensitivity is low. Seeing this type of enthusiastic selling should give you confidence that the bears will be in control for a few more days after the long black candle appears, and you can capitalize on that.

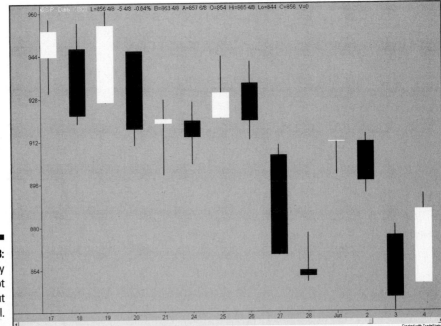

Figure 5-13:
A dragonfly
doji not
working out
too well.

Understanding long black candles

A long black candle is created when the bears seize control at the start of a day and push until the day's end. Figure 5-14 is a picture of a typical long black candle.

Figure 5-14:
A long
black candle.

For some quick insight on the numbers involved, have a look at Figure 5-15, which is an intraday chart of price action that creates a long black candle. Keep in mind that the figure is just one example, and that there are several other intraday patterns that can produce a long black candle on a daily chart. Basically, any pattern that begins near the high of the day and ends near the low of the day results in a long black candle, even if the action that got the price to the low occurred in just a couple of the 30-minute bars. The potential intraday action is limitless; the important thing is to know the bears pushed hard and down, and the bulls weren't able to hold up the price.

REMEMBER

The most important thing to *bear* in mind (pardon the pun) is that the long black candle indicates that the bears were in charge for the majority of a day. The day begins with the bears controlling the activity, and it ends the same way.

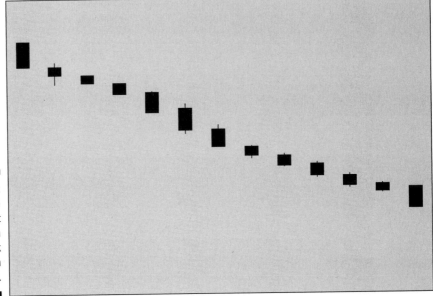

Figure 5-15:
A 30-minute
chart that
produces a
long black
candle on a
daily chart.

A useful rule of thumb for the long black candle is that the candle section should cover at least 90 percent of the candlestick. The wicks should be barely visible or completely missing.

The long black candle also usually indicates that many price levels have been covered over the course of one day. A reversal is very possible in the short term, but the long black candle shows the bears are being aggressive and suggests that this aggression will continue.

Identifying black marubozus

Like the long white candles described earlier in this chapter, there are marubozu versions of the long black candle, which are cleverly called *black marubozus*. The black marubozu features an open equal to the high and a low equal to the close. Figure 5-16 is a black marubozu, or as my toddler son would say, a black rectangle.

Just like their bullish counterparts, there are three variations of the black marubozu. Figure 5-16 is the first variation, which is a marubozu that opens on its high and closes on its low. The second is the closing black marubozu. You can spot a closing black marubozu by recognizing that there's no wick on the candlestick at the bottom or closing end of the candlestick. The close is equal to the low, while the open is a little bit lower than the high for the day. Figure 5-17 is a closing black marubozu.

Figure 5-16:
A black
marubozu.

Figure 5-17:
A closing
black
marubozu.

The third variation is the opening black marubozu. This pattern is created when the open is equal to the high of a day, and the close is just above the day's low. A small wick appears only on the bottom of this candlestick. Figure 5-18 is an example of a typical opening black marubozu. The appearance of a small wick on the bottom of this candlestick indicates the possibility of some late-day buying or that the low price of the day enticed some buyers. This source of speculation leads some to regard the opening black marubozu as the least reliable of the three black marubozu variations.

Figure 5-18:
An opening
black
marubozu.

Trading based on long black candles

Now it's time to see how you can trade using long black candles in the real world. Figure 5-19 is near and dear to my heart because it represents a trade I actually executed while writing this book. This is a chart of the November soybean futures contract that trades at the Chicago Board of Trade. At the time, I wanted to take a short position in the soybean contract, but was waiting for a confirming trading signal or bearish chart pattern before I executed my position. The long black candle highlighted in Figure 5-19 provided the short signal I sought.

Getting a good bearish signal from a long black candle

I've noticed in the past that long white or black candlesticks are generally followed by continuations of their up or down moves more often with commodities than with stocks. Futures on commodities tend to have strong trends. This tendency makes me quicker to initiate a position in futures than in stocks. And by the same token, I'm usually quicker to concede that I'm wrong on a futures trade than on a stock trade. Keep these differences in mind and use them to your advantage. (Chapter 11 covers trends in more detail.)

Back to my soybean trade. For fundamental reasons, I was looking for a signal that told me to short the soybean futures contract. When I saw the long black candlestick on a particular day, I put on a short near the close of that day. I was quickly rewarded the next day, as another very bearish day followed.

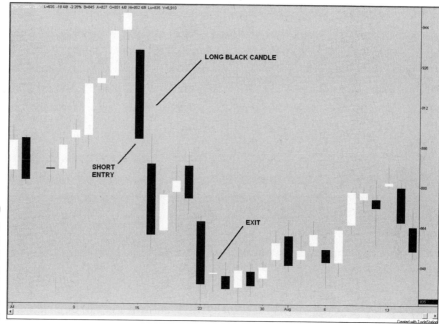

Figure 5-19:
A long black
candle that
provides a
nice sell
signal.

If things hadn't worked out as I'd planned, I still wouldn't have suffered big losses, because I also entered a protective order called a *buy stop,* which is the opposite of the sell stop mentioned earlier in this chapter (see "Understanding long white candles"). My buy stop level was the high of the long black candle — the resistance level that if broken, would negate the sell signal given by the long black candle.

Keep in mind that resistance levels are where chartists believe sellers will be brought into the market and keep prices from going higher. In candlestick charting, resistance is generally the highest level of one of the candlesticks that created a sell signal. After this resistance level is broken, the signal isn't considered valid anymore.

Luckily, that level was never reached, and the trade turned out to be a profitable one. I continued to monitor the short position from day to day and exited on the day indicated on the chart. The pattern for that day is a regular doji, which often signals the reversal of a trend. I cover regular dojis in more detail in Chapter 6.

A long black candle failing as a short signal

As with long white candles, and any candlestick patterns for that matter, long black candles don't always work out perfectly. Long black candles do fail, as you can see in Figure 5-20. In fact, this figure includes two instances of long black candle failures!

Figure 5-20 contains a chart of the futures contract trading on crude oil from the summer of 2007. If you were involved with any oil or other energy-related commodity trading during that time, you'll remember that shorting was a hard row to hoe then.

Two long black candles appear in Figure 5-20. Both fail. One crashes and burns after a few days, and the other follows suit the very next day. For clarity's sake, I labeled them #1 and #2:

✔ Long black candle #1 was followed by an up day, but this up day didn't break resistance or the high of the signal candle. It managed to stay below resistance for a few days before breaking out and then trading higher for several days in a row. Note that if you didn't get out of a short position on the day that resistance was broken, you never had a shot to get out at that level again. Without a protective buy stop at the failure level, your losses would've continued to pile up.

✔ Long black candle #2 doesn't work out too well either, but at least it failed quickly. The possibility for a successful trade was clearly over at that point, and if you were involved, you could've moved on to the next trade. The trait that #2 shares with #1 is that if you didn't exit when the resistance level was violated, you basically didn't have a chance to get out at a lower level to limit your losses. Your losing trade would've just gotten worse. Getting out of trades quickly is just as important as finding and executing winning trades.

The Bearish Gravestone Doji

The doji is one of the most significant candlestick formations and is created when the open and close for a day are equal. It doesn't matter where this occurs on a wick for a candlestick to be classified as a doji, but the location dictates what kind of doji it is.

Identifying the gravestone doji

When the open and close are both equal to the low of the day, the result is the most bearish of doji: the gravestone doji. Figure 5-21 is a good example of a bearish gravestone doji.

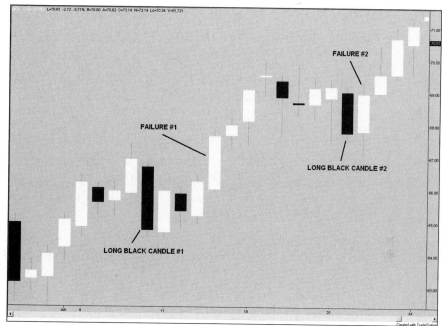

FAILURE #2

FAILURE #1

LONG BLACK CANDLE #2

LONG BLACK CANDLE #1

Figure 5-20:
A long black
candle as a
failing sell
signal.

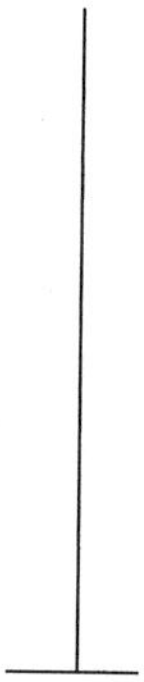

Figure 5-21:
A bearish
gravestone
doji.

The price activity that creates a gravestone doji begins and ends at the low of
a day. The progression for the day includes the following:

1. **A security opens and trades up during the day, as the bulls dominate
   the activity.**

2. **Higher prices attract sellers, and the selling becomes strong enough to
   overwhelm the bulls.**

3. **As the bears take over, the price is moved back down to the open,
   which was also the low of the day.**

Closing at this level after trading up during a day doesn't bode well for the bulls in the near term. Figure 5-22 provides an example of such a day, which would be a fearful one for the bulls.

Trading based on gravestone dojis

Take a look in this section at a couple of examples of gravestone dojis that have popped up in the real world and what happened afterward. The two examples I provide are for stocks, not commodities. The first example, which you can see clearly in Figure 5-23, is a gravestone doji that offered a useful sell signal followed by lower prices.

I included several days of price action to show a combination of interesting factors:

- ✔ First, notice that this gravestone doji signals the beginning of a pretty prolonged downtrend in the stock.

- ✔ Second, notice that during the downtrend, there are a couple of smaller gravestone dojis. If you'd shorted on the first gravestone doji and kept on the short position, you would've been pretty happy with the results. The appearance of a couple more bearish formations would've given you the confidence to maintain your short position.

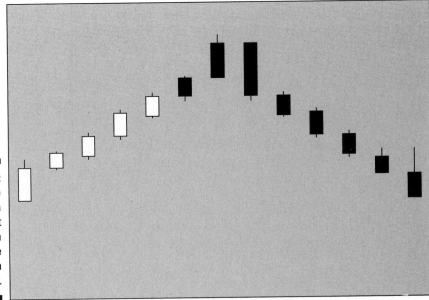

Figure 5-22:
A 30-minute chart of a day that creates a gravestone doji on a daily chart.

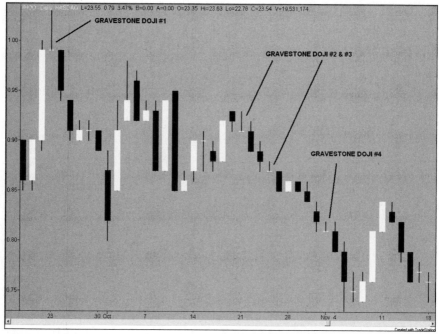

Figure 5-23: A great example of the gravestone doji working as a sell signal.

✔ Finally, there's a fourth gravestone doji toward the end of the downtrend. Notice that it fails fairly quickly, as the following day has a high equal to the original gravestone doji's high. If you'd ridden the stock price down to this level and seen a sell signal fail, it would've been time to buy the stock back, take your profit, and move on to the next trade. That would be a profitable outcome for you.

The next example shows what can happen if you're not as fortunate. Figure 5-24 is a chart of Apple Computer's stock (AAPL). A gravestone doji appears in the middle of the chart and during an uptrend. Dojis are often associated with a trend change, and seeing the bearish doji in an uptrend may be a signal of a trend change to the down side. Unfortunately for anyone trading this sell signal, things don't work out so well.

The gravestone doji is initially followed by a couple of down days, and it does appear that the trend may be changing. However, a couple of positive days put this trend change in doubt. A couple of days later resistance is tested and broken, and the uptrend continues. The sell signal failed, but a nimble trader would've placed a buy stop to limit the losses on this failure.

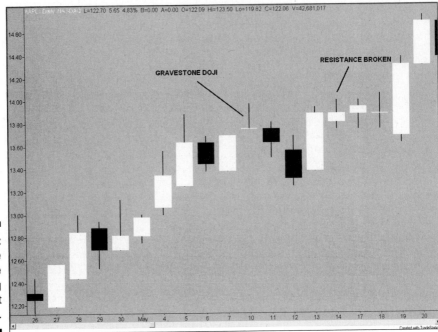

Figure 5-24:
The
gravestone
doji failing
on a chart
of AAPL.

Chapter 6

Single-Stick Patterns That Depend on Market Context

*I*n Chapter 5, I cover a few of the more basic and easily defined single-stick candlestick patterns, which are either bullish or bearish indicators regardless of their location on a chart. For those patterns, the price action that occurs during the previous few days just isn't that significant.

But not all single-stick patterns are that straightforward. Some extremely useful single-stick patterns rely heavily on their location on a chart. Making yourself familiar with these patterns and how to identify and trade based on them is another way that you can add a versatile weapon to your trading arsenal. That's what this chapter is all about. Also, context is essential to the single-stick patterns that are covered in this chapter. This isn't always the case, but for this chapter, you need to know the market environment before deciding if a signal or pattern is valid.

A variety of single-stick patterns can provide some terrific trading opportunities if you can spot them in the right market environment. I begin this chapter by quickly touching on how you can define a market environment, and then I cover some of the most significant single-stick patterns that you can exploit for profitable trading.

Understanding Market Environments

In order to take full advantage of single-stick patterns that rely heavily on the market context in which they appear, you first need to know how to quickly and effectively determine the market environment. Being aware of the current market environment is key to properly using most candlestick patterns in general, but especially for the ones I describe in the rest of this chapter.

The three market states

A market or stock is usually defined as being in one of three states:

- ✔ **Bullish:** Price behavior trending up
- ✔ **Bearish:** Price behavior trending down
- ✔ **Range bound:** No discernable trend

Deciding which of the three states a market is in can be as easy as looking back a few weeks on a chart and spotting a general direction or drawing a line that shows the market's trend. It may also be as complicated as using a technical indicator to reveal the direction of the market. These indicators are covered extensively in Chapter 11, but for this chapter, I use examples where the market trend is easy to decipher.

Identifying the market trend

For a quick visual representation of what an uptrend or downtrend looks like on a chart, check out these figures; it doesn't get much clearer. Figure 6-1 shows an uptrend.

Figure 6-2, conversely, shows a downtrend.

At times, the market environment may not be completely apparent or obvious. Either different people may see the trend or lack of trend in a different way or the time frames participants are using may cause different traders to have differing views of the trend or lack of trend. If that's the case, then pass on any trades you're considering. The uncertainty is just too high, and there will always be another trading opportunity in the future.

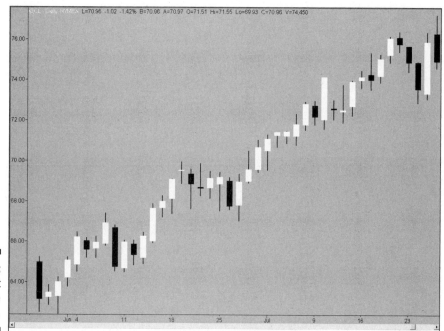

Figure 6-1:
A chart
with a nice
uptrend.

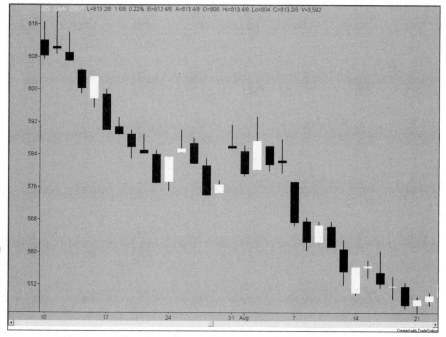

Figure 6-2:
A chart
with a nice
downtrend.

Delving Into Dojis

A *doji* is a single-stick pattern in which the open and close for a day are equal (see Chapter 5 for more discussion on dojis). This level of exactness is a rarity, though, and some candlestick chartists are flexible and say that if the open and close are very near each other, it's still considered a doji. I agree, although I do think that they need to be the same in the case of the dragonfly and gravestone — two dojis that are indisputably bullish and bearish, respectively. But there are other varieties of dojis for which the market context is critical, and I cover a few of the significant ones in this section.

Dojis are often associated with the reversal of a trend and can serve as outstanding reversal indicators. If a doji appears in an uptrend, it could very well indicate that the trend may be changing to a downtrend soon, especially if the doji is a gravestone doji. Likewise, if a doji (especially a dragonfly doji) appears during a downtrend, there's a good chance that things will look up soon.

The long legged doji

In addition to the dragonfly and gravestone dojis (covered in Chapter 5), one last doji is significant enough to merit a specific name. This one is cleverly called the long legged doji.

A long legged doji is considered a reversal signal when appearing in an uptrend or downtrend. This doji indicates that there has been much uncertainty in the market after a period of directional certainty. This change of conviction often results in a change in trend.

Identifying long legged dojis

The long legged doji has a fitting name: It features a small stick with very long wicks (or legs) on each end. The small candle on a long legged doji is normally located very close to the center of the candlestick. Check out Figure 6-3 for a classic example of a long legged doji.

In addition to its unique appearance, the long legged doji is singled out due to the unusual price action that causes the formation of this candlestick pattern on a daily chart. Figure 6-4 provides a look at a 30-minute chart that translates into a long legged doji.

Figure 6-4 just looks like a roller coaster ride. Imagine trying to trade during a day like that and ending up where you started. You can really lose (or win) big on such a day.

Figure 6-3:
A long
legged doji.

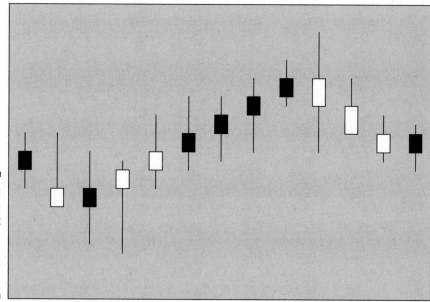

Figure 6-4:
A 30-minute
chart that
creates a
long legged
doji on a
daily chart.

If you've just started trading or don't feel quite comfortable with your trading abilities yet, it's probably best for you to steer clear of day trading on extremely volatile days. I've been trading for years, and I have taught myself to lay off the day trading when things are particularly hairy.

Using long legged dojis as buy signals

As I mentioned earlier in this section, the long legged doji may be a buy or sell signal depending on prior price action. In a downtrend, the signal can forecast a change to an uptrend and act as a buy signal, and in an uptrending market, the long legged doji can indicate that the uptrend is coming to an end and serve as a sell signal. I provide a couple of examples where a long legged doji is a good buy signal and then demonstrate where it doesn't work out too well.

The long legged doji giving a good buy signal

Figure 6-5 is a long legged doji that occurred in late 2002 on the futures contract of the Canadian dollar. It occurred after three very bearish days in a row and was followed by a very nice uptrend. This example shows how a long legged doji works when it signals the end of a down move. Unfortunately, I didn't trade this particular scenario, but I definitely will if I see the same pattern in the future!

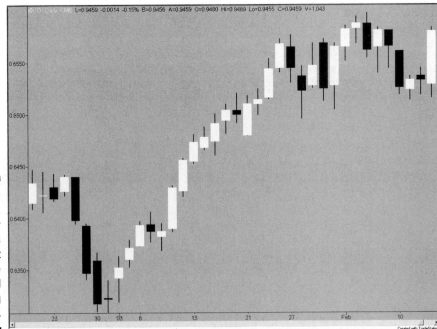

Figure 6-5:
Canadian dollar futures contract with a nice buy signal from a long legged doji.

Notice that the doji buy signal in Figure 6-5 works almost immediately — what's expected of a trend changing signal. If the signal doesn't seem to be working very quickly, beware.

Trading against a trend is a very dangerous prospect. You need to be sure you're prepared to take a loss and move on quickly to the next trade if things go sour.

A failing long legged doji

Now on to the bullish long legged doji that didn't work too well. In all honesty, it was difficult to find a good real-world example. The long legged doji is fairly rare, and when it shows up during a trend, it usually does signal an impending trend change. It does happen, though, and Figure 6-6 is an example of a long legged doji that didn't signal a change in trend.

Figure 6-6 features price action for a stock with a long legged doji showing up after a few downtrending days. The price trends up for the next day or two and things look fine, but then the long legged doji's low is broken, and the signal is no longer valid. If you were trading this stock and didn't get out at that critical point, where a stop order should've been placed or an exit trade should've been executed, you would've endured some pretty painful losses.

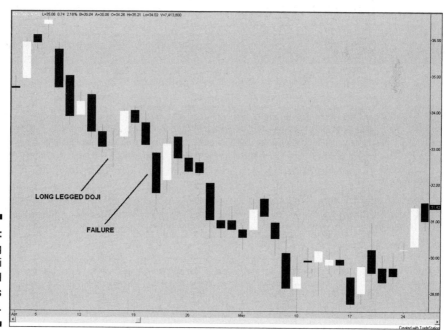

Figure 6-6:
A long legged doji buy signal that fails quickly.

Be sure you're prepared to get out of a trade immediately after the signal you're trading goes bad. Use that as a rule, and follow that rule regardless of how much it may hurt. To help me remember the importance of these rules, I taped the following quote from *Zen in the Markets* by Edward A. Toppel to the monitor on my trading desk: "You can break the rules and get away with it. Eventually the rules break you for not respecting them."

Using long legged dojis as sell signals

Just as a long legged doji that appears during a downtrend can be considered a buy signal or the end of the downtrend, a long legged doji that appears in an uptrend may be considered an uptrend reversal or sell signal that can be extremely helpful if you're looking to short a security.

Sometimes in the market no trend is obvious or exists. If you see a long legged doji during one of these times, do nothing. The long legged doji is only useful as a signal when it appears during a trend.

Seeing a good short signal on the long legged doji

Have a look at Figure 6-7 for an example of a long legged doji that provides a useful signal for shorting. This daily stock chart is for Gap, Inc. (GPS). The long legged doji appears in the middle of an uptrend. Notice that there wasn't much of a chance to get out of a long position, and although the opportunity to put on a short was definitely there, you would've had to have been on your toes to pull it off. The stock opened up slightly the next day, and then the bears took over and dominated most of the day. Even the bears that were late to the party toward the end of the day were rewarded with a substantial gap down the next day.

The long legged doji sells signal failing

As always, an example that didn't work too well is in order. Figure 6-8 is a chart of the futures contract that trades on the Canadian dollar. In the center of the chart is a nice long legged doji that appears in an uptrend that may seem to be rolling over. *Rolling over* means that the price action on a chart has been strong but is starting to top out. I've highlighted the uptrend and then where the price begins to roll over or top out. Toward the right side of this rolling price action, a long legged doji appears. Things look good for a little while, and then the high of the doji is overtaken, and the price is off to the races once again.

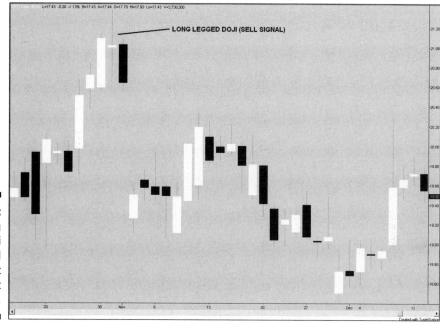

Figure 6-7:
A long legged doji sell signal on GPS that works out quite well.

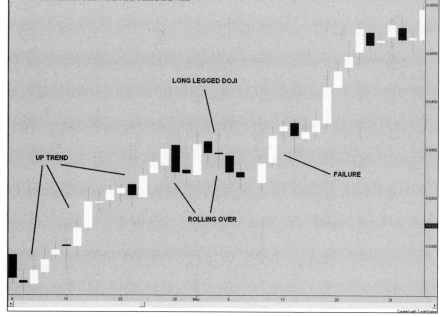

Figure 6-8:
A long legged doji sell signal on Canadian dollar futures that fails.

Other dojis

The long legged doji, bullish dragonfly doji, and gravestone dojis are powerful but rare. You're more likely to see a doji with an open and close that appear somewhere other than the center or one of the ends of a wick. These dojis are still useful as reversal indicators, and because they appear more often than the named dojis, they offer more trading opportunities. Figure 6-9 highlights a variety of dojis.

When evaluating a doji, I look for the candle to appear on the top half of the wick if I'm using the doji as a buy signal or on the bottom half of the wick if I'm using it as a sell signal. With the open and close near the high, I feel that the bulls are winning the day, and if the open and close are near the low, I feel that the bears are coming out on top.

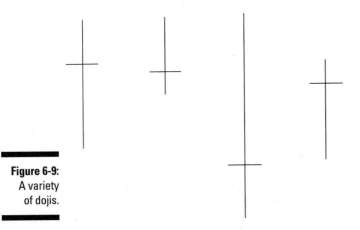

Figure 6-9:
A variety
of dojis.

Figure 6-9 looks like a chart that my three-year-old created while she was learning how to write the letter *t*. Basically dojis just look like *t*'s or upside down *t*'s.

Using regular dojis to trade long

Figure 6-10 is a chart of the stock Capital One Financial Corp. (COF). Notice the long doji on the left. After that doji, the stock takes off on a very nice uptrend. The doji is a great example because the candle that marks the open and close is clearly in the top half of the price action for the day. I really have more comfort buying a doji signal when the price closes near the high; I just feel that more bulls are on my side.

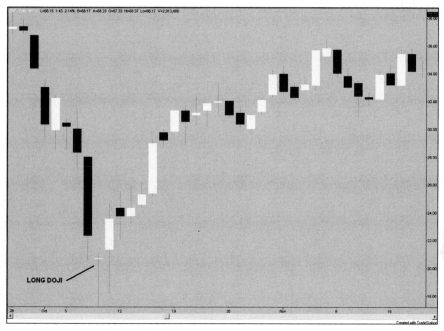

L=68.15 1.43 2.14% B=68.17 A=68.23 O=67.33 Hi=68.37 Lo=66.17 V=2,913,486

Figure 6-10:
A regular
long doji
appearing
on a chart
of COF.

LONG DOJI

Created with TradeStation

For an example of a failing doji signal, see Figure 6-11. It's a chart of the futures contracts that trade on the Japanese Yen. In the center of the chart is a doji appearing during a definite downtrend. The signal is negated the following day with a violation of the low of the day in which the doji appeared. Once again, if you traded this signal and you didn't call it quits after the violation and signal failure, you'd be in for a painful ride down.

Using regular dojis to short

Regular dojis work well in short or selling situations, too. Figure 6-12 shows a short doji formation in an uptrend that quickly reversed for a nice short selling opportunity in the U.S. Treasury bond futures. The short doji is highlighted, along with another doji. The day after the short doji, the rarest of all dojis appears on the chart: the four-price doji, which occurs when the open, high, low, and close are the same on a chart. This occurrence is very rare and usually happens on a very low volume day. The incidence may also represent a data error. In this case, having a source to double-check the data behind the chart would be very helpful. (See the "Data Integrity" sidebar in this chapter for more details.)

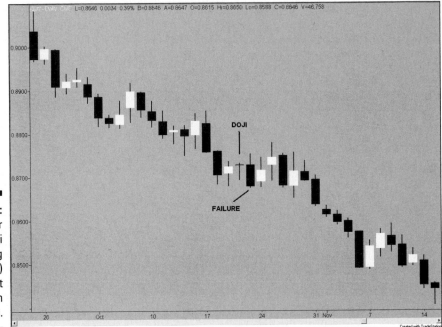

Figure 6-11:
A regular long doji appearing (and failing) on a chart of the Yen futures.

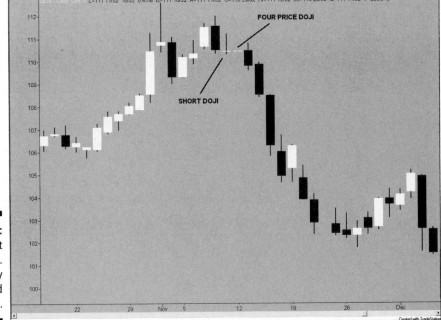

Figure 6-12:
A short doji on U.S. Treasury bond futures.

The signal doji in Figure 6-12 meets the criteria of appearing in an uptrend and then also appears to have the open and close in the bottom half of the day's price action. No violation negates the signal, and the signal is quickly followed by a downtrend lasting several days. I wish all my trades were so easy to identify and profit from.

Like all other signals, short dojis aren't perfect. Have a look at Figure 6-13, a chart of IBM. This figure shows two failures of a short doji signal within the span of just a couple of weeks. Both are highlighted on the chart, and both fail pretty quickly.

This leads me to another fact I've picked up over the years. Each market or stock may have its own individual trading characteristics. Although shorting a doji formation in an uptrend may be a highly successful trading method for the majority of financial instruments, there may be some out there who continuously shrug off this sell signal. Unfortunately, knowing what works well in various markets is just a matter of putting in time and gaining experience.

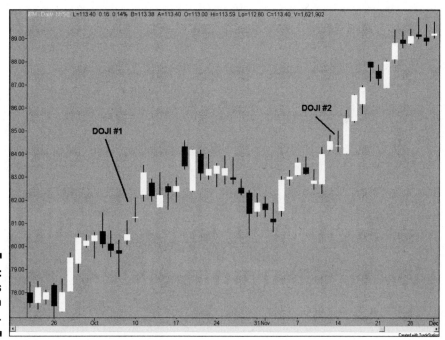

Figure 6-13:
Short dojis
failing on
IBM.

Data integrity

With so many financial products trading in the world today and so much data floating around, data errors are bound to occur. In the case of a four-price doji, having a second source to check the price action of the day is extremely valuable. As a professional trader, I use multiple charting software packages and data sources to assure that the data I'm using accurately reflects the price action that occurred in the past. With fewer resources, you may want to consult an exchange's Web site for data accuracy or free data sources such as Yahoo! (www.yahoo.com) or MarketWatch.com (www.marketwatch.com). (Flip back to Chapter 4 for more information about online and electronic sources of charting information.)

MarketWatch.com has a terrific function that allows you to enter a stock symbol and a specific date to check for accuracy. Either way, when you see some price action that looks out of place on a chart, doing a double check can save you frustration and money in the long run.

Looking At Other Patterns: Spinning Tops

Like the doji, the *spinning top* is another single-stick pattern that depends on market context and reveals a tight battle between bulls and bears. Whenever the bulls-versus-bears battle is close, eventually one side has to give, and when this happens, an explosive move in one direction is possible. My favorite analogy for that scenario is a coiled spring being pushed hard on both sides. Eventually one side gives in, and that's the direction the spring flies.

The key is picking the right direction, and considering the market environment where you find your pattern helps you make the right pick. For spinning tops or any other patterns that indicate a tight battle between bulls and bears, if the bulls have been in charge for some time leading up to the pattern, it usually indicates that the bears are starting to gain some strength. And the reverse is also true: If the pattern appears during a bearish trend, it generally indicates that the bulls are going to make a run (and you don't have to be in Pamplona to run with them).

Identifying spinning tops

To qualify as a spinning top, a candlestick should have a small body and wicks that stick out on both ends. The body should appear close to the center of the range of the day's price action. Also, the wicks should both be at least as wide as the candle section of the candlestick. For a clear picture of what a spinning top looks like, check out Figure 6-14.

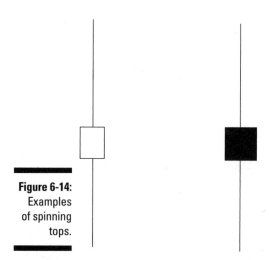

Figure 6-14:
Examples
of spinning
tops.

The color of a spinning top's candle isn't terribly important, although it's nice to see a dark body if you're expecting a reversal of an uptrend (sell signal) or a white body if you're expecting a reversal of a downtrend (buy signal).

One of the best features of spinning tops as compared to dojis is that spinning tops appear much more frequently. Dojis are powerful signals, but they can be pretty rare. I scanned many charts to come up with the examples for this book, and it was much, much easier to find good examples of spinning tops than it was to track down dojis. And with more appearances come more chances to trade and make more profits!

Using spinning tops for profitable trading

Like dojis, spinning tops are nice indicators that a trend may be about to change direction. Catching an early trend change can be a very profitable endeavor, and in the sections below, I give you an idea of how you can execute some fruitful trades by using spinning tops.

Recognizing a buy signal with a spinning top

Figure 6-15 is a chart of the futures contracts that trade on the Standard & Poor's 500 Index (S&P 500). The low of a downtrend culminates with a spinning top, and a trader who recognizes this signal is rewarded with a nice up move if she shows a little patience.

For this reversal pattern, I wanted to use a chart that appeared to be failing initially. Although the futures contract in Figure 6-15 didn't immediately reverse to an uptrend, it also didn't match the low of the signal day. The contract came close, but the low was never broken, so the signal was never violated. Such a case may test your patience, but sticking with this buy signal would've been rewarded after a few days of watching it go nowhere.

Looking at an example of a failing spinning top

On the flip side, take a look at Figure 6-16, which is a chart of the futures contracts that trade on the ten-year U.S. Treasury notes. I've highlighted a spinning top that appears in a downtrend. The next day shows a quick failure, with the downtrend continuing for several days afterward. Although the appearance of the spinning top on this chart may have been a hopeful sign for someone choosing to go long, that hope was dashed pretty quickly.

Getting a nice short signal from a spinning top

Spinning tops may also be used quite effectively to recognize a shift from an uptrend to a downtrend. Figure 6-17 is a chart of the futures contract on the Euro currency. A spinning top appears just as an uptrend is rolling over, which is a favorite situation of mine. The next day's high comes very close to penetrating the high of the spinning top signal day, but doesn't quite get there. The result is a downtrend that lasts almost a month.

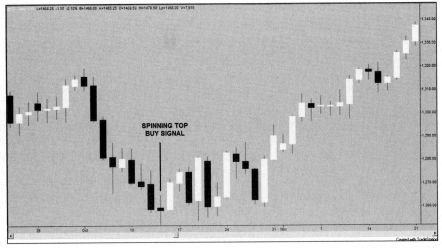

Figure 6-15:
A long spinning top on S&P 500 futures contract that yields a nice profit.

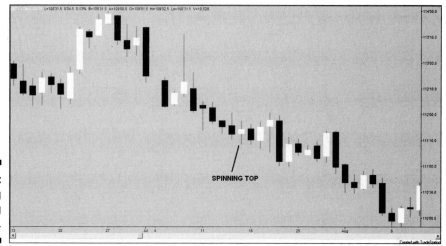

Figure 6-16:
A long
spinning
top that fails.

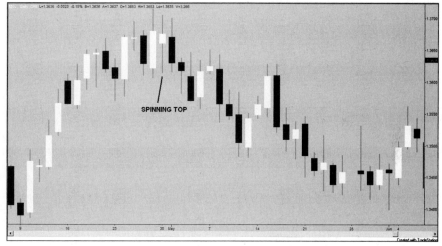

Figure 6-17:
A short
spinning
top on Euro
futures
indicates the
beginning
of a
downtrend.

To capitalize on the scenario presented in Figure 6-17, you would initiate a
short position on the futures contract either near the close of the day on
which the spinning top appeared or the next day, when the spinning top was
validated by the fact that the day's high didn't violate the high of the
previous day.

Seeing a failing spinning top short

Figure 6-18 shows a chart where spinning tops just keep failing. This chart is of the stock for Yahoo!, which carries the symbol YHOO. I've highlighted three spinning tops that appear after some small uptrends. Each fails pretty quickly and miserably.

Discovering More about Belt Holds

More single-stick patterns that depend on market context *and* offer outstanding trend reversal signals are *belt holds*. But wait — if you read Chapter 5, you and belt holds have already been introduced, although you may know them by a different name.

Belt holds are exactly the same as marubozus that have no wick on the opening end of the candlestick formation. As with the other patterns in this chapter, the difference is that the usefulness of belt holds as trend reversal signals depends heavily on the market environments in which they appear.

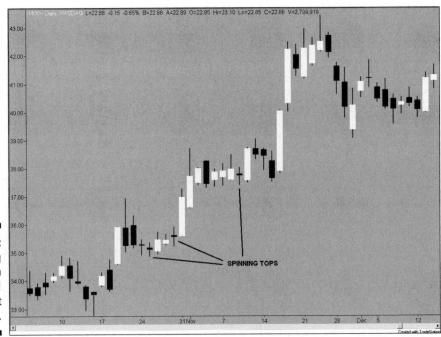

Figure 6-18: Spinning tops on a Yahoo! chart that don't pan out.

Spotting belt holds on a chart

There are two types of belt holds: bullish and bearish. Bullish belt holds feature an open equal to the low and a close near the high, which leaves a small wick on the top of the candle. Bullish belt holds appear during downtrends. For an ideal example of a bullish (long) belt hold, take a peek at Figure 6-19.

Bearish belt holds, on the other hand, open on their highs and close near their lows, thus leaving a small wick on the bottom of the candle. Bearish belt holds show up in the midst of uptrends. You can find a picture perfect version of a bearish (short) belt hold in Figure 6-20.

Buckling down for some belt hold-based trading

It's time to investigate what it's like to trade signals. These are pretty powerful and common patterns that can be used. The dramatic reversal from the opens they represent often does show a trend change occurring over the course of just one day.

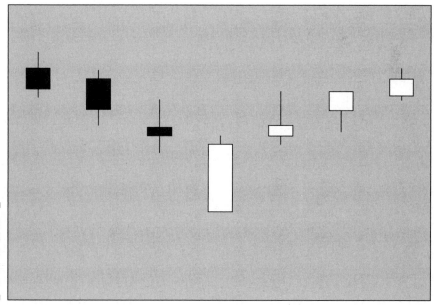

Figure 6-19: Textbook example of a long belt hold.

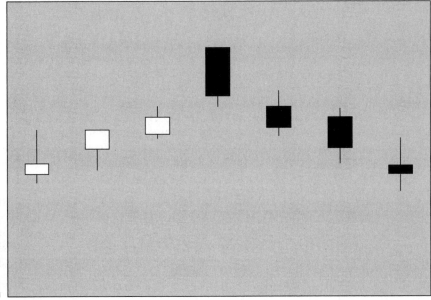

The price action behind a belt hold is pretty directional. For example, a stock in a defined downtrend may open on its low and then spend most of the day rallying. As a downtrend presents itself, the bulls have finally had enough and start buying. Prices reach a low enough level to encourage not just buying, but aggressive buying.

Belt hold as a long signal

Figure 6-21 is a chart of Wal-Mart stock. The long belt hold pattern actually shows up on the chart on the day after Christmas in 2006. I like this chart because in addition to this being the company's most important time of year, it shows how sentiment changed relative to the retailing environment right after the crucial holiday season had ended.

Two factors contribute to the strength of this long belt hold.

✔ **The sheer length of the candlestick:** Very aggressive buying is exhibited by the size of the candle and overall candlestick.

✔ **The fact that the gap from the opening price was filled:** Also, you can find another bullish indication in the fact that that the stock gapped lower than the previous low on the open (it means that the price attracted buy interest immediately). Notice that the whole price action of the previous day was covered. That's bullish stuff.

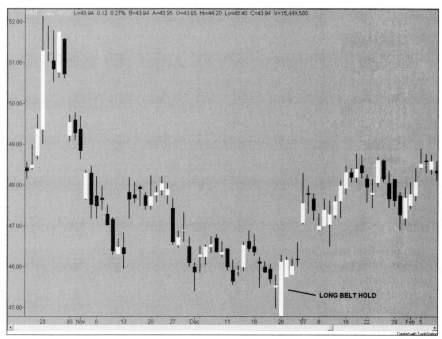

L=43.94 0.12 0.27% B=43.94 A=43.95 O=43.65 Hi=44.20 Lo=43.40 C=43.94 V=15,449,500

LONG BELT HOLD

Figure 6-21:
Chart of a
long belt
hold in Wal-
Mart stock.

Belt hold failing on the long side

Want to know what happens when bullish belt holds go bad? Look at
Figure 6-22. This figure is a chart of the futures contract that trades on
soybeans. The bullish belt hold comes on the heels of some pretty bearish
trading that occurred over the course of a few weeks. For the sake of full dis-
closure, I'll fess up and say that I actually traded this signal because I was
looking for a short-term bottom and was encouraged by the price action of
that day. However, I was a little less wealthy the next day because the signal
failed. Happens to the best of us.

Bearish belt hold signals occur when there's an obvious uptrend with a day
that opens on its high and closes very near its low. This signal appears as a
dark candle with just a small part of the wick appearing on the bottom. It's
a day when the bears rule for most of the day after being pushed around by
the bulls for several days prior.

Bearish belt hold working out

For a nice bearish belt hold scenario, look at Figure 6-23. This chart of
exchange traded funds represents a basket of biotech stocks also known as
the Biotech Holders (BBH). The BBH bears had been overtaken by the bulls,
but the short belt hold reveals that the bears are clawing their way back into
the action.

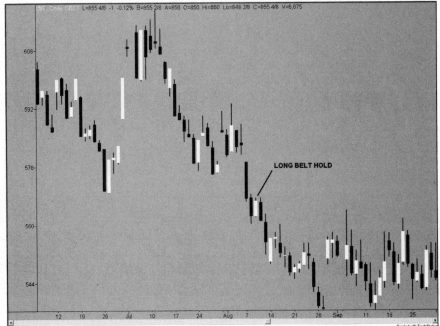

Figure 6-22:
Chart of a failing bullish (long) belt hold in soybean futures.

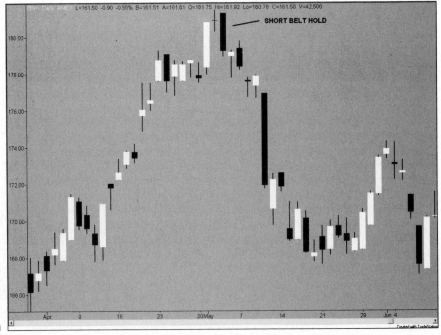

Figure 6-23:
Chart of a nice short belt hold signal on the BBH.

Take a closer look at Figure 6-23. Notice any additional bearish patterns? I chose this chart specifically to try to push you to start looking beyond what I highlight on a chart. Give yourself a pat on the back if you notice the doji the day before the belt hold. Give yourself two pats if you notice the doji's short signal was intact while you received a short signal from the belt hold. I'd give you a chance to give yourself three pats on the back, but that can be hard on your rotator cuff.

A failing bearish belt hold

Just so you'll know what to look for if you suspect that a bearish belt hold may be failing, check out Figure 6-24. It depicts the futures contract that trades on the Japanese Yen.

It's a really nice bearish belt hold pattern, except that it just doesn't work out. The belt hold appears during an uptrend that's been in place for several days, and it's pretty encouraging that lower trading occurs during the next few days. However, seven days after the signal appears, the Yen futures trade over the high of the belt hold day and then trade much higher pretty quickly.

Sometimes signals take a few days to fail. They don't immediately show signs of failure, so stay on your toes and keep your eyes out for signs of trouble.

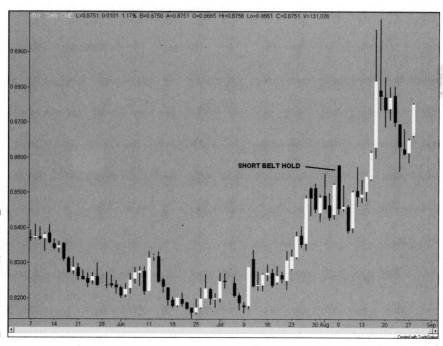

Figure 6-24:
Chart of a bearish belt hold on the Japanese Yen that fails.

SHORT BELT HOLD

Deciphering between the Hanging Man and the Hammer

The last single-stick patterns that rely on a specific market environment that I present in this chapter are the hanging man and the hammer. I paired them together in this section because they appear exactly the same. Don't be fooled, though — the two patterns aren't identical. The hanging man is considered bearish, and the hammer is considered bullish, and the difference between the two is where they appear on a chart.

Spotting and distinguishing the hanging man and the hammer

The first step in working with the hanging man and the hammer is understanding how to spot them on a chart. The pattern is fairly distinctive, so identifying it usually isn't a problem.

The hammer or hanging man is recognized by a small candle that appears at the very top of the pattern. There's usually a pretty long wick on the bottom. If you see this pattern at the bottom of a downtrend, you're looking at a hammer. If it appears at the top of an uptrend, it's considered a hanging man. (Both cases assume that the patterns are actually good signals, of course.) Also, in less than ideal cases, it's possible for a small wick to be sticking out of the top of the candle.

For a classic example, look at Figure 6-25.

Figure 6-25:
A hammer or hanging man (depending on the market context).

Although the hammer and the hanging man are individual patterns, there's one extra step to them: the confirmation of the pattern. The confirmation comes on the following day's opening price. If the opening price on the very next day is in the direction of the signal, you're working with a true hammer or hanging man. If you think you have a hanging man appearing in an uptrend, you wouldn't trade on it unless it's confirmed the next day with an opening price lower than the previous close. By the same token, if a hammer appears during a downtrend, you need to confirm it with an opening price on the next day that's higher than the hammer's close.

Trading on the hanging man and the hammer

To better illustrate the intricacies of the hanging man and the hammer, I show you examples of both patterns that were either confirmed the next day or not confirmed. If you're planning to dig into later chapters and read more about complex patterns, get used to the idea of confirming patterns, because it pops up continually throughout the rest of the book.

Going long with a hammer pattern

Figure 6-26 is a chart of Dell, Inc. (DELL) stock with a hammer that pops up during a downtrend. The following day, the stock opens higher than the close of the previous day for DELL. That's the confirmation that indicates that the hammer is a good long signal, and you'd be very wise to wait for it before buying. Be patient and wait for the confirmation, even if you're completely convinced that it's hammer time!

The confirmation may cost you a little in profits because you pay a slightly higher price, but Figure 6-27 shows what it may cost you if you choose not to wait.

Figure 6-27 is also a chart of DELL. This one contains a potential buy hammer that isn't confirmed on the next day. In fact, the opening the next day is lower than the low that occurred on the day that the hammer appeared. Not only would you have saved yourself the effort of trading in and out of this stock by waiting for confirmation, but you'd also have saved yourself a little in losses.

If a candlestick signal calls for some sort of confirmation, always wait for the confirmation. Don't try to get ahead of the confirmation day by trading in early. In the long run, it catches up with you!

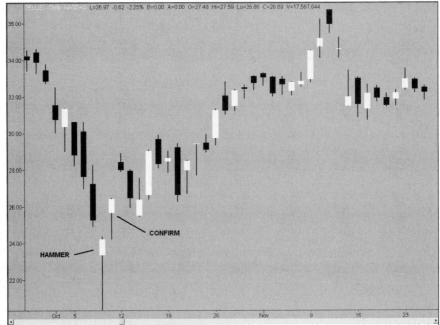

Figure 6-26:
A hammer with confirmation on a chart of DELL stock.

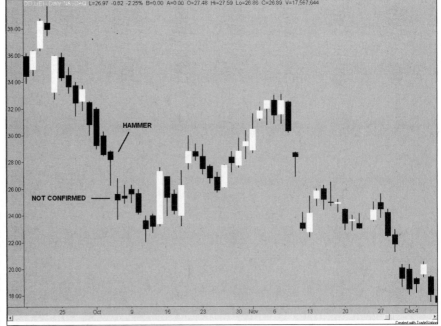

Figure 6-27:
A hammer with no confirmation on a chart of DELL stock.

Shorting with a hanging man pattern

Now for a look at a successful hanging man. Figure 6-28 is a chart for the stock of Toll Brothers, symbol TOL. If you aren't familiar with Toll Brothers, it's a homebuilder focusing on the higher end of the housing market. If you remember what happened to the housing market in 2007, you can see why this is a good short example.

Figure 6-28 shows how you could have made money when the housing market first started to tank. I'm not saying that trading housing-related stock is the way to offset any potential losses in the value of your home, but this was a chance to take advantage of the fall in value of a home-building company as it anticipated the drop in housing prices and home sales activity.

Right at the very peak of a trend in the TOL stock, a hanging man appeared. If you happened to already own this stock (also called *being long*), that was a pretty scary signal that may have suggested that it was time to take your profits and move on to a less risky investment. If you were in the market looking for a stock to short, that would've looked like a swell opportunity. After the hanging man, a very dramatic reversal occurred, and the downtrend continued for several weeks.

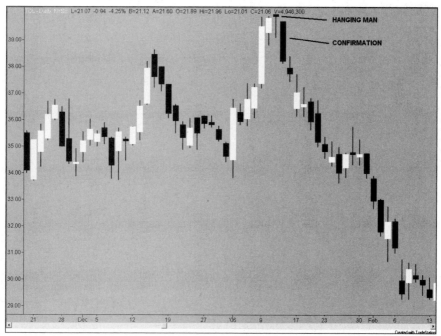

Figure 6-28: A hanging man short signal on TOL.

Finally, I provide you with a hanging man that doesn't get confirmed. Sorry for the abundance of examples using retail stocks, but I've had a profitable history with them, and they often make good examples. Figure 6-29 is a chart of the stock for Kohl's Stores (KSS).

A very encouraging hanging man appears on the chart in a defined uptrend. However, after waiting patiently overnight for confirmation of the end of the uptrend and a shorting opportunity, a trader is surprised to see a gap opening and a continuation of the uptrend. If she's following the rules (as she should be) and waiting for the confirmation of the hanging man, all she gets is disappointment. But it could be worse: If she'd jumped the gun and sold, it would've cost her even more.

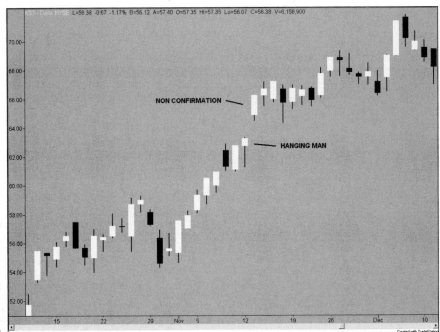

Figure 6-29:
A failing hanging man short signal on KSS.

Chapter 7

Working with Bullish Double-Stick Patterns

In This Chapter
▶ Understanding double-stick patterns that signal a trend reversal
▶ Working with double-stick patterns that tell you a trend will continue

Compared to the single-stick patterns in Chapters 5 and 6, double-stick patterns are difficult to come by. But these patterns can be very powerful and profitable if you put in the time and effort to monitor them.

I tackle a number of double-stick patterns in this chapter, and each of them consists of two days. I'll refer to the first day as the setup day, and I'll call the second day the signal day. When you're looking for double-stick patterns, you'll have to start paying attention to the possibility of a pattern developing on the setup day, and you'll react (trade) if you see what you need to see on the signal day.

In this chapter I cover some double-stick patterns that signal a trend reversal and a few that signal a trend continuation. The reversal signals are more fun, because they help you to outsmart the crowd and buy near the end of a trend. The trend confirming signals are useful if you're already on the right side of a trend, or if you're considering going against a trend, and you're looking for a signal that can kindly tell you to reconsider.

If you want to go hunting for double-stick patterns, I must warn you that you're bound to suffer some disappointments. Often, you see the beginnings of a double-stick pattern on the first day, but you can get discouraged when the pattern doesn't shape up correctly on the second day. Your patience may be tested, and you may want to bag it and work only with single-stick patterns, but doing so is like playing the game without all the equipment you need to play it well.

Bullish Reversal Patterns

A wide variety of two-day patterns signal the end of a downtrend and the beginning of an uptrend, and those patterns are the focus of this section. There's an old saying in trading that "the trend is your friend." It's based on the idea that getting (and staying) on the right side of the trend is the best way to make a profit in the market. I don't disagree with that sentiment, but plenty of traders make a good living catching changes in trend. It's not the easiest type of trading, but it can be rewarding. This type of trading basically involves trying to pick a top or bottom of a trending move. Because this involves going against the current type of market and against the majority of participants, it's a difficult process.

If your trading strategy is dependent on catching trend changes, make sure that you're humble and quick to acknowledge when you're wrong about a trade. Use orders that force you to take a small loss before you rack up big losses.

Throughout this section, I include patterns that work and ones that fail, and I point out where a trade starts to go wrong. In these examples, you can see how bad a trade can get if you don't play it safe and take a small loss to prevent losing big.

Bullish engulfing pattern

The first two-stick pattern is the bullish engulfing pattern. The pattern's name comes from the fact that the signal day engulfs the setup day. Both the wick and the body of the second day completely cover the same ground as the first day and then some. Also the first day of this bullish pattern is a down day, with the second day starting out looking like there's going to be more bearish trading, but this selling is reversed by the emergence of buying — so much buying that the previous day's open and highs are both surpassed. (There's also a bearish version of this pattern, and it's covered in Chapter 8. In fact, most of the bullish two-stick patterns I discuss in this chapter have a bearish counterpart.)

Spotting the bullish engulfing pattern

To find the bullish engulfing pattern, take these steps:

1. **First look for a setup day with a dark candle.**

2. **Then look to see if the signal day is bullish.**

   If so, you're on the right track, but the following statements must also be true in order for your pattern to be a full-fledged bullish engulfing pattern:

- The wick of the signal day is longer than the wick of the setup day.
- The high of the signal day is higher than the high of the setup day.
- The low of the signal day is lower than the low of the setup day.
- The candle of the signal day is longer than the candle of the setup day. (In this case the signal day's close is higher than the setup day's open, and the open of the signal day is lower than the close of the setup day.)

Figure 7-1 includes two days that create a bullish engulfing pattern.

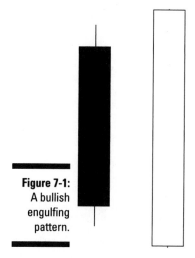

Figure 7-1:
A bullish
engulfing
pattern.

The trading activity that creates this pattern is extremely bullish:

✔ On Day 1 (the setup day) the bears dominate.

The open is near the high, and they push the price down all day until the close ends up near the low.

✔ On Day 2 (the signal day) the bears are at it again and move the price a bit lower before the bulls come roaring in.

They arrive on the scene and immediately start pushing prices up, and they don't stop. The bulls exceed the prices from the previous day and even push the closing price up over where trading commenced the previous day.

When a bullish engulfing pattern occurs in a downtrend, that indicates that the bulls have been pushed around for some time before the pattern developed and that they're geared up to continue their buying assault on the bears for days to come.

Using the bullish engulfing pattern for savvy trading

If you're vigilant and lucky enough to spot a bullish engulfing pattern, trading on it can yield some very appealing results. Figure 7-2 is a real-world example of the bullish engulfing pattern on a chart of the ETF that represents the members of the Dow Jones Industrial Average (DJIA), which is known as the Diamonds because its symbol is DIA. (An ETF or *exchange traded fund* is a security that trades like a stock, but represents a basket of stocks or an index.)

The DIA is a popular trading vehicle among short-term traders who try to profit from the direction of the Dow Jones Industrial Average from day to day and also among long-term investors who seek exposure to all DJIA stocks without having to buy all 30 of them individually.

Although it's not picture perfect, Figure 7-2 is a useful example of how the bullish engulfing pattern develops and how it can work out profitably. The bears dominate the setup day, leaving the close near the low. On the signal day, the DIA opens lower than the previous close and appears to trade lower — bad news for the bulls. But at some point during the day, the bulls rally with some strong buying and push the DIA much higher, to the point where the close of the day is higher than the high of the setup day. The resulting price action includes several days where the bulls are firmly in the driver's seat.

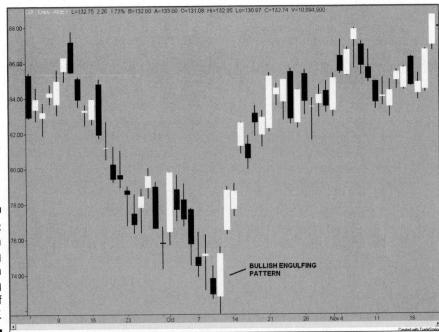

Figure 7-2:
A bullish engulfing pattern developing on a chart of the DIA ETF.

That leads me to an important question: How do you know when the bullish engulfing pattern's signal is no longer valid? My rule of thumb is if the low of the setup day is violated, then the signal is no longer good. To work this rule into your trading strategy, place a sell stop on the low of the setup day, not the signal day. Other traders may suggest that the sell stop be placed on the closing price of the setup day or even the opening price of the signal day, and you may want to consider those options as you get comfortable trading on the bullish engulfing pattern. Keep in mind, though, that things can get pretty miserable if you hold onto this trade for too long.

A failing bullish engulfing pattern

Figure 7-3 is an example of what happens when good bullish engulfing patterns go bad, using the Euro currency futures contracts to show the price action when the setup day's low is violated a few days after the pattern arises.

The setup day in this example is very encouraging. There's a definite down-trend, and all the other bullish engulfing pattern criteria check out. But things sour quickly. The bulls lose the fight, and the result is a very bearish day. No matter what you choose to be your failure level, this day should be when you throw in the towel.

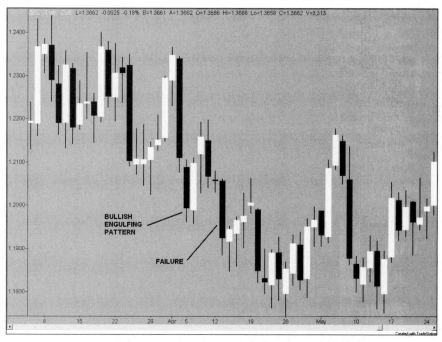

Figure 7-3:
A bullish engulfing pattern that fails on a Euro currency futures chart.

As I was compiling real-world examples for this book, I had an extremely tough time finding a bullish engulfing pattern that didn't work out profitably if it was correctly traded. Bullish engulfing patterns don't *always* work, but finding one is an exciting prospect, and the chances are very good that if you trade on it wisely, the result will be bright.

Bullish harami

In general, a *harami* is a two-day pattern with the candle of the setup day that's longer than the candle of the signal day. This pattern can almost be considered the opposite of the bullish outside day and be called a bullish inside day.

The first day is very bearish and occurring in a downtrend. On the second day, the bulls take a shot at moving prices higher. There's not too much success because although the second day closes up slightly, it closes lower than the first day's open, and the first day's high is never surpassed. However, it's a day where the bulls may have started to take a stand and stop the current downtrend, because the second day is an up day and the low of the first day isn't penetrated.

Harami is the Japanese word for *pregnant;* if you draw an outline of the harami pattern, it looks like a pregnant woman.

Identifying the bullish harami

If you want to identify a true bullish harami, the pattern and the market must have the following features:

- The relevant market or stock is in a downtrend.
- The setup day has a longer candle than the signal day.
- The setup day has a black candle, with the open greater than the close, and that candle is fairly long.
- The signal day's candle has an open lower than its close.
- The open of the signal day is higher than the close of the setup day.
- The low of the setup day is lower than the signal day's low, and the high of the setup day is higher than the high of the signal day.
- The signal day's open is higher than the setup day's close.
- The signal day's close is lower than the setup day's open.

Figure 7-4 is a picture of two days that create a bullish harami. ***Note:*** The high and low of both days don't come into play on this pattern — just the open and close.

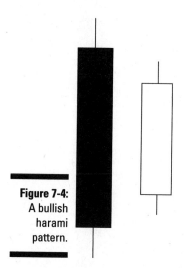

Figure 7-4:
A bullish
harami
pattern.

The setup day of the harami is a down day that follows a bearish trend. On the signal day, the open is up from the first day's close, and the bulls rule the day, because the close is higher than the open. Since there has been a downtrend, the bulls may be a bit timid, worried that the bears are going to come back and push to new lows. The confidence the bulls gain when this doesn't occur should translate to more buying, and a reversal of the downtrend that culminated in the bullish harami.

Trading based on the bullish harami

Now for a couple of examples of the bullish harami that help you figure out what to do (or not do) when you spot one on your own. I start with a successful appearance of the pattern at the end of a downtrend. The result is an attractive trend reversal.

Getting a nice buy signal on the bullish harami

Figure 7-5 is a chart of the futures contract that trades on the Australian dollar. The bears push the price down from the open until the close for eight days in a row. Finally, on the signal day of the bullish harami, the bulls find a level where they're ready to start buying. This day is the first of many days where the bulls push prices back up from the depths where the bears had pushed them.

Notice in Figure 7-5 that the high of the signal day is a little higher than the setup day. This example helps me make the point that the bullish harami is just the opposite of the bullish engulfing pattern. (See the earlier section entitled "Bullish engulfing pattern".) With a bullish engulfing pattern, all four price components of the candlestick are involved, but only the open and close matter when you're working with a harami.

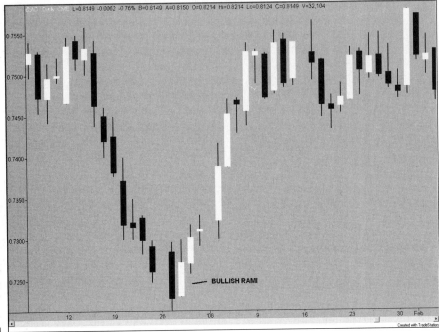

Figure 7-5:
A bullish
harami on a
chart of the
Australian
dollar
futures.

Seeing a bad example of the bullish harami

Like most other patterns, the bullish harami can go awry. Figure 7-6 is a chart
of IBM. A bullish harami appears because IBM's stock has been trending
down slowly. Some up days exist, but most are down days for a few weeks
leading up to the harami pattern. Any bullish inklings from the harami don't
last very long.

The failure level of a bullish harami can vary depending on your preference.
I use the open of the signal day as my stop level, and I suggest you use the
same level in your trading efforts. In Figure 7-6, this level holds up for less
than a day, and although there's some sideways trading for a few days, the
downtrend resumes in time.

Bullish harami cross

Much like the doji with all its variations, the harami has more than one version.
A doji pattern has an open that's higher than the close of the setup day and a
close that's lower than the open of the setup day. This section covers the bullish harami cross — a special variety of harami — which actually involves a doji
pattern, which is covered in Chapter 6, but should always be considered an
indicator of a potential reversal.

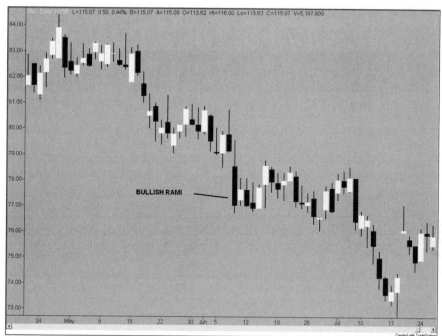

BULLISH RAMI

Figure 7-6:
A bullish
harami on a
chart of IBM
followed by
bearishness.

Recognizing the bullish harami cross

The bullish harami cross starts out just like its cousin the bullish harami (see the previous section, "Bullish harami"), and it must contain the following characteristics:

- ✔ It appears during a downtrend.
- ✔ Its setup day is a long black candle.
- ✔ Its signal day is a doji.

It's much easier to understand the specifics of the bullish harami cross if you see a good example, so check out Figure 7-7.

Using the bullish harami cross for profitable trading

The bullish harami cross isn't a common pattern, but when it appears, the trend reversal may be pretty abrupt. Also, if the pattern doesn't hold and the downtrend continues, this failure usually happens quickly.

A nice buy signal from the bullish harami cross

To get an idea of how you can trade to turn a profit with the bullish harami cross, look at Figure 7-8. That's a chart of the Australian dollar futures, with a bullish harami cross that successfully signals a trend reversal. I actually traded this pattern, and the results were strong.

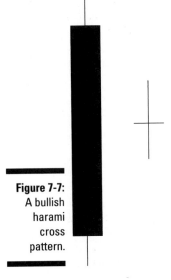

Figure 7-7:
A bullish
harami
cross
pattern.

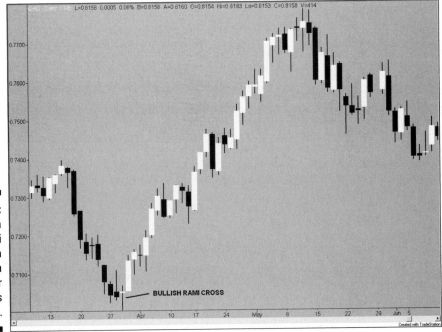

Figure 7-8:
A bullish
harami
cross on an
Australian
dollar
futures
chart.

When this pattern reared its head, I was looking for an entry point for trading long on the Australian dollar futures contract. I had been monitoring it for a while, and I bought near the close of the bullish harami cross's signal day. This pattern adheres to the rules for a buy signal because it's at the bottom of a downtrend, and the doji's open and close fall within the setup day's open and close. Soon after I got in, I was happily rewarded with an uptrend that lasted for several weeks, and you can enjoy the same kind of results if you spot the bullish harami cross in a similar environment.

Failing to give a good buy signal

Look again closely at Figure 7-8. There was a failed harami cross a few days before the successful one. I noticed this pattern, and it cost me a little before I profited from the one that worked so well. Figure 7-9 adds a highlight where the failed signal occurred.

For this failed signal, I placed my sell stop on the low of the doji day. I know that contradicts what I said in the regular bullish harami section earlier in this chapter, but since the open and close of the signal day on a bullish harami cross are in such a small range, I generally use the close of the previous day as a stop.

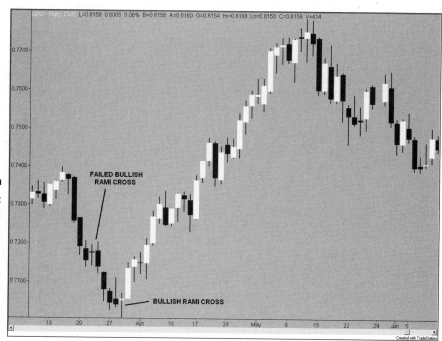

Figure 7-9:
A failed bullish harami cross on an Australian dollar futures chart.

Sometimes using stops that don't allow for some market fluctuation gets you out of a successful trade too quickly. On the other hand, placing a stop with too much wiggle room can get you out of a bad trade long after it would've been prudent. Placing stops is as much an art as a science; it's one of the more difficult parts of trading. See Chapter 5 for a quick refresher on stops.

Bullish inverted hammer

The bullish inverted hammer is a fairly rare pattern. This pattern occurs in a downtrend, and the first day (setup day) is a bearish candle — usually a long bearish candle. The second, or signal, day is actually the inverted hammer; this is the rare part because the price action that creates an inverted hammer is fairly rare.

In order to get the inverted hammer as the signal day, you should start with gap down and end with a close near the opening gap price. Usually with much volatility associated with a gap opening, it would be rare to have the open and close in the same price proximity.

In this section, I demonstrate what the two days that create the bullish inverted hammer look like.

Spotting the bullish inverted hammer

Like many bullish patterns, the bullish inverted hammer is preceded by some sort of downtrend. The setup day is a down day — a continuation of the prevailing downtrend. The signal day is the inverted hammer. I explain the hammer in Chapter 6, and this pattern is just an opposite version of it.

The inverted hammer has a long wick on the top, and its candle takes up a small part of the bottom of the whole candlestick. The body may be white or black, but because the high is way above the rest of the candlestick, you can tell that most of the trading activity occurs in a small area near the low. The low serves as a support level for upcoming days. Take a look at Figure 7-10 for a handy visual representation.

Understanding how to trade on the bullish inverted hammer

To initiate a trade using the bullish inverted hammer, wait until the open of the subsequent day. Initiate a position only if the open of that day is higher than the low of the inverted hammer day.

Think of it this way. For the bullish inverted hammer to be considered valid, it needs to be confirmed by the open of the day immediately after its appearance. If that open is higher than the signal day's low, you're clear to buy, and you should put your stop in at the same time.

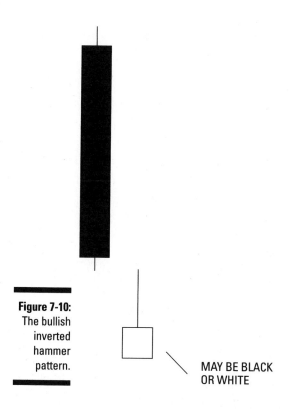

MAY BE BLACK
OR WHITE

Figure 7-10:
The bullish
inverted
hammer
pattern.

Checking out a successful bullish inverted hammer

Figure 7-11 is a chart of an ETF that focuses on financial stocks. The official name is the Financial Select Sector SPDR, and the symbol is XLF. I'm going to stick with XLF for simplicity's sake. The inverted hammer appears after a down day and is confirmed by a higher opening. I chose this specific chart because there's no question that the open on the day after the pattern confirms the bullish signal. If you see a bullish inverted hammer confirmed like this, you should put on a long trade quickly because an uptrend is likely on the way.

The bullish inverted hammer often appears, and the following day's open won't confirm the bullish signal. If you see that develop, wash your hands of any trades involving that pattern immediately.

Seeing a failed confirmation

Figure 7-12 is a chart of an unconfirmed bullish inverted hammer of the stock for Caterpillar, Inc., the manufacturer of large construction equipment that trades under the symbol CAT. With a downtrend in place and after a down day, a bullish inverted hammer appears. But on the following day, the opening price isn't higher than the previous low or the low of the inverted hammer. The pattern's bullish signal isn't confirmed, and no trade should be initiated.

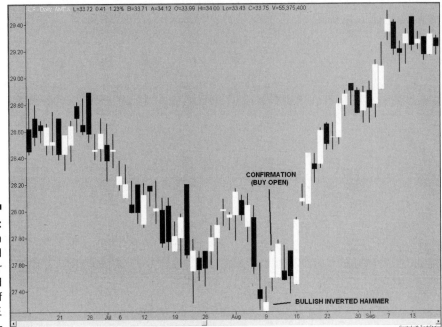

Figure 7-11:
The bullish
inverted
hammer
confirmed
on a chart of
the XLF ETF.

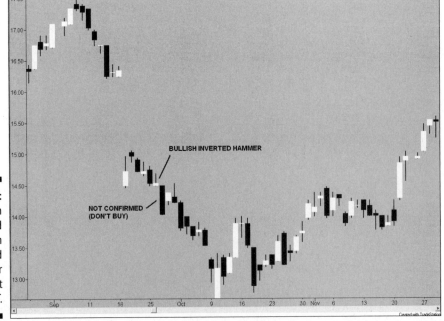

Figure 7-12:
An
unconfirmed
bullish
inverted
hammer
on a chart
of CAT.

You may be asking, "Why look at a signal that ends up not being a signal at all?" This won't be the last candlestick pattern that requires some sort of confirmation on the opening or even the closing of the day after the pattern appears, so it's worth getting used to the concept. And you can also rely on similar confirmations when trading on some of the patterns I cover in previous chapters of this book. Instead of buying a close on a bullish signal, you can wait until the next day and buy the opening if it appears to be going in the same direction of the signal or doesn't negate the previous day's signal.

Finally, although I spend all my working days in front of monitors looking at charts and markets, most new or casual traders don't. Being able to look at charts outside of market hours and then being prepared to initiate a trade the next day can be very appealing for traders who can't or won't be glued to a monitor all day.

Bullish doji star

The bullish doji star is very similar to the bullish inverted hammer. (See "Bullish inverted hammer" earlier in the chapter.) It occurs in a downtrend and signals that the bulls have had enough. The doji pattern always indicates that the battle between bulls and bears was a tight one, and when it appears as the second day of a two-day bullish doji star pattern, it means that the bulls are starting to seize control.

Identifying a bullish doji star

A bullish doji star is a two-day pattern with a doji appearing on the signal day, and it must appear during a downtrend. A genuine bullish doji star must also include the following features:

- A down setup day, preferably with a long black candle.

- A signal day that includes an open and close that are equal or very nearly equal, preferably in the middle of a relatively short trading day. (This indicates an almost equal battle between the bulls and bears, where neither faction can claim victory.)

- A gap down opening between the long black candle of the setup day and the doji of the signal day.

    This last feature shows that a gap down is met with buying but only enough buying to keep the price stable.

Figure 7-13 shows two days of trading activity that creates the bullish doji star.

Figure 7-13:
The bullish
doji star.

Wishing (and trading) on a bullish doji star

Figure 7-14 shows a bullish doji star working out in a downtrend reversal for the stock Hewlett Packard Co., symbol HPQ. Notice the doji that appears after the gap down from the previous day, which was a down day. The low of the doji is never violated, and a buyer is handsomely rewarded with a huge day for the bulls three days after the pattern appears. If only all buy signals resulted in a 10 percent up day!

Failing on a long signal

Unfortunately, some bullish doji stars are more like falling stars than shooting stars. Check out Figure 7-15 for an example. It's a chart of the futures contract that trades on U.S. Treasury bonds. A doji star appears after a down day and in the midst of a downtrend. Very encouraging! For the next couple of days, the downtrend looks like it has come to an end. But just when the bulls think they are going to make a move, the bears come in with a vengeance and push prices lower than the low of the doji signal day. The downtrend kicks right back into gear.

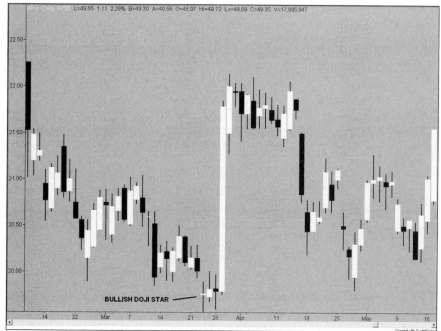

Figure 7-14:
The bullish
doji star
working
well as a
buy signal
on a chart
of HPQ.

BULLISH DOJI STAR

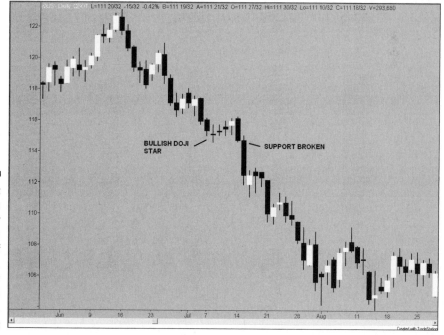

Figure 7-15:
The bullish
doji star
failing on
a chart of
the U.S.
Treasury
bond
futures.

BULLISH DOJI
STAR

SUPPORT BROKEN

Bullish meeting line

The bullish meeting line is another great example of a pattern that offers a heads-up that a trend reversal is on the way. It's an interesting (and rare) pattern.

Recognizing a bullish meeting line pattern

The setup day of this pattern is a long black candle, and the signal day is a long white candle. The closing prices of the two days are equal or nearly equal, which indicates that the bears controlled the setup day. There's also a gap down opening, which shows that the bears are still in control at the beginning of the signal day, but the bulls soon arrive on the scene. As the signal day progresses, the low opening price brings in buying activity and a close that reaches the previous day's close and eliminates the gap that was created on the opening.

Figure 7-16 is a picture of how bullish meeting lines appear on a chart.

Making a successful trade using bullish meeting lines

For a successful example of trading on the bullish meeting line pattern, I use an example of Post Properties, Inc., a real estate company specializing in apartment complexes (and a former landlord of your author). The company trades under the symbol PPS.

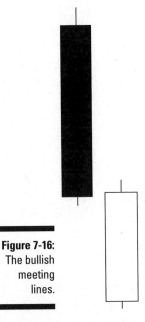

Figure 7-16:
The bullish
meeting
lines.

The chart in Figure 7-17 reveals a pattern that shows up during a downtrend, and the setup day is very bearish. The signal day has a gap opening on the down side, but after trading lower, appears to recover and close near the previous day's close, completing a bullish meeting line pattern. The following day has a threat of support being broken as the stock trades lower than the signal day's open, but the low of that day holds. The result is a few days of very bullish trading. Spotting the bullish meeting lines and getting in at the right time would yield some substantial profits in a case like this.

To give you an idea of what failing bullish meeting lines look like, check out the chart of U.S. Treasury bond futures in Figure 7-18. True to form, the contract is in a downtrend, and the pattern shows up where I've highlighted on the chart. The pattern appears to be validated as the next couple of days aren't necessarily bullish, but the low of the signal day isn't violated. However, on the third day after the pattern is completed, the bears take over again, and the downtrend is back in place. Again, putting a wise sell stop in place at either the low or the open of the signal day would served as a nice tourniquet.

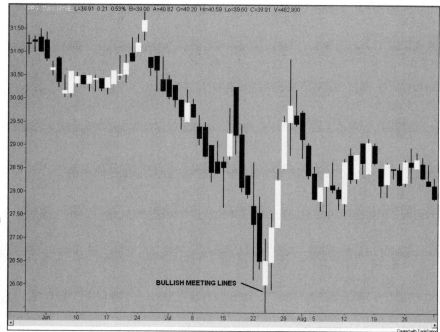

Figure 7-17:
The bullish meeting line pattern on a chart of PPS.

BULLISH MEETING LINES

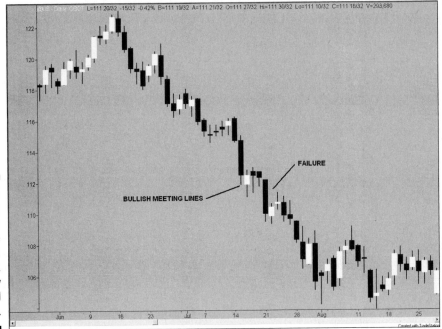

L=111 20/32 -15/32 -0.42% B=111 19/32 A=111 21/32 O=111 27/32 Hi=111 30/32 Lo=111 10/32 C=111 18/32 V=293,680

FAILURE

BULLISH MEETING LINES

Created with TradeStation

Figure 7-18:
A failing
bullish
meeting line
pattern on a
chart of U.S.
Treasury
bond
futures.

Bullish piercing line

The bullish piercing line is one more bullish double-stick pattern that signals
a trend reversal. Just like the other patterns discussed earlier in this chapter,
it's crucial that the bullish piercing line appears during a downtrend for it to
be considered valid.

Identifying a bullish piercing line pattern

Like the bullish meeting line pattern (see the previous section), the bullish
piercing line consists of a long black candle on the setup day and a long white
candle on the signal day. The open of the signal day should be lower than the
low of the setup day. This means that bearishness persists on the setup day,
and then the open of the signal day reveals more selling because the open is
lower than the setup day's low. The signal day's close is much higher than
the open, which means that the bulls came in as a reaction to the lower opening price and pushed prices higher. The tide, therefore, has turned in favor of
the bulls.

Figure 7-19 is a good example of what a bullish piercing line looks like.

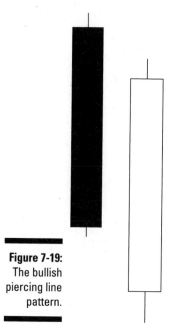

Figure 7-19:
The bullish piercing line pattern.

Trading on the bullish piercing line

The bullish piercing line pattern combines a setup day that's a long black candle. The signal day is a bullish candlestick that opens with a gap down, but closes well within the range covered by the first day. This is a case where the bulls show up after a bearish open and decide it's time to take charge and push prices up.

Figure 7-20 is an example of a bullish piercing line appearing on the chart of a railroad stock for Burlington Northern Santa Fe Corp., which trades under the symbol BNI. You can't beat this example for a clear representation of the bullish piercing line pattern showing up and signaling the end of a downtrend. The setup day is a long black candle, and the signal day has a gap opening before the bulls show up and make a solid bullish run. Notice that the signal day doesn't have a high that exceeds the high of the first day. If it did, and if its close exceeded the setup day's open, this would be a bullish engulfing pattern. (I cover the bullish engulfing pattern earlier in this chapter.)

The bullish piercing line failure example I provide here occurs on a chart of FedEx Corporation (symbol FDX). In this case, the bullish piercing line doesn't deliver. As you can see in Figure 7-21, in the midst of a downtrend, a bullish piercing line appears. The following day, the low price of the bullish piercing line is violated by that day's low. This sign is clear that the bullish activity from the previous day isn't as strong as the long white candle day indicated. It takes a couple of days, but the downtrend in FDX continues.

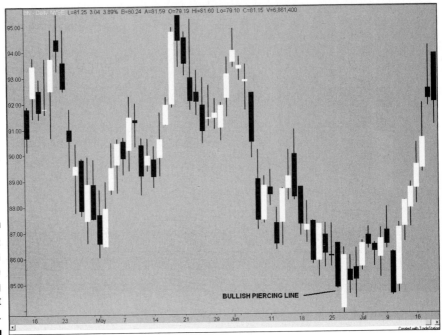

Figure 7-20:
The bullish piercing line appearing on a chart of BNI.

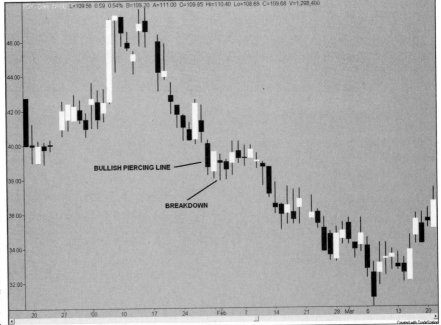

Figure 7-21:
A failing bullish piercing line on a chart of FDX stock.

Bullish Trend-Confirming Patterns

Not all double-stick patterns indicate that a trend reversal is forthcoming. Some of them actually tell you that the market is going to continue in the direction it's already going. It may not sound very exciting, but there are some benefits to getting confirmation that a trend is going to stay in place.

First, if you're considering selling a stock because you believe the price is close to peaking, the appearance of a pattern showing the trend is still in place may help you improve your exit price. After all, it's always frustrating to sell and then watch as a stock continues to climb in value. Also, everyone has heard that the way to make money buying securities is to buy low and sell high, but there are plenty of traders that buy high and sell higher.

These people are known as *trend followers,* and they can embrace these trend confirmation signals to the tune of some outstanding returns. Think you may want to join their ranks? If so, read on for a few examples of bullish double-stick patterns that do a terrific job of confirming the continuation of a trend.

Bullish thrusting lines

The first trend-confirming pattern I cover here may be a bit difficult to pick out of a chart at first glance, but it's worth understanding and looking out for it. Unlike the double-stick patterns I describe in the preceding sections in this chapter, it's critical that the bullish thrusting line pattern appears during an uptrend, not a downtrend, because this pattern would be confirming the direction of an uptrend, but wouldn't have much significance during a downtrend.

Recognizing a bullish thrusting line pattern

The setup day of a bullish thrusting line is a long white candle, bullish in pretty much any market. The signal day is a black candle. This black candle should have a gap opening higher than the high of the setup day and a close near the day's low. However, the close of the signal day should be above the midpoint of the first day. For a bona fide bullish thrusting line, check out Figure 7-22.

Trading on a bullish thrusting line

On the setup day of a bullish thrusting line (and for several days before that), the bulls have been in charge of the price action. On the signal day, the bulls push a stock to a gap opening, which brings in some sellers, but the sellers don't push hard enough to get the closing price under the midpoint of the previous day. This means that the bulls are still around and poised to take control. That can be a big help if you're considering buying, because the bullish signal from this pattern can give you a chance to get on board at a reasonable price before the stock continues to go up.

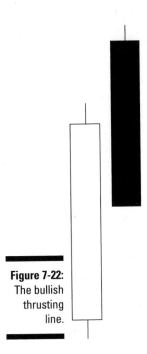

Figure 7-22:
The bullish
thrusting
line.

Figure 7-23 is an example of the bullish thrusting line showing up on a chart of International Paper Co., symbol IP. The setup day is an up day, followed by a gap opening. The stock trades off a bit on the signal day after opening higher, but it manages to close above the midpoint of the first day of the pattern (hooray!). For a few days after this signal, the stock trades sideways, but then resumes the uptrend.

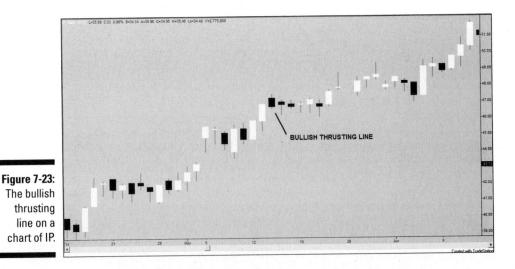

Figure 7-23:
The bullish
thrusting
line on a
chart of IP.

Notice that the stock doesn't violate the low of the first day of the pattern — that's the stop level I use when trading on this pattern. I suggest that you use the same, and you can see why in the next example.

Failing to indicate the continuation of an uptrend

Figure 7-24 is a chart of the investment banking firm The Bear Stearns Companies, Inc. (symbol BSC). A bullish thrusting line pattern develops in an uptrend, but the following day, the low violates the low of the pattern's setup day. Some bullish trading occurs after this violation, but a few days later, a pretty ugly downtrend begins.

If you bought BSC based on that bullish thrusting line and failed to put a stop at the low of the setup day, you lost more than you could bear. A failing trade like that can make even the most grizzled traders want to curl up and hibernate.

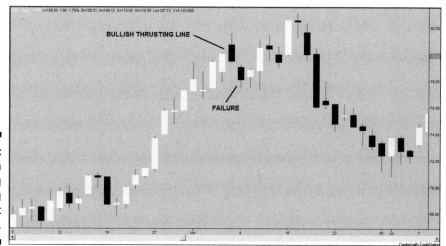

Figure 7-24:
The bullish thrusting line failing on a chart of BSC.

Bullish separating lines

For another double-stick pattern that confirms a trend, consider the bullish separating lines. It isn't exactly what it sounds like, because the lines involved may actually overlap a bit, but it's a useful pattern and certainly one worth understanding in depth.

Singling out the bullish separating lines

Like all its trend-confirming relatives, the bullish separating lines pattern must appear during an uptrend. The setup day of the bullish separating lines is a down day and usually a long down day at that. The signal day is an up day, bullish right from the open. The unique feature of this pattern is that the opens of both days are equal or almost equal. Figure 7-25 is a terrific example.

Understanding how to trade on the bullish separating lines

The bullish separating lines confirm uptrends, but the signal day of the pattern is actually a bearish day. The bears decide that the price is right to start selling, and they dominate the bulls, pushing prices lower throughout the day. On the signal day, the bulls come in and are ready to start buying again. There's so much bullishness that the opening price of the signal day is equal to the opening price of the setup day, and from that point on, the bulls dominate the day, and the uptrend remains intact.

The bullish thrusting lines and a trend that comes to an end

Figure 7-26 is a chart of the stock for Transocean, Inc., a company that builds large drilling machinery for extracting oil in deepwater environments. Not coincidentally, its symbol is RIG. (Looks to me that the symbol assignment was rigged.) I've highlighted the pattern forming at the beginning of an uptrend.

I love this example because the pattern occurs early in an uptrend, so a trader may feel that he hasn't completely missed the bull run by using this signal as an entry point. If he kicks himself for missing a buy at a lower price but still has some interest in getting in on a trade, this pattern may give him the confidence to step up to the plate and buy the stock.

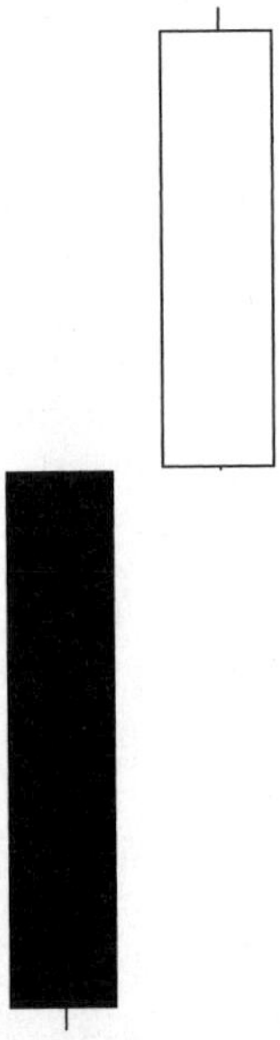

Figure 7-25:
The bullish separating lines.

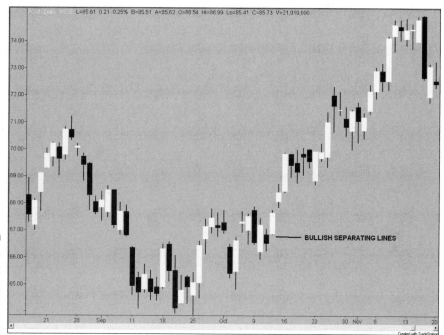

BULLISH SEPARATING LINES

Figure 7-26:
The bullish separating lines on a chart of RIG.

Conversely, Figure 7-27 is an example of the bullish separating lines showing up at the end of an uptrend. The stock charted is for The Home Depot, Inc. (HD), a store I seem to visit every weekend. If you bought HD based on the pattern in this figure popping up during an uptrend, you wouldn't have taken too bad of a loss. The stock doesn't change to a downtrend, but instead, it just starts to trade aimlessly in a nontrending fashion. Using a stop wouldn't have saved you massive amounts of cash, but it would've saved you the angst of trying to figure out if the trend was reversed or just flat.

You have a few options when it comes to determining failure for the bullish separating lines. You may choose the low or close of the setup day or the open or low of the signal day. It really depends on how aggressive you feel and how certain you want to be that the pattern's signal has failed.

In the case of the HD example in Figure 7-27, the day before failure would take out the signal day close while the following day (the day highlighted as a failure) would take out all the other options.

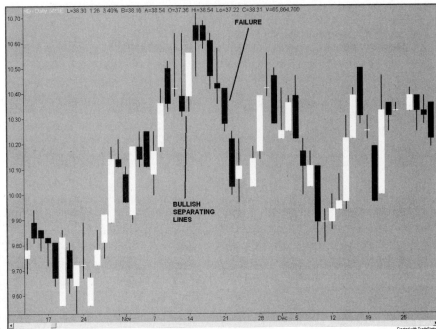

Figure 7-27:
The bullish
separating
lines failing
on a chart
of HD.

Bullish neck lines

The *bullish neck line* is a trend confirmer and more of a classification than a distinct pattern. There are two neck line patterns: the *in neck* and the *on neck* patterns. At times it may be difficult to tell them apart without getting out a magnifying glass to look at a chart. But because they look very much alike, I decided to group the two together in this section. Keep in mind that the bullish neck lines I describe must occur during an uptrend to have any real significance.

Identifying bullish neck lines

The setup day of the bullish neck line pattern is a long white candle that indicates a lot of buying, and the signal day is a black candle that may be long or short. The close of the signal day will be very near the close of the setup day. If that's the case, it may be said that it's "on neck." If the close of the signal day is a little lower than the close of the setup day, the pattern is instead said to be "in neck." You can see examples of both in Figure 7-28. Notice that they're pretty similar.

Both the on neck and in neck bullish neck line patterns tell the same story, so it's not necessary to separate them for discussion. As I mentioned, they occur during an uptrend. The signal day has a gap opening that brings in sellers, but there's not enough selling to trade too much (or at all) below the previous day's close. You may recognize these patterns as more bullish versions of the bullish thrusting lines discussed earlier in this chapter.

Trading on the bullish neck line pattern

This section gives an example of the bullish neck line working well to signal a trend that continues to the upside as the bulls push back and hold prices near the close of the first day of the pattern when the bears try to make a push.

Figure 7-29 is a chart of Amgen, Inc., one of the world's largest biotech companies. It trades under the symbol AMGN. The bullish neck line appears during a small pullback during a longer term uptrend. It's slightly in neck, almost to the point that it may not qualify as a bullish signal. However, a trader that takes this as a buy signal and places a stop at any appropriate level would be handsomely rewarded with a continuation of the longer term uptrend. In this case, the potential stop levels would be the low of the setup day or the low of the signal day. I'm always placing stops very close to the entry point, so I probably would've chosen the low of the signal day, or the higher of the two choices.

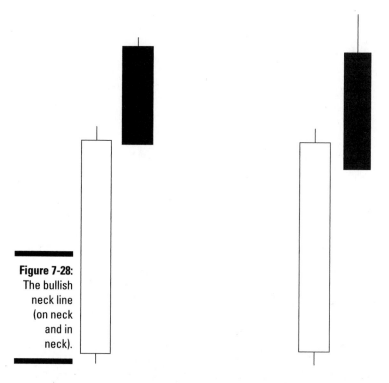

Figure 7-28:
The bullish neck line (on neck and in neck).

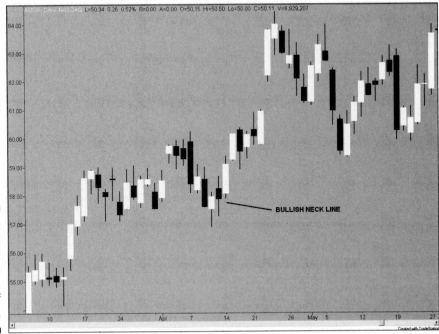

Figure 7-29:
The bullish
neck line
working
well on a
chart of
AMGN.

Bullish neck line fails to signal a trend continuation

I hate to end the chapter on a down note, but I need to show you what it looks like when the bullish neck line pattern fails. Figure 7-30 is a chart of the U.S. Treasury bond futures. A bullish neck line appears near the top of this bullish move. There's only one day where the bulls are happy for making a move based on this signal, and then the tide turns quickly. The only positive I can say about this scenario is that it happened quickly, so you can move on to the next trade without a long and painful failure. And any stop level you picked would've been taken out by that ugly black bar.

That's it for the bullish double-stick patterns for now. In later chapters they come back, teamed up with technical indicators that may signal it's time for a reversal or that a strong trend is in place.

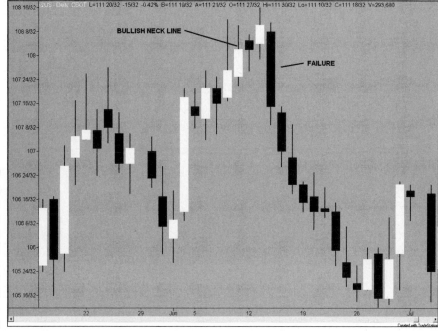

Figure 7-30:
The bullish
neck line
failing on
a chart of
the U.S.
Treasury
bond
futures.

Chapter 8

Utilizing Bearish Double-Stick Patterns

In This Chapter

▶ Working with bearish double-stick patterns that signal a trend reversal

▶ Predicting the continuation of a downtrend by using bearish double-stick patterns

*I*n Chapter 7, I discuss the nature and usefulness of bullish double-stick patterns, but they aren't the only double-stick show in town. As with most bullish patterns, bearish two-day counterparts exist, too, and you should know how to recognize and trade them, and that's what I focus on in this chapter. These patterns work as effective sell signals, and keep in mind that when a sell signal pops up, even if you don't have a long position on, you can use the opportunity to initiate a successful short position.

Just like the bullish patterns in Chapter 7, the bearish double-stick patterns in this chapter may appear as reversal patterns (signaling that an uptrend is coming to an end) or as continuation patterns, which tell you that a prevailing downtrend will continue. These bearish examples have two parts: the first day, which I refer to as the setup day, and the second day, which I call the signal day.

Understanding Bearish Reversal Patterns

I'm definitely biased toward bearish reversal patterns. I've always been a bit of a countertrend trader, and because many candlestick patterns signal trend reversals, I've always found plenty to use in my trading. But trading in anticipation of trend reversals isn't always a cakewalk. In fact, it almost put me out of the business during the strong bullish markets that have become known as the dot.com bubble. I managed to keep from going broke during that period, and I learned some expensive lessons about money management and using stops that I include in my explanations throughout this chapter.

A bit of a warning about using short reversal patterns: First, remember that in theory, a short has an unlimited loss. Also, keep in mind that when you're shorting stocks, you're working against a general long-term uptrend in stock prices. Some successful traders are exclusive shorts, but they're pretty rare. Don't get me wrong. I do believe that shorting should be part of any trading or investing program, but please use shorting as part of a larger trading strategy, not as your primary way of working the markets.

You can use many extremely useful patterns for shorting, as signals for exiting from a long, or as exercises in patience before buying. Take a look at this section, which covers those patterns.

The bearish engulfing pattern

The bearish engulfing pattern is one of the best patterns to start with because of the dramatic nature of the bearish second day that appears on the pattern. The pattern involves the bears taking control after an extended period of bullishness, and the trend is definitely one to watch.

Identifying the bearish engulfing pattern

Check out Figure 8-1 for an example of the bearish engulfing pattern.

Leading up to and including the setup day of this pattern, the bulls have been in the driver's seat. On the open of the signal day, the sellers or shorts finally have had enough, and they decide that the price has gone up enough to bring them into the action. They push the price down dramatically and quickly (in one day). But these bears aren't finished with their selling, and the close of the signal day is near that day's low. That will most likely continue — to the point where a downtrend develops — because the sellers aren't done putting pressure on the stock or market.

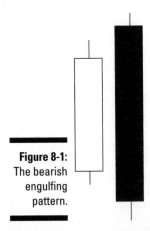

Figure 8-1:
The bearish
engulfing
pattern.

Trading on the bearish engulfing pattern

For a real-world example of a bearish engulfing pattern that can be used for a profitable trade, have a look at Figure 8-2. Here you see the pattern appear on a chart of the exchange-traded fund (ETF) that represents the 30 stocks that trade in the Dow Jones Industrial Average (DJIA).

On this chart, there's a bearish engulfing pattern right at the end of a nice uptrend. The bulls control the setup day; an uptrend is in place, and those bulls keep it going. At the start of the signal day, the bulls continue on their buying spree and cause the opening to be higher than the setup day's close. Then the bears come in and push hard — so hard in fact that although the price had opened higher than the setup day and even traded above that day's high, the bears are still able to push things down below the setup day's low. Those bears mean business!

The overwhelming push by the bears that stops an uptrend dead in its tracks is the key to the bearish engulfing pattern. The DIA (the symbol of the ETF that trades based on the level of the DJIA) chart in Figure 8-2 is a great example of a bearish engulfing pattern scenario that can lead you to profitable results. After the bears reverse the uptrend, the signal holds, and the next day's trading doesn't come near the pre-reversal prices. If you short at the end of the pattern and ride the downtrend for a while before buying back, you have a profitable trade.

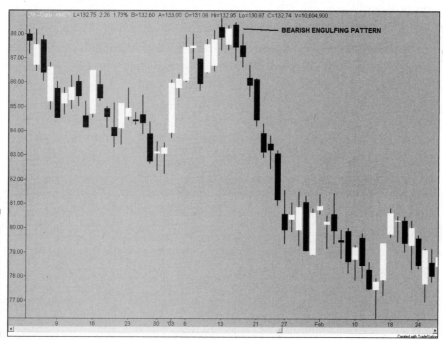

Figure 8-2:
A bearish engulfing pattern signaling a sell on the DJIA ETF.

The bearish engulfing pattern fails

I provide an example of a failing pattern for every successful pattern in this book, and in Figure 8-3, I highlight what can happen when a bearish engulfing pattern goes wrong. This unfortunate outcome occurs on a chart of the Japanese Yen futures. The bearish engulfing pattern shows up but fails pretty quickly, and the uptrend just keeps going higher.

This scenario looks ripe for a bearish engulfing pattern: A clear uptrend is in place and actually appears to be slowing a bit (a good sign). The bulls continue the trend on the setup day, and then on the signal day, a small gap opening appears. At first the bulls push prices much higher, but then the bears take over, and when they start selling, it's powerful enough to cover the setup day's bullishness, and then some. If you see this pattern on a chart, you may have good reason to get excited, but things go sour quickly.

The day after the pattern appears, the bulls get back in on the action, and the price closes higher than the opening of the signal day. The pattern clearly fails, but if you trade on it, you can avoid heavy losses if you place a stop at the right level.

When working with bearish engulfing patterns, I place my stops at the open of the second day. That's when I can tell that the bulls have again seized control of the price action, and I know that can continue for some time. It's always prudent to have a stop in place, and that may be a good level to choose to put your stop. I advise you to place your stops at the same level.

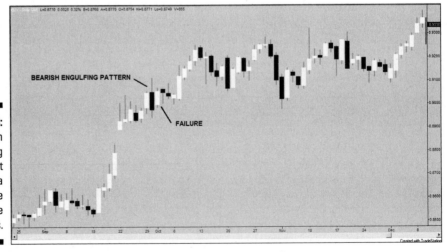

Figure 8-3:
A bearish engulfing pattern that fails on a chart of the Japanese Yen futures.

The bearish harami pattern

The bearish harami pattern can tip you off that an uptrend is about to be reversed. Loosely translated from the Japanese, *harami* means *pregnant*. If you use your imagination and squint a little, you can see in Figure 8-4 how the pattern got its name. I guess if you draw a line to circle the area that a harami covers, you end up with something that resembles the outline of a pregnant woman. Okay, so it's not going to fetch much at an art auction, but it can pay off if you understand how to identify and trade on it.

Spotting a bearish harami

The setup day of a bearish harami pattern is a continuation of a prevailing uptrend — a strong up day. At first glance, the signal day isn't much to jump up and shout about, either. It's a day where the price action doesn't stray outside of the high and low of the setup day, and it indicates that the bears take over on the open, and neither side makes much progress pushing around the price action. But since this trend occurs after a bullish day and during a marked bullish trend, it can very well serve as a sign that the bears are starting to take control of the price action. Figure 8-4 shows an extremely straightforward illustration of the bearish harami pattern.

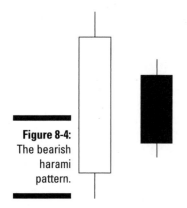

Figure 8-4:
The bearish harami pattern.

Another name for the signal day in this pattern is an *inside day,* where the high is lower than the previous high, and the low is lower than the previous low. When they occur on their own, inside days indicate a lack of conviction by both the bulls and the bears. But combine an inside day with a preceding bullish day and a bullish trend in place, and the combination can show you that the bull run is coming to an end.

When a prevailing trend starts to fade away into indecision, the next dominant trend is likely to go in the opposite direction.

Using the bearish harami pattern for a clever trade

For a good look at what the bearish harami looks like on a real chart, check out Figure 8-5. The chart is of the ETF that represents a group of the largest retail stocks, including Wal-Mart, Home Depot, and Walgreens. The trading symbol for this ETF is RTH. I have an affinity for retailers because I covered them fundamentally, and I've traded them at various firms. I also like this ETF and individual retailers as trading vehicles because their performances are closely linked to the state of the economy. With fluctuations in economic opinion comes volatility in these stocks, and with volatility comes trading opportunities!

The setup day of this two-day bearish harami pattern is a very strong up day that occurs in the midst of an uptrend that's been in place for several weeks. The signal day is an inside day that's a little on the bearish side. After that day the price falls quickly, back to the level where the uptrend began. The fall occurs much more quickly than the ascent, which is often the case with downward moves. They tend to happen much more quickly than uptrends. I guess fear is stronger than greed in the stock market.

A failing bearish harami pattern

Figure 8-6 provides a solid example of how the bearish harami can fail, because it happens twice in a row on this chart. This double dose of pattern failure should open your eyes to what can go wrong when the bearish harami doesn't play out favorably.

Figure 8-6 is a chart of the futures contract that trades based on the price of crude oil. As you can see, the bearish harami appears twice in a row. The setup day of each pattern is a nice up day (in the middle of an uptrend), and both of the signal days are inside days with dark candles that indicate bearish trading. These two patterns have something else in common, as well. They both fail immediately! Both patterns crash and burn the day after they appear on the chart. If you trade these patterns and take a small loss, I bet the next time a bearish harami rears its head, you think twice before putting on a trade.

The setup day of the second bearish harami on this chart is actually the same day that the first pattern fails. I define a bearish harami failure as a violation of the high of the signal day. This violation occurs on both patterns in Figure 8-6, and both fail the day after the pattern appears. (My definition for failure on a bearish harami pattern isn't the only one; a failure can also be a violation of the close of the setup day, or even the high of the setup day.) After trading achieves any of these levels, the prevailing uptrend becomes apparent. You need to figure out your level of risk tolerance and decide for yourself what level to use as a failure point for the bearish harami, but using my definition (the violation of the signal day's high) is a good starting point. This level is a good one to place a stop order to avoid a loss getting out of control.

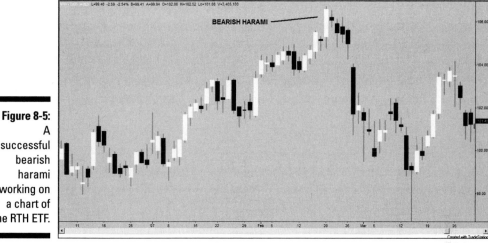

Figure 8-5:
A successful bearish harami working on a chart of the RTH ETF.

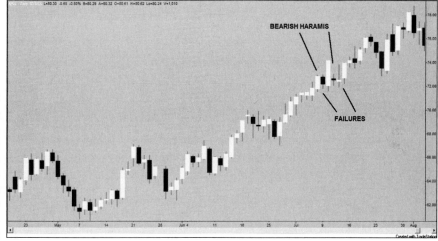

Figure 8-6:
A bearish harami pattern failing twice on a crude oil futures chart.

The bearish harami cross pattern

The next bearish two-day pattern is closely related to the pattern I discuss in the previous section ("The bearish harami pattern"), and it can be used in a similar manner. This pattern — the bearish harami cross — also marks the first return of the doji in this chapter. A *doji* is a candlestick pattern that looks like a cross and usually indicates some sort of indecision in the market. (Dojis are covered more in Chapter 6.) When this indecision occurs in a trend, it may signal that the trend is preparing to reverse.

Recognizing the bearish harami cross

The bearish harami cross occurs in an uptrend and consists of an up setup day followed by a doji for the signal day. The signal day doji must be both a cross and an inside day. Take a look at Figure 8-7 for an illustration of the bearish harami cross.

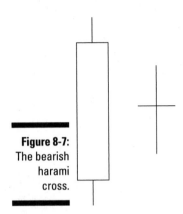

Figure 8-7:
The bearish harami cross.

Because the doji indicates that indecision ruled the day, I actually prefer the bearish harami cross to the plain old harami reversal pattern. Dojis are rare, and the occurrence of a bearish harami cross pattern is more of an event than the appearance of the bearish harami.

Trading on the bearish harami cross

The chart in Figure 8-8 gives you an idea of how the bearish harami cross can spell market success for you. This figure shows the pattern appearing on a chart of one of my favorite commodity contracts: frozen concentrated orange juice, or OJ.

In the movie *Trading Places* (one of my favorites), commodities are being explained to ersatz trader Eddie Murphy. There's a table that displays several traded commodities (including orange juice), and when the conniving old Dukes brothers get to the OJ, one of them says, "orange juice, like you may have had for breakfast this morning" in a tone he could've used to explain the concept to a first grader. The look Eddie Murphy gives the camera is priceless.

Anyway, Figure 8-8 shows the bearish harami cross appearing in a choppy uptrend. The setup day is clearly an up day, and the contract reaches new highs. The cross or doji day follows, and the bulls are clearly running out of steam. After that, you see a very bearish day with no violation of the high for the setup day, which is what I like to use as the failure level for this pattern, and then a downtrend that lasts a few weeks. If you put on a short position and ride the downtrend for a while, you end up with an attractive profit.

For a failing bearish harami cross, I use Transocean Offshore (RIG). This company builds drilling rigs for use in deep water. The stock is a great trading vehicle due to the company's exposure to the energy markets.

Signaling a losing trade

In Figure 8-9 you can see that during an uptrend, a little cross appears after a bullish day. This cross or doji is actually a slight up day, but a doji just the same in my book. Much like the price of energy, the stock prices of energy-related stocks have been on a tear, and RIG is no exception. This bearish harami fails pretty quickly, and the uptrend stays intact.

Figure 8-8:
A bearish harami cross that produces a favorable result on a chart of OJ.

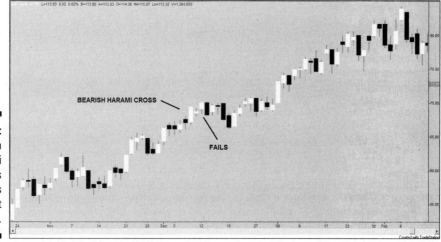

Figure 8-9:
A bearish harami cross pattern fails on a chart of RIG.

You may notice that although this signal failed, there were a few days after the failure where the chart still appears to reveal a change in trend. This confusing start-stop-start situation is part of the game.

Signals sometimes fail and trades get stopped out temporarily, only to eventually reveal price action that could've produced profitable results. These occurrences are frustrating, but I've never been upset with myself for following trading rules or signals, even when it's clear a few hours or days later that I could've made money if I had overridden a stop or ignored a failure signal. When I consistently follow the rules, I can't second guess myself, but if I don't follow the rules and a trade fails, I can only blame myself. I suggest that you adopt the same philosophy, especially if you're just starting to trade.

I can't emphasize enough that sticking with a trading plan and following your rules may be the most key components to becoming a successful trader.

The bearish inverted hammer pattern

Like many of the bearish reversal patterns described in this chapter, the bearish inverted hammer is set up with a long white candle that occurs during an uptrend. Then there's a gap opening and even more buying to start the signal day. However, at some point the bears are called to action and start to push prices lower, and if you keep your eyes peeled for that move and trade accordingly, you should be able to turn a profit.

Identifying the bearish inverted hammer

The bearish inverted hammer is depicted in Figure 8-10. The inverted hammer is actually the second day of the pattern. The setup day is a long white candle, which indicates a very bullish day. The start of the signal day (also called the hammer day) sees a gap opening and continued bullishness; that process carries on for part of the day, and higher prices are achieved. At some point during the signal day, the bears have had enough and selling begins. The bearish action pushes prices down below the opening price, and the close is equal to or very near the day's low.

Using the bearish inverted hammer in your trades

To provide you with a winning scenario for the bearish inverted hammer (Figure 8-11), I offer a pattern that actually came up while I was searching for an example for this section. This chart is for the Financial Select Sector Fund, symbol XLF, which is an ETF that represents a handful of large financial stocks such as Citigroup, American International Group, and Bank of America. You can see the bearish inverted hammer near the top of the chart. When I saw the pattern, I figured I should put my money where my mouth is. I knew that even if the trade didn't work out, I'd still have an example of a failing pattern for later in this section. Luckily, though, that wasn't the case.

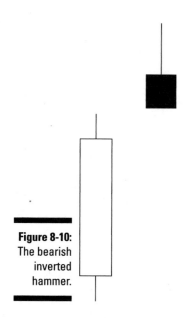

Figure 8-10:
The bearish
inverted
hammer.

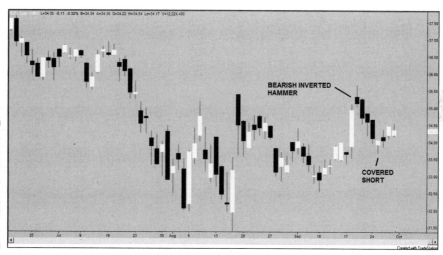

Figure 8-11:
A bearish
inverted
hammer
that works
on a chart of
the XLF ETF.

I shorted the XLF on the signal day of the pattern, held it for four days, and exited on the first up day. I also placed a buy stop order at the open of the signal (or hammer) day. That's a very tight stop, but this trade was outside of my normal trading activity, and I felt it was prudent to place a close stop. More aggressive traders may have chosen the high of the signal day for their stop.

The example in Figure 8-11 is doubly useful because it also shows you how to exit a trade. I don't discuss exiting trades much in this book — too many methods and goals exist once a trade has been initiated to cover here — but this situation is definitely worth pointing out. I chose my exit in this trade because the reciprocal version of the bearish inverted pattern appeared. I saw the bullish pattern, and I was happy to exit and take a profit of just over a dollar on one hundred shares — I'll let you do the math — and take my wife to dinner on the proceeds. I ended up with material for this book and a nice dinner for Merribeth. Now that's a perfect trade.

Recognizing a losing trade

On a somewhat gloomier note, have a look at Figure 8-12 for an example of a couple of failing bearish inverted hammers. Figure 8-12 is a chart of the ETF that represents the 30 stocks that comprise the Dow Jones Industrial Average and trade with the symbol DIA, sometimes called the Diamonds. Luckily for this author and trader, there wasn't a real-life trade involved with this example.

Both patterns appear in an uptrend, and both feature an up setup day followed by a gap opening and strong activity during the signal day that reverses with a lower close. Although usually an indication of a reversal, both times these signals were proven to be false fairly quickly.

In the case of the first pattern, all possible resistance levels were violated and the uptrend continued. For the second pattern, I highlight two failures:

✔ One is a violation of the open of the hammer day.

✔ The other is a violation of that day's high.

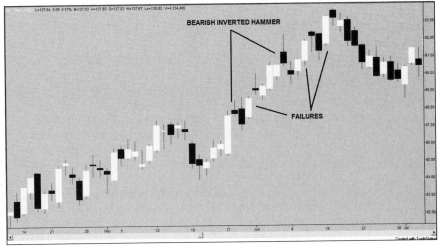

Figure 8-12:
Two bearish inverted hammer failures on a chart of the DIA ETF.

The second pattern takes a little longer to fail, but it does eventually. The second pattern is interesting because it does occur toward the end of the uptrend. But the signal is violated, and a trader following the rules would have exited the short. This additional illustration shows how you sometimes have to just follow the rules and move on, even when it's clear later that you could've turned a profit if you'd stuck with the position. Don't look back and say "what if?" Be confident in the fact that you followed set rules and that over the long haul, following the rules results in more consistent trading profits.

The bearish doji star

The bearish doji star is another bearish reversal pattern that contains — you guessed it — a doji. This pattern is also an extension of the bearish inverted hammer, which I discuss in the previous section.

Spotting the bearish doji star

The bearish doji star always occurs in an uptrend, and the setup day is an up day. The signal day is a doji that's sort of hanging out there by itself, because the opening of the signal day is gap down from the previous day's price action. Figure 8-13 is an example of how the two days that make up a bearish doji star appear together on a chart.

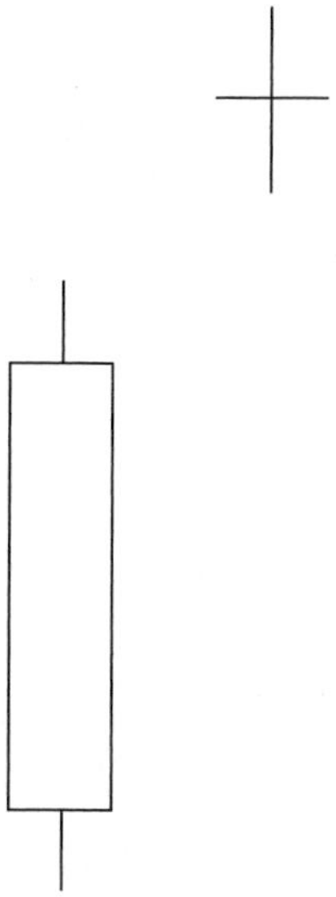

Figure 8-13:
The bearish
doji star
pattern.

Understanding how to trade using the bearish doji star

Figure 8-14 is a chart that shows the bearish doji star in action. In this example, this doji star pattern is working well to signal an impending drop in the stock for microchip maker Intel (symbol INTC). An uptrend is in place, and the setup day of the pattern is a bullish day in accordance with the trend. The signal day is a doji, with the combined open and close outside of the range covered by the setup day's trading activity. After all the bullishness of the previous few days, the bears are finally making a stand.

The day after the pattern is a very bearish day, so if a trader didn't put on the trade during the doji day, he doesn't have a chance. Then the day after the long black candle appears, the stock gaps down tremendously. This change is a quick victory for any sellers that are attracted to short this bearish doji star.

Failing to give a good short signal

For the losing example of a bearish doji star, I present Figure 8-15, which is a chart of the stock for Apple Computer (symbol AAPL). The bearish doji star I highlight in the figure showed up during a bullish trend, and you can see that this chart includes a nice up day followed by a doji. All the bearish doji star criteria are in place, but the pattern fails swiftly and mercilessly, and the trend continues with a very strong up day directly after the pattern. The potential Apple trade goes rotten.

My failure level for a bearish doji star is the high of the signal day, as opposed to that day's open or close. Using the combined open and close area of the doji doesn't provide much room for volatility on a stop. If the stock opens just slightly up the next day, then it will hit the buy stop, which is very likely to happen even in the case of a trend reversal. In order to avoid regular market noise forcing me out of a trade, I prefer to rely on the high of the signal day for my stop exit.

The bearish meeting line

Although rare, the bearish meeting line pattern is worth understanding as you build your arsenal of double-stick bearish patterns that signal a trend reversal. This line can be a clear indication of a change in trend due to the stark contrast of the two days that combine to form the pattern.

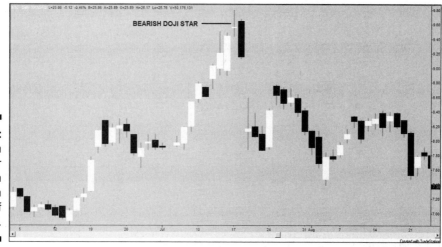

Figure 8-14:
A bearish
doji star
pattern
working on
a chart of
INTC.

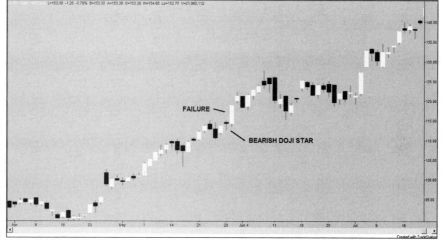

Figure 8-15:
The bearish
doji star
pattern fails
on a chart of
AAPL stock.

Understanding how to identify the bearish meeting line

If you're looking for an ideal visual representation of the bearish meeting line, it doesn't get any better than Figure 8-16.

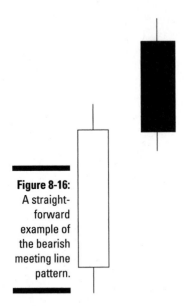

Figure 8-16:
A straight-forward
example of
the bearish
meeting line
pattern.

On the setup day of the bearish meeting line, as with most of the two-day bearish patterns, you see a strong up day. Then, on the signal day, you notice a gap opening, which quickly entices some sellers. The selling continues until the close. A long black candle is the result, with the close of the day being very near its low. The close of the signal day also happens to be very near the close of the setup day, and the meeting of these lines gives the pattern its name.

Trading on the bearish meeting line

For an example of the bearish meeting line pattern producing a scenario that's ripe for a successful trade, see Figure 8-17. That's a chart of the aluminum maker Alcoa (symbol AA). As a producer of a material used in many everyday products, Alcoa is another stock that has strong ties to the overall economy. AA is a volatile stock at times, creating both long and short opportunities.

A definite uptrend exists on this chart — the first criteria for keeping any eye out for a bearish reversal signal. The setup day is a very nice up day, and then the signal day opens with a gap higher. The bulls are ruling the trading activity, and the situation is perfect for a successful bearish meeting line pattern.

If you were watching this pattern develop, you'd be pleased to see that sellers come in and push prices lower than the previous day's close, and although the stock rebounds a little, the price settles on the signal day near where the stock closed on the setup day.

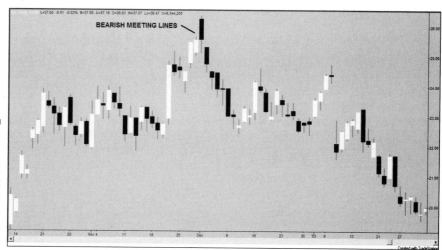

Figure 8-17:
A bearish
meeting line
pattern that
turns out
well on a
chart of AA.

Then the trend reversal begins. And what a trend reversal it is! Six black candles line up in a row, signaling that the uptrend has definitely ended. Any trader not prepared on the day the signal was completed misses out on a good part of the outstanding downtrend.

To get in on the close of a day that a pattern is completed, watch for the patterns as they develop during a trading day. Usually, with five to ten minutes left in a trading day, you can tell whether a pattern is forming or not. The problem for you if you're a new or part-time trader is that you probably have a job or other responsibilities that may prevent you from being available to trade during these important time periods. Be sure to factor in your own availability when developing your trading strategy.

An unsuccessful bearish meeting line

An example of the bearish meeting lines failing to signal an uptrend reversal appears in Figure 8-18, which is a chart of the futures contract that trades on the level of the Euro currency versus the U.S. dollar. The uptrend is in place, and the formation appears as it should. This pattern is very encouraging for a trader who's been waiting for a good time to short. In this example, however, that enthusiasm from a short seller is fleeting.

The day that follows the pattern proves it to be invalid. Prices trade higher than both the open and the high of the pattern's signal day, making it clear that the pattern is a bust.

When shorting based on the bearish meeting line pattern, I usually place my stops on either the high of the signal day or the open of the signal day.

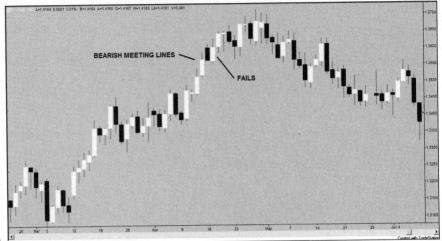

Figure 8-18: The bearish meeting line pattern fails on a chart of Euro currency futures.

The bearish piercing line or dark cloud cover pattern

Another two-day bearish reversal pattern is the bearish piercing line, also known as the dark cloud cover, because some say that the signal day is an ominous dark cloud that hangs over the setup day. It requires a little use of your imagination.

Identifying the bearish piercing line pattern

You can see a straightforward illustration of the bearish piercing line in Figure 8-19. Just like all the bearish two-stick reversal patterns I describe in the preceding sections of this chapter, this pattern must appear in an uptrend. Also, in keeping with the other bearish reversal patterns, the setup day for the bearish piercing line is a bullish day. The signal day is a long black candle with an opening that's higher than the setup day's high. The signal day indicates that some sellers came rushing in, pushing prices down through the setup day's opening price and below its midpoint.

Making trades based on the bearish piercing line

The bearish piercing line pattern can be used to put on a profitable short, as you can see in Figure 8-20. This chart shows the bearish piercing line on a chart of Intel (INTC).

The pattern occurs in what appears to be the late stages of an uptrend. The price is still working higher, but not with as much momentum as it did where I've pointed out the first stage of the uptrend. If you see a reversal pattern when you believe a trend is starting to lose steam, that's more encouraging than when the pattern appears in a strong trend. In later chapters I discuss how to use indicators to make these distinctions (see Chapters 11, 14, and 15).

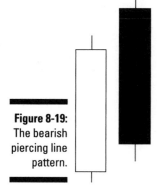

Figure 8-19:
The bearish piercing line pattern.

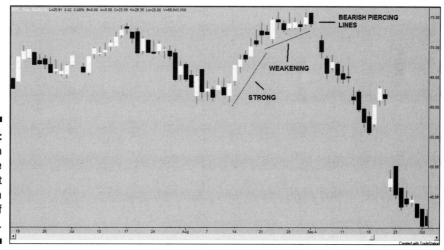

Figure 8-20:
The bearish piercing line pattern at work on a chart of INTC.

Falling short with the bearish piercing line

This INTC chart is another example of the limited amount of time you may have for initiating certain trades. Unless you keep a close eye on the chart, you miss your chance to put on a successful short. So what does a bearish piercing line pattern look like when the pattern fails? For an answer, see Figure 8-21.

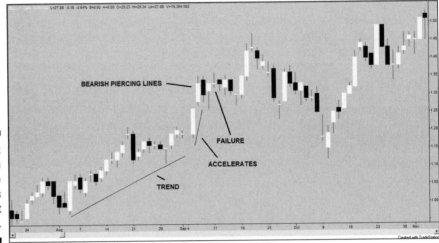

Figure 8-21: The bearish piercing line pattern fails on a chart of DELL.

Figure 8-21 shows a chart of the stock for another technology company, Dell Inc. (symbol DELL), which was founded by Michael Dell. (Maybe I'm too focused on the market, but how cool would it be to have your name become a stock symbol?) Here you can see a bearish piercing line that occurs during an uptrend. The uptrend continues on, and the failure of the pattern (and the appearance of higher prices) takes a couple of days. If you jump the gun on this pattern and put on a short without a smart stop, you see some losses.

Making a Profit with Bearish Trend Patterns

In addition to double-stick patterns that tell a trader it's time to sell or put on a short after an uptrending move, some patterns also indicate a downtrend continuation is on the horizon. These patterns can tell you when you still have room to profit on a short. You can also turn to them when you're looking to buy a stock that's been in a downtrend and looks to be "getting cheap." A bearish double-stick trend continuation pattern can let you know that a stock is going to get cheaper and can therefore be had at an even lower price.

A quick note on trend strength

Allow me to point out an interesting side note and comparison of Figures 8-20 and 8-21. The successful bearish piercing line occurs when the trend appears to be moderating. On the DELL chart, which contains the failing pattern, the opposite occurs. The trend is strong, but the pattern appears after an acceleration of momentum. This burst of uptrend momentum can indicate to an observant trader that even though a bearish pattern has appeared, it's probably smart to use caution when putting on a short. It can also signal that a quick exit may very well be in order. Remember to keep on the lookout for these increases in trend strength. To help you train your eye, I've highlighted the relevant area in Figure 8-21.

All the two-day bearish trending patterns covered in this section require that the market or stock in question be in a down-trending mode. Determining the trend can be subjective and can also be a matter of the time frame in which you're trading. I go into great detail on determining trend in later chapters (especially Chapter 11), but for this section, just concentrate on the pattern and don't worry as much about whether you agree with my assessment of the prevailing trend.

The bearish thrusting lines

The first two-day pattern that indicates the continuation of a downtrend is the bearish thrusting lines pattern. I like this pattern because the signal day is an up day. You may scratch your head and wonder why I would like an up day that indicates the continuation of a downtrend. At first blush it does sound counterintuitive, but the presence of an up day on the signal day of this pattern means that a great opportunity exists to put on a short at prices higher than the previous day of the downtrend.

Understanding how to spot the bearish thrusting lines

Figure 8-22 shows you exactly what the bearish thrusting lines look like on a chart. Again, the prevailing trend should be down, and the setup day is a long black candle. On the signal day, prices open weak, but then the bulls come in and try to reverse the trend and take over. They seem to be succeeding, but they're not quite strong enough to get prices to the upper half of the candlestick that was created by the setup day's trading. This activity means that although the bears don't completely control the day, they're still around and are eager to reassert themselves in the coming days.

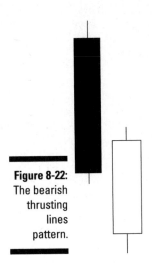

Figure 8-22:
The bearish thrusting lines pattern.

Trading on the bearish thrusting lines

For an example of the bearish thrusting lines working well, turn to Figure 8-23 and a chart of the stock for the Toll Brothers (symbol TOL), which is a high-end home-building company. During the recent contraction of real estate prices, the publicly traded home-building stocks lost a lot of ground, and TOL was no exception.

The bearish thrusting lines actually pop up three times on this chart, and for each of those three occurrences, the stock's price drops for days after the pattern appears. For the sake of emphasis, I added a downtrend line to show the continuing downtrend.

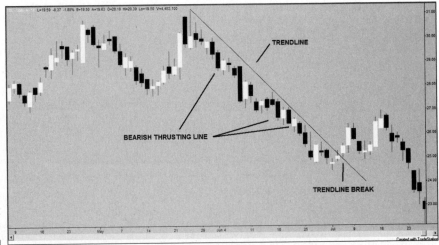

Figure 8-23:
The bearish thrusting lines pattern works on a chart of TOL.

A successful trade based on the bearish thrusting lines in this chart starts with the close of the first pattern's signal day. If you're short from the top of this downtrend, you definitely feel like a skilled trader. You can easily monitor the continuation patterns and follow the trend as it heads down. But where would you exit the short?

An exit would be prudent when the price trades over the hand-drawn line on the chart. (See Chapter 11 for more information on how to draw trendlines.) At that point the downtrend has been broken, and the easy money on the short has been made, so be smart and take your tidy profit and move on.

Recognizing a disappointing bearish thrusting line pattern

Want to see what happens when the bearish thrusting lines fail? Look no farther than Figure 8-24, which is a chart of the futures contracts that trade based on the level of the Japanese Yen versus the U.S. dollar. You can see that toward the end of this downtrend, two double-stick patterns actually fail to indicate the end of the downtrend. Both two-day patterns and the failing days are highlighted on the chart.

I hate to see the patterns in Figure 8-24 fail. They both start out with so much promise! Both patterns appear in downtrends and meet the criteria of having a long black candle setup day followed by an up signal day that retraces some of the long black candle day's area but doesn't close higher than its midpoint. The failures occur when the highs of the signal days are violated on the days that follow each pattern. You can even say that the violations occur when days that follow the patterns have prices that exceed the midpoint, open, or high of the setup day. It doesn't matter which level you choose — they all get violated, the patterns fail, and the trends turn upward quickly.

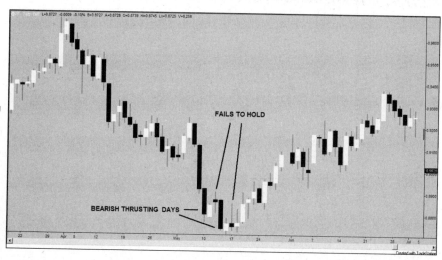

Figure 8-24:
The bearish thrusting lines fail at the end of a downtrend on the Yen futures.

FAILS TO HOLD

BEARISH THRUSTING DAYS

The bearish separating lines

The next continuation or trending pattern is referred to as the bearish separating lines pattern. If you flip back to Chapter 7, you can read all about this pattern's bullish counterpart.

Identifying the bearish separating lines

The setup day of the bearish separating lines pattern is a long white candle, which can make some bears or shorts a bit nervous when it appears in a downtrend. A little relief for those factions comes on the signal day, however, when the opening price is near the setup day's open. That relaxes them a bit, and they decide that the up day wasn't justified, so they keep right on selling on the open of the signal day. But what happens to the bulls that had a ball on the setup day? They can't take the heat, so they sell their positions, and the price just keeps on trending lower and lower. For a graphical representation, check out Figure 8-25.

This pattern is somewhat rare because it's unusual for the open of the signal day to be equal or near the setup day's open. It really amounts to a gap down opening, with all the prices from the setup day not even trading on the signal day. Short-term buyers on the setup day hardly have a chance to get out with a profit on the signal day, which is a very discouraging prospect for a buyer.

Understanding how to trade on the bearish separating lines

The example I use in Figure 8-26 for illustrating how you can use the bearish separating lines for your trading purposes is an unusual stock chart for this book. The stock represented is Inco (symbol N), a large producer of the metal nickel. The model is uncommon because Inco merged out of business with another company at the beginning of 2007, and it doesn't trade publicly in the U.S. anymore. Still, though, the example is a sound one, and it shows you how the bearish separating lines can really sing when the conditions are just right.

Figure 8-26 clearly shows a downtrend in place, but then a couple of white candles appear and make the shorts a little twitchy. The second white candle in the highlighted area is the setup day of the bearish separating lines pattern. It reveals that either some bulls think the price is right to buy or the shorts are starting to take their profits and get out. However, the signal day of the pattern shows the price opening near the open of the setup day. Behold the bearish separating lines! That means the bears aren't done selling, and they push the price lower throughout the day and keep the downtrend going.

The pattern in Figure 8-26 is very well formed, but it may not be the best pattern to rely on if you're interested in initiating a new trade. If you trade it on the close, you sell at the bottom of a long black day, so quite a bit of ground will be covered in the direction you want to trade. This particular pattern is best used as a confirmation that the downtrend is intact, and you're lucky to see it if you want to hold onto a short position for a little while longer.

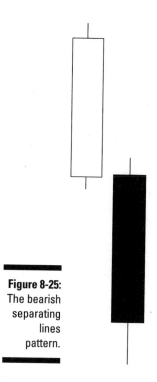

Figure 8-25:
The bearish
separating
lines
pattern.

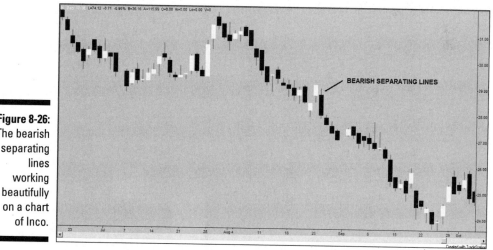

Figure 8-26:
The bearish
separating
lines
working
beautifully
on a chart
of Inco.

The failing bearish separating line

Just when you thought you'd always love the bearish separating lines, here I
come with an example of what happens when they go bad. Figure 8-27 is a
chart of General Electric (GE), a conglomerate that stretches from the NBC

television networks to appliances to aircraft engines. You'd be hard pressed to find someone who hasn't been exposed to a branch of GE at some point in his life. (I say that, of course, with my CNBC on in the background.)

The downtrend on the chart in Figure 8-27 is a strong one, and when the pattern appears, it looks like the downtrend has been underway for several weeks. The setup day of the pattern is an attempt by some buyers to pick a cheap place to buy. Then, on the signal day, the bears take over from the open and push prices lower. But notice that on the day immediately after the pattern, the open and high of the signal day are both violated. That's a pretty good sign that the pattern may not be indicating that the trend will continue.

Shortly after the pattern in Figure 8-27 is violated, a trend reversal occurs. If you're considering buying before you see the bearish separating lines, that pattern may keep you from doing so. If you're short and you see the pattern, you may have waited to cover. Because the pattern didn't hold and the trend was broken, buyers can change their minds more easily and start buying. That's certainly the case here, and you can see that the price of GE heads higher for several days as a result.

The bearish neck lines

The last bearish double-stick pattern in this chapter is the bearish neck lines, and just like its bullish counterparts from Chapter 7, this pattern is more of a pattern classification than one single pattern.

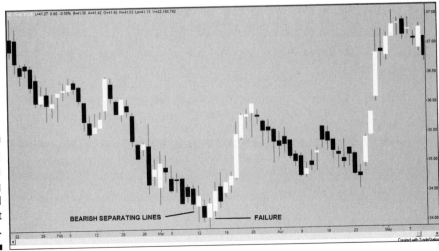

Figure 8-27:
The bearish separating lines fail on a chart of GE.

Recognizing bearish neck lines

Bearish neck lines have two types: bearish *on neck* lines and bearish *in neck* lines. The difference between the patterns is so small that you don't have to separate them out into two sections.

Figure 8-28 includes both bearish in neck and bearish on neck patterns. The only difference is that the wick of the in neck setup day may overlap some with the signal day of the pattern. Both variations have a long black candle for the setup day followed by a gap down and a rebound attempt that manages to trade back only to the close of the setup day. The bears hold their ground at this level.

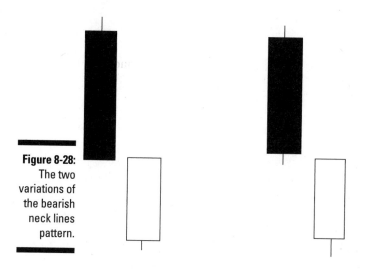

Figure 8-28: The two variations of the bearish neck lines pattern.

Using the bearish neck lines for profitable trading

Figure 8-29 shows a chart of the futures contract that trades based on the prices of 30-year bonds issued by the U.S. Treasury. The bearish neck lines on this chart are in neck because the setup day overlaps with the signal day. The bulls try to rebound the futures price, but they're met with bearish resistance at the previous opening price. Then you see a brief battle between the bulls and bears followed by a continuation of the downtrend.

This pattern is valid even though prices don't immediately continue down on the following day. The trend doesn't really break, and the price levels of the long black day aren't violated. The next couple of days may be nerve-wracking for bears, but those that hold their ground on a short are rewarded with lower prices.

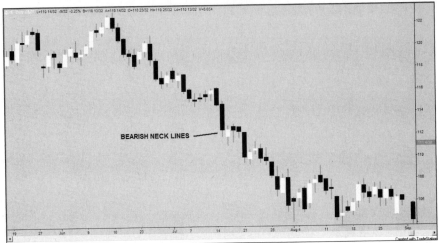

Figure 8-29:
The bearish
neck lines
working on
a chart of
the U.S.
Treasury
bond
futures.

Noticing an unsuccessful bearish neck line

Just like the rest of the two-stick patterns in this chapter, the bearish neck lines can fail. Refer to Figure 8-30.

Figure 8-30 is a chart of the stock representing ownership in U.S. Steel (symbol X). Because U.S. Steel is such a large producer of an eminently vital material, the company is very economically sensitive, and its stock is volatile for trading both long and short.

The bearish neck lines appear during a downtrend, and the other criteria are in place; the setup day is represented by a long black candle, which is followed by a gap down. Prices then rebound, but the bears hold the price steady. All appears to be well, but then a couple of days after the pattern appears, the bulls get rolling on a more successful run and the trend changes.

I point to two days as failure days in Figure 8-30. Choose whichever resistance level you want, but when a long black candle day is involved, picking the midpoint may be prudent if you hope to get out of a short or buy before the trend is in full swing and the prices you're facing aren't too steep. The first failure day trades through the midpoint, the second trades over the high, and then the uptrend is in place.

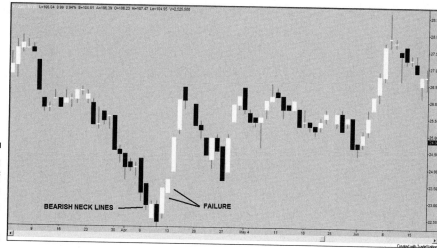

L=106.04 0.99 0.94% B=105.81 A=106.39 O=106.23 Hi=107.47 Lo=104.95 V=2,526,500

BEARISH NECK LINES ───── ─── FAILURE

Created with TradeStation

Figure 8-30:
A failure of
the bearish
neck lines
pattern.

Part III
Making the Most of Complex Patterns

The 5th Wave   By Rich Tennant

"I was so into my charts that one day she came in and told me she was running away with the pool boy. Now there's a trend I didn't see coming."

In this part . . .

Rome wasn't built in a day, or even two, and many candlestick patterns share that construction schedule. Some of the most useful and interesting candlestick patterns take three days to form. I call these complex patterns, and I cover them throughout Part III with explanations of how you can spot the patterns and use them to inform your buying and selling decisions. To close the part, check out the explanations of a few technical indicators, which can complement your candlestick charts and enhance your results.

Chapter 9

Getting the Hang of Bullish Three-Stick Patterns

In This Chapter
▷ Three-day patterns that signal the end of a downtrend
▷ Predicting an uptrend continuation using three-day patterns

*T*he addition of three-stick candlestick patterns to your trading arsenal makes your trading strategies more complicated, more interesting, and hopefully, more profitable. In this chapter, I cover some of the bullish three-stick patterns that you can use to make effective and efficient trades.

The three-stick patterns are a little more of a challenge than their one- and two-stick counterparts because there are several rules that each must follow in order to emerge as a valid signal. Three-stick patterns can also be a bit frustrating. You may watch the first two days of your favorite (and most reliable) pattern begin to emerge only to see it fizzle out on the third day. But if you're up to the challenge and willing to deal with the occasional annoyance, these patterns can be valuable tools when trying to predict trend reversals or confirm that a current trend is going to stay in place.

Understanding Bullish Three-Stick Trend Reversal Patterns

The three-stick patterns in this section offer you a heads-up when a downtrend is about to switch gears and turn into an uptrend. Many of these three-stick patterns exist, and in the pages that follow I cover many of the most common ones. With three days needed to complete each pattern, you have time to watch as the patterns shape up, and you should be focused in when the third day rolls around, and you've noticed some interesting developments during the two preceding days.

When working with three-day patterns, be prepared by closely monitoring days that follow two days of promising price action. If a pattern is completed as you'd hoped, you need to be ready to put on the appropriate trade and stop order near the close of the day on which the pattern is completed.

The three inside up pattern

The three inside up pattern is a good place to begin my discussion of the bullish three-stick patterns that can let you know when a downtrend is about to be reversed. This pattern is a straightforward pattern that you can recognize with just a little practice.

Identifying the three inside up pattern

The three inside up pattern has a peculiar name, but a quick look at Figure 9-1 should give you a good idea of where the name originated. The *three* part comes from there being three days involved in creating the pattern. There are three sticks, and the second day is an inside day relative to the first day, which is a long down day. The final day is an up day that closes higher than the open of the first day.

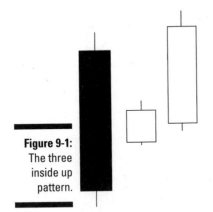

Figure 9-1:
The three inside up pattern.

The trading activity that results in a three inside up pattern involves a gradual shift of power from the bears to the bulls. I like this pattern and the way it develops because it usually gives a trader time to put on a trade before too much of the reversal has occurred. Traders can always buy high with the intention of selling higher, but it's nice when buying high doesn't mean they're buying *too* high.

Making effective trades using the three inside up pattern

The chart in Figure 9-2 gives you a very good idea of how the three inside up pattern can tip you off as to when to buy in advance of a forthcoming uptrend. It's a chart of the futures contracts that trade based on the ten-year Treasury bonds issued by the U.S. government. It's one of the most actively traded futures contracts, and it's a very economically sensitive security.

This chart shows an extended downtrend in the price of the ten-year futures. There have been a couple of attempts to change the course of the trend, and before the pattern arrives, it appears that the downtrend has been moderating. I include a couple of trendlines on the chart as an illustration.

If you're looking for trend reversal patterns, a good sign is when you see that the prevailing trend is starting to moderate. When you spot a moderating trend, be sure to keep your eyes peeled for a candlestick pattern indicating that a trend reversal is on the way.

The first day of the three inside up pattern in Figure 9-2 is a long black candle, which is followed by a slight up day that's an inside day relative to the first day. The third and final day is a strong up day that closes above the open of the first day of the pattern and completes the bullish signal. Then it's off to the races, and the trend starts shooting upward.

Are you wondering where you may place a wise sell stop order when you're working with the three inside up pattern? If so, good question. You have several choices. In most cases, I use the open or low of the second day. If those levels are violated, I regard the pattern as invalid. You can also use the open or low of the third day; both are viable alternatives.

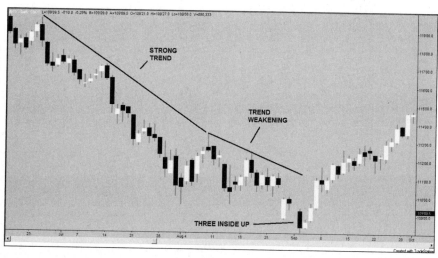

Figure 9-2:
The three inside up pattern offers a useful buy signal on a chart of ten-year U.S. Treasury bond futures.

Avoid using the first day, because if the security breaks through the lows of the first two days, then there's a good chance that the first day levels are going to be tested if not violated. Wouldn't you rather be out of the long trade before this occurs?

The three inside up pattern not working out too well

This section gives you an example of what can happen when a three inside up pattern fails. Take a look at Figure 9-3, where you can see a three inside up pattern that appears in a downtrend but doesn't signal a trend reversal. It's a chart of the futures contracts that trade based on the level of the Australian dollar versus the U.S. dollar. This isn't the most liquid of currency futures pairs, but it's still active enough to make money on both the long and short side.

The first day of the pattern in Figure 9-3 is a down day, and the second day shows a gap up but doesn't have a low that violates the low of the first day. The second day's close is also higher than its open, but the second day's close stays between the open and close of the first day. And if you're thinking that the second day is an inside day, you're absolutely right! Finally, the third day is also an up day — a long white bar — with an open that's higher than the open of the second day. So where does the pattern go wrong?

The day after the pattern is the culprit. On that day, a long black candle violates anything a savvy trader considers a support level, and that's all she wrote. Even though the pattern fails, the failure day can be a blessing for buyers who have solid stops in place, because that little bit of failure (and the subsequent stop-induced end of the trade) would save them from the effects of a downtrend that continues for several days.

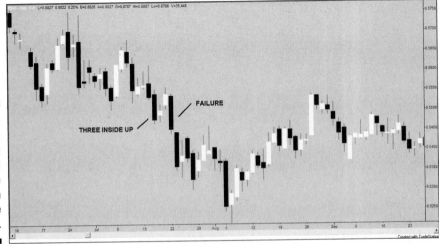

Figure 9-3: The three inside up pattern fails on the Australian dollar future contracts.

The three outside up pattern

The three outside up pattern is another relatively simple three-stick reversal pattern that you can pick up on with a little patience and a basic understanding of the necessary components. This section gives you the full scoop.

Spotting the three outside up pattern

Like all bullish reversal patterns, the three outside up should occur in the midst of a downtrend. Here is how the days play out:

1. **Day one: The pattern's first day is actually a down day, but just a slight down day.**

2. **Day two: The second day opens with a gap down from the first day, but prices don't stay down for long.**

   This day creates an "outside day" relative to the first day with the high being higher, the low being lower than the first day. Also, the open of the day is lower than the previous close, and the close of this second day is higher than the open of the first day.

   The bulls take over at some point during the second day and push prices higher until the close is near the day's high. The second day is a long white bar, and it's an outside day relative to the first day. *Outside* means that the price action for the second day traded outside of the high and low of the first day.

3. **Day three: The third day completes the pattern with another up day.**

   On the third day it's clear that the bulls aren't done, and the day closes higher than the high of the second day. The trend has definitely turned, and it's headed up, up and away.

For a straightforward example of the three outside up pattern, see Figure 9-4.

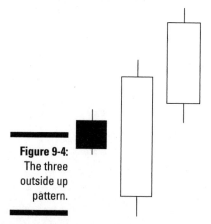

Figure 9-4:
The three outside up pattern.

Trading on the three outside up pattern

For a real-world example of the three outside up pattern, I use a chart of the stock for a company that helps its customers escape the real world. The chart is in Figure 9-5, and the company is Electronic Arts (ERTS), which produces some of the world's top video games. Its Madden Football games comprise its flagship series, and the company's stock is great on both the short and long side because it has many volatile moves based on the popularity of individual games and the platforms on which the games are played.

On the chart in Figure 9-5, ERTS stock appears to have found a bottom, and it looks like an uptrend is on the horizon. When you're working with three-day reversal patterns, try to buy at the beginning of a trend when prices are relatively low compared to recent history. The pattern plays out fairly well: The trend is down, and a down day — albeit not a very convincing one — occurs on the first day. It's followed by an outside up day, and then the third day is an up day that outpaces the bullishness of the second day.

The three outside up pattern comes before more bearishness instead of bullishness

The three outside up pattern is a thing of beauty, but Figure 9-6 shows you the pattern's potential for ugliness when it goes bad. The chart is for Hewlett Packard (HPQ). The pattern shows up in a downtrend, and the first day is indeed a down day. The second day is an up day, and it's an outside day relative to the first day. Very promising! Then, to top it all off, the pattern is completed with an up day on the third day that exhibits some bullish behavior.

Figure 9-5:
The three outside up pattern makes for a winning trading scenario on a chart of ERTS.

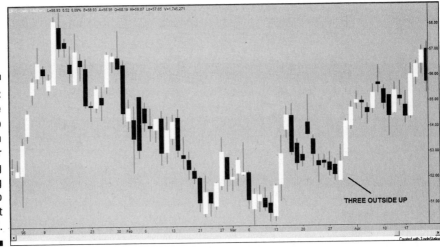

THREE OUTSIDE UP

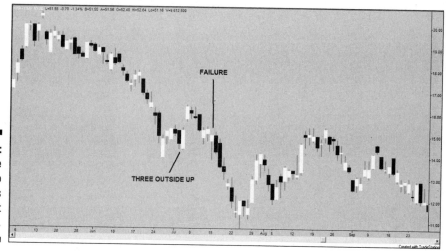

L=51.55 -0.70 -1.34% B=51.55 A=51.56 O=52.45 Hi=52.64 Lo=51.16 V=9,612,500

FAILURE

THREE OUTSIDE UP

Created with TradeStation

Figure 9-6:
The three outside up pattern fails on a chart of HPQ.

But the bullishness isn't meant to last. On the very next trading day after the pattern appears, the stock never even gets over the previous day's closing price. The gap is quickly filled, and then in a few days anything that may be considered a support level is compromised. Easy come, easy go.

The three white soldiers pattern

The three white soldiers pattern includes three bullish candles in a row. If the pattern occurs with a downtrend in front of it, you can consider it a possible signal that the bulls have had enough and are buying in force.

WARNING!

Although it's a nice indication to buy, a small drawback to the three white soldiers is the amount of ground that's already been covered at the completion of the pattern.

Recognizing the three white soldiers

To locate the three white soldiers on a chart, look for three consecutive up days that occur in a prevailing downtrend. Then look closer. If the open, high, low, and close of the second day are higher than those of the first day, and those four points are also higher on the third day than the second, then you're looking at the three white soldiers pattern. Make sense? Have a look at Figure 9-7 for a visual.

The price action behind these days is dramatic, and it normally indicates a quick shift from a downtrend to an uptrend. The three white soldiers mean that the bulls are in control for three straight days beginning with the open of the first day.

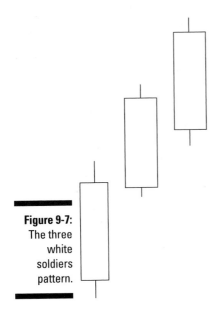

Figure 9-7:
The three
white
soldiers
pattern.

Using the three white soldiers to make a profitable trade

The example I use to show you how to make trades based on the three white soldiers pattern is near and dear to my heart. It's a chart of the futures contracts that trade on the level of the Euro, and I executed a successful trade based on this very pattern. Prior to spotting the pattern, I'd been looking for an indication that the downtrend was coming to an end, and so I was delighted to see the three white soldiers shown in Figure 9-8.

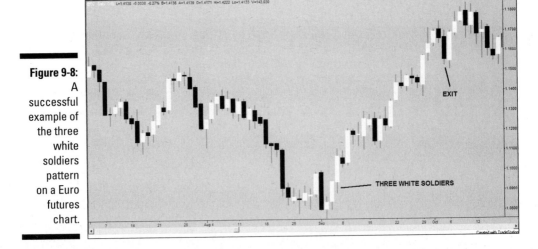

Figure 9-8:
A
successful
example of
the three
white
soldiers
pattern
on a Euro
futures
chart.

After such a dramatic move, there's sometimes an opportunity for a pullback (a small trend down from a higher level), but I bought the Euro futures very close to the closing price of the third day of the pattern. I had a plan in place to buy the Euro when it appeared the downtrend was coming to an end, so I was a little more aggressive than I needed to be. With a little patience I could've gotten a better price the next day, but I didn't want to risk missing the trade altogether — something that can sometimes feel worse to me than losing money.

I also highlight on the chart in Figure 9-8 where I chose to exit the position. The trend had been in place for a few weeks, and the long black candle broke the low of the two previous days. I'd been using a sell stop order and continued to move the stop higher as the futures contract price increased. My stop was in place at the low of the day that came two days before the long black candle because I felt this level would indicate the trend was starting to fade. I also kept an eye out for any problematic reversal formations, which you should also do if you find yourself in a similar situation.

Although I exited the trade before the trend reversed again, I was still very happy with this trade. I had a plan, executed it, and profited from it. Why can't all trades be as easy as this one?

The three white soldiers fail to signal bullishness

The three white soldiers is a pretty strong bullish trend reversal pattern, but like all other patterns, it does have the potential for failure. Figure 9-9 shows you what can happen when the three white soldiers doesn't fare so well in battle. It's a chart for the stock that represents ownership in Disney (DIS). I'm assuming that most people have some familiarity with Disney. With a three-year-old in the house, I'm more familiar with the company these days than I want to be.

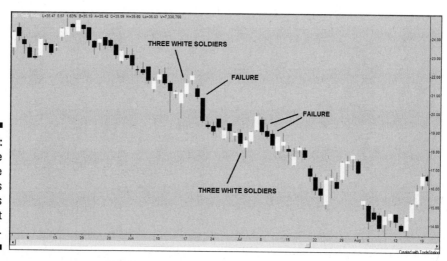

Figure 9-9:
The three white soldiers pattern fails on a chart of DIS.

The three white soldiers pattern actually fails twice on the chart in Figure 9-9, and both failures are highlighted. If you see this situation developing and make the decision to trade on it, you'd be smart to place your initial sell stop at the low of the pattern's second day. Most traders cover a lot of ground before they put on a trade, so some retracing of the new uptrend should be expected. Placing a liberal sell stop allows for that.

The morning star and bullish doji star patterns

The morning star and bullish doji star are recognized as separate patterns, but because they have very similar characteristics, I've grouped them together in this section.

Identifying the morning star and bullish doji star

You can see basic examples of both the morning star and bullish doji star patterns in Figure 9-10. The only real difference between the two patterns is the second day. The second day of the bullish doji star is a true doji, while the second day of the morning star pattern is *almost* a doji.

The price action behind these two patterns is very similar. The first day for both patterns is a down day, which is to be expected in a bullish reversal pattern. The second day for both patterns starts with a gap opening, indicating that the bears are continuing to push down the price. Then the rest of the second day is made up of very tight price action between the open and close. The third day is very bullish, with prices rising to cover some or all the ground from the down day. When you spot one of these patterns in a down-trend, it usually means that the trend is ready to reverse.

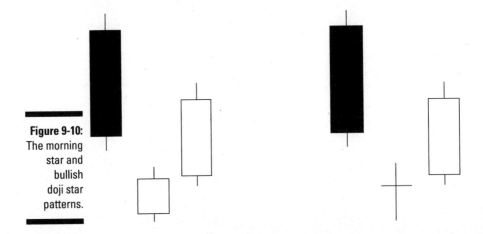

Figure 9-10:
The morning star and bullish doji star patterns.

Trading on the morning star and bullish doji star patterns

Figure 9-11 is a chart of the Euro futures, and it's a good example because the bullish doji star pattern in the chart indicates that the trend has reached the bottom. Keep in mind that the bullish doji star here could just as easily be a morning star pattern, and the result would be the same.

The days play out in the following pattern:

1. **The first day of the pattern is actually the third of three bearish days.**

   Leading up to this pattern, the bears are ruling the price action.

2. **The second day features a gap opening that's a little lower than the low of the first day, and the day ends up forming a doji after some back and forth between the bulls and bears.**

   The doji has pretty long legs, indicating an intense battle for price action during the day.

3. **The third and final day of the pattern is a white candle, indicating that the bulls ruled the day.**

   It closes high and into some of the range covered by the first day. The two days after the pattern see a bit of bearish price action, but no significant support levels are violated, and then three days later the bulls really get rolling, and it's clear that an uptrend is in place. And what an uptrend it is!

To take advantage of this type of bullish doji star pattern (or a morning star pattern in the same situation), you should either try to buy near the end of the pattern, or possibly attempt to put on a long position on any sort of near-term price weakness that doesn't violate a stop level.

Figure 9-11:
The bullish doji star pattern performs favorably on the Euro futures chart.

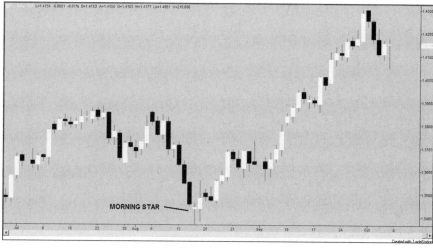

MORNING STAR

As you can see, raking in a profit on a trade based on the bullish doji star or morning star is a definite possibility if you keep your eyes open and place your trades wisely. But the pattern can also fizzle out and cause losses.

The bullish doji star not working too well

Figure 9-12 is a chart with a morning star pattern that has the potential to cause some heartbreak. It's a chart of the stock for Janus Capital Group (JNS), which is an asset manager of over $150 billion in investments. Yes, that's *billion*, with a *b*. Keep in mind that this could also be a bullish doji star because the patterns are extremely similar and basically interchangeable for your trading purposes.

The morning star arrives after a downtrend has been in place for a few weeks. The trend appears to be moderating a bit — an encouraging sign if you're looking to buy a stock. The pattern is completed in textbook fashion, with just one exception. The stock doesn't change trend very quickly. The price levels established by the pattern that you may use as stops are violated a few weeks after the pattern appears; you may want to bail out on this trade long before that.

Another factor that may be used when you're determining when to exit a trade is time. A violated price level isn't the only way a pattern can fail. You can also consider a pattern a failure due to the passage of time. If you see a promising pattern that doesn't fail but the hoped for price action doesn't occur, feel free to call it a failure and get out. How long you wait before bagging it is up to you, but using a time stop is a very useful trading tool.

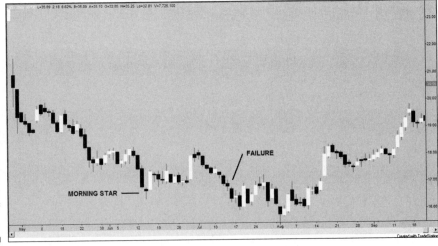

Figure 9-12: The morning star pattern fails on a chart of JNS.

The bullish abandoned baby pattern

The next bullish three-stick trend reversal pattern I cover in this chapter is the *bullish abandoned baby pattern*. It's a close cousin of the morning star and bullish doji star patterns, and although its name sounds sad, you can end up very happy with the results if you trade it wisely.

Identifying the bullish abandoned baby pattern

The bullish abandoned baby gets its name from the second day of the pattern, which just kind of floats out on the chart by itself like it's been abandoned by the first and third days. The second day is also smaller than the other two candlesticks, so it's the baby of the pattern. Look at Figure 9-13 for an example.

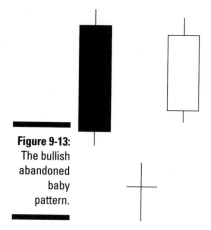

Figure 9-13: The bullish abandoned baby pattern.

The first day of the pattern is a bearish day. The second day gaps lower and has pretty tight price action, especially compared to the other two candlesticks in the pattern. Day three is a very bullish day that gaps higher than the second day.

Making a trade based on the abandoned baby pattern

For a look at a bullish abandoned baby pattern that provides a great buying signal, see Figure 9-14. It's a chart of ITT Corporation, a conglomerate with businesses in a variety of industries. Its products range from electronics for defense systems to solutions to treat wastewater.

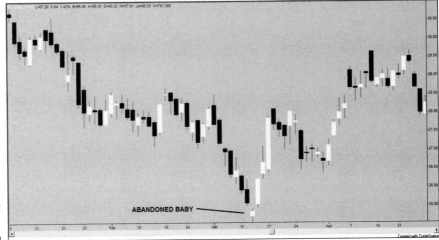

Figure 9-14:
The
abandoned
baby pattern
behaves as
expected
on a chart
of ITT.

The pattern develops with a bearish day in the midst of a downtrend. The second day opens with a gap down, and the price action for that day occurs in a fairly tight range. (A gap on a chart occurs when there's an area or price action that isn't covered by two consecutive bars. The area or price range where no trading occurs is known as the gap.) The high of the second day never goes higher than the low of the first day, leaving a gap on the chart. The final day gaps up above the high of the second day, and that gap isn't filled. The final day is also a very bullish day, and anyone watching can see that the bulls are in the driver's seat.

The gap openings in the abandoned baby pattern may remind you of the old rule of thumb that "gaps always get filled." That nugget does hold true, but for this pattern it's quite possible that the gap won't be filled for quite some time. It can take months, or even years — long past the points at which you can profit from the trade.

The abandoned baby that didn't work too well

In addition to successful examples of the abandoned baby pattern signaling a trend reversal (see the preceding section), in some cases you'd be better off, well, abandoning a trade involving this pattern.

Figure 9-15 is an unusual chart to say the least, but a good example of an abandoned baby that didn't work and probably shouldn't have been traded in the first place. The stock represented on this chart is for Edison International (EIX), a power company that does business primarily in southern California.

Even before the pattern on Figure 9-15 emerges, this stock doesn't necessarily look like one you'd want to trade. There are several gaps on the chart before the pattern emerges, indicating that it's not the most liquid stock in the world.

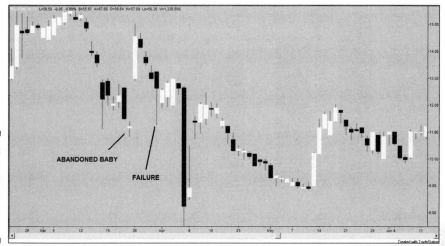

ABANDONED BABY

FAILURE

Figure 9-15:
An
abandoned
baby pattern
fails on a
chart of EIX.

The second day of this bullish abandoned baby does appear after a few down days and a bearish move of over 40 percent, so the pattern is complete. But it comes very close to recent highs and reaches a level that the stock has had a difficult time exceeding in the past. Because of this distance covered by the last day of the pattern, I recommend avoiding entering on the close of the third day, and I'd probably ignore this pattern altogether. I know that's easy to say when the results are readily available, but truthfully, that's enough information for me to shy away from the trade.

The bullish squeeze alert pattern

The bullish squeeze alert pattern is one of my very favorite bullish patterns. It's a versatile three-stick pattern, and it pops up on a relatively frequent basis, meaning that the opportunities to trade it are more common than some of the other patterns I discuss.

Spotting the bullish squeeze alert pattern

The rules that govern the formation of a bullish squeeze alert allow for a little wiggle room. The strictest rule is that the first day of the pattern must be a down day. After that, the second day has to be an inside day of the first and the third an inside day of the second. Beyond that, though, the rules are kind of flexible. The second and third days can be up days, down days, or a combination of the two. The only strict criteria governing the second and third days are that they must be inside days, and they have to form a triangle.

Figure 9-16 shows a variation of the bullish squeeze alert that includes black candles for the second and third days.

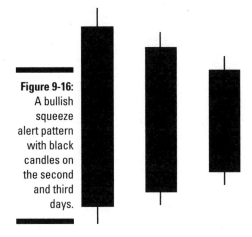

Figure 9-16:
A bullish
squeeze
alert pattern
with black
candles on
the second
and third
days.

I love this pattern's versatility, and it owes that attractive trait to the presence of a triangle. Regardless of how they're formed, I've found that triangles usually lead to some volatile moves. Keep on the lookout for triangles as you scan your candlestick charts. A triangle formed on a chart shows that prices are coiling together and will soon be ready to spring in one direction or the other.

Executing trades with the bullish squeeze alert

You can see the bullish squeeze alert at its bullish best in Figure 9-17. It's a chart of Southern Company (SO), which is a power company or utility that serves customers in Alabama, Florida, Georgia, and Mississippi.

Utility stocks aren't the most exciting stocks to trade, but the advantage is that you generally won't rack up massive losses on a trade in this sector that doesn't work out.

The pattern appears during a downtrend, and the first day is a long black candle. The second day is an up day, but also an inside day relative to the first day. The final day is a down day, but according to the rules, it's also an inside day relative to the second day. I chose this chart to show that the second and third days don't have to be specifically down or up, but do have to be days that are inside days of the preceding day.

The pattern forms a triangle, which means you can expect quick price moves in either direction. Because of this high level of volatility, I like to use the low of the pattern's first day as my sell stop. That gives the security the opportunity to move without being stopped out just before a move in the right direction. This pattern is followed by some lower trading, but then the stock takes off like it should.

The bullish squeeze alert failing to bring on higher prices

If you want to see a bullish squeeze alert pattern in a failure situation, look no farther than Figure 9-18. The figure features a chart of Target (TGT) stock. The days go like this:

1. **The first day of the pattern is a very long black candle.**

2. **The second day is a very encouraging (for the bulls) white candle, which is an inside day relative to the first day.**

3. **Finally, the pattern is capped off with a down day, but it's an inside day relative to the second day, so the pattern is complete.**

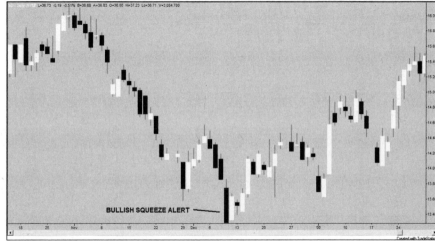

Figure 9-17:
The bullish squeeze alert pattern performs well on a chart of SO.

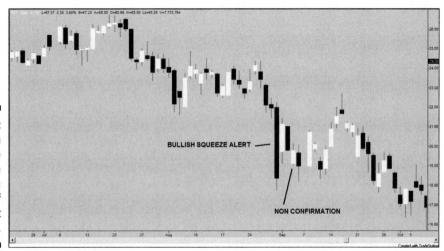

Figure 9-18:
A bullish squeeze alert pattern fails on a chart of Target stock.

The stock shows lackluster trading for a few days after the pattern appears, and although the high of the pattern's third day isn't violated, the lack of uptrending action may indicate that the pattern is a dud. There's no real need to wait around for lower prices to get out; it's probably best just to exit and move on, or if you wait on confirmation, just bag the idea of a trade and start looking elsewhere. You should try to be liberal with your stops on the bullish squeeze alert, but sometimes it's best to also require some confirmation that the squeeze is going in the desired direction a couple of days after the pattern appears. If it's not, feel free to stop waiting around and go on to your next trade.

Working with Bullish Three-Stick Trending Patterns

In addition to the trend reversal patterns that take three days to develop, there are also a handful of three-day trending patterns. These patterns usually include a long white candle followed by a gap of some sort. Generally, the gap or the low of the first day of the pattern may serve as a useful support level to let you know when the prevailing trend is still intact.

Three-day patterns have three uses for traders as follows:

- ✔ If you're considering buying a stock but hate to pay up when the price has been rising, three-day bullish trending patterns can give you confidence that the price you pay is as good as the price is going to be for a while.

- ✔ If you're interested in shorting, a three-day bullish trending pattern can tell you when to hold off for just a little longer to allow for the trend to provide you with a better price to use in your trade.

- ✔ If you're shorting a stock, a three-day bullish trending pattern can tell you that it's time to buy back and move on, because the trend definitely isn't your friend.

In this section I describe a number of three-stick trending patterns and how you can incorporate them in your trading strategy.

The bullish side-by-side white lines pattern

The first bullish three-day trending pattern is the bullish side-by-side white lines pattern, and it's about as bullish as it gets. If you see this pattern on a chart, you can feel pretty confident that the prevailing uptrend is going to continue in grand fashion.

Spotting the bullish side-by-side white lines pattern

To locate the bullish side-by-side white lines pattern on one of your charts, first look for a day with a long white candle that's followed by a gap opening on the second day. That second day should develop into an up day that never retraces prices down to the high of the first day. Finally, look for an up third day that basically covers the same ground as the second day and definitely doesn't retrace to close the gap to the high of the first day. Sound confusing? The straightforward example in Figure 9-19 should clear things up.

Trading on the bullish side-by-side white lines

I provide a solid scenario for trading the bullish side-by-side white lines pattern in Figure 9-20, which is a chart of Tyson (TSN). Tyson is a large distributor of chicken, beef, and pork products. Because these commodities' prices vary due to tastes, weather, or competition, TSN can actually be a pretty interesting stock to trade.

The pattern in Figure 9-20 emerges in an uptrend that hasn't been in place for long. This sign is a positive in my book because the longer the trend, the more likely it will be reversing in the near future. The first day of the pattern is a white candle, followed by two more white candles that cover similar ground but don't close the gap with the high of the first candle. It's obvious that the bulls have been moving the price in their direction and the bears are continuing to lose the battle. And as you can see, that action continues for quite some time.

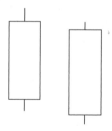

Figure 9-19:
The bullish side-by-side white lines pattern.

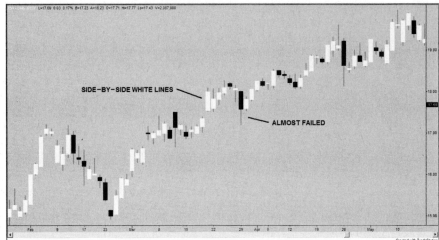

SIDE—BY—SIDE WHITE LINES

ALMOST FAILED

Figure 9-20:
The bullish
side-by-side
white lines
pattern
works well
on a chart
of TSN.

Created with TradeStation

Although it can be considered a bit liberal, I like to use the low of the first day as a stop for this pattern. I choose that level because there's a gap involved in the formation of the pattern. Gaps are made to be filled, and I know that the bears will try to make a run at a gap like this. I would prefer not to be stopped out until they've succeeded in running the price below the low of the first day. On the chart in Figure 9-20, I highlight where the bears make a run at the bulls, but the bulls push back, and the uptrend remains in place.

REMEMBER

When you spot a trending pattern that includes a gap, there's a possibility for some aggressive trading. There's a chance that the gap will be filled with the trend still in place, so you can place an order to buy in the gap and a stop at the low of the pattern. This strategy is aggressive because you can buy and sell in a short period of time as the bears take over. But if you can execute the move properly, it'll allow you to enjoy a very good entry price in the midst of an uptrend.

The bullish side-by-side white lines failing to indicate more bullishness

Even though the bullish side-by-side white lines pattern is generally a bullish powerhouse, it's possible for the pattern to fail. For an example, take a look at Figure 9-21.

Figure 9-21 is a chart of Analog Devices Inc. (ADI), a producer of semiconductors used in products that range from computers to DVD players. Because its chips are used in several products that can be considered discretionary purchases, its stock — as well as the stocks for just about every other company that makes semiconductors — hinges on the overall economy and is therefore very volatile.

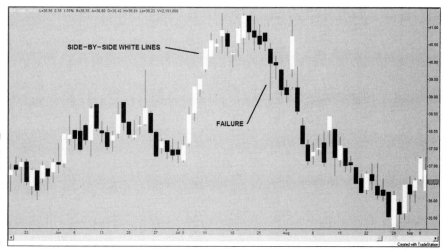

SIDE-BY-SIDE WHITE LINES

FAILURE

Figure 9-21:
The bullish
side-by-side
white lines
fails on a
chart of ADI.

The pattern in Figure 9-21 emerges at what appears to be the beginning of a very strong uptrend. There are a few strong up days followed by a gap up and two more white lines, which make up the pattern in this case. Because so much ground was covered so quickly by the pattern, it may be prudent to place a buy order in the gap that was created with the pattern, because there may be some price retracement where a better buying point would occur. Then you may place a sell stop below the low of the first day. It turns out to be a lousy prospect because the gap and the low were both taken out on the day I labeled as the failure day, but those losses pale in comparison to what you could expect if you bought at the end of the pattern.

The bullish side-by-side black lines pattern

The bullish side-by-side black lines pattern occurs during an uptrend, and although it includes some bearish trading, it doesn't violate the uptrend's validity. It has some bearish undertones, but it's still a fairly bullish indication of an uptrend continuation.

Recognizing the bullish side-by-side black lines pattern

The first day of the bullish side-by-side black lines is a long white candle that occurs during an uptrend. The second day opens with a large gap relative to the first day and then trades off some during the day. However, a gap is established between the first and second days even though prices trade down during the second day. The third day opens higher, much like the second day. Prices trade lower during the first day, but the gap that was established between the first and second days stays intact. The picture in Figure 9-22 is worth more than a thousand words in this case.

It may seem a bit odd that a three-day bullish pattern has two black candles as the final two days, but that's what it takes to create the bullish side-by-side black lines. It works out because the bullishness of the prevailing uptrend and the first day of the pattern are strong enough to keep the bears from closing the price gap.

If you choose to enter on the completion of the side-by-side black lines pattern, your entry point will be a lower price point than if you made the same decision with the bullish side-by-side white lines.

Using the bullish side-by-side black lines for a profitable trade

For an example of the bullish side-by-side black lines paying off in a real-world trading scenario, take a look at Figure 9-23. It's a chart of Gannett (GCI), publisher of *USA Today* and operator of several high profile Web sites including CareerBuilder.com.

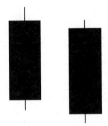

Figure 9-22:
The bullish side-by-side black lines pattern.

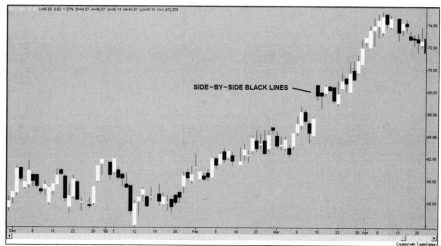

SIDE-BY-SIDE BLACK LINES

Figure 9-23:
The bullish
side-by-side
black lines
pattern pays
off on a
chart of GCI.

The days play out as follows:

1. **The first day of the pattern is a white candle that occurs during a small pullback of the prevailing uptrend.**

   The trend appears to remain intact, but it can be moderating.

2. **The second day has a gap opening and a little selling during the day.**

   A gap is established between the first and second days.

3. **The third day of the pattern has a slightly higher opening, and some selling takes place during the day.**

   The gap still exists, and the day closes slightly below the open. It takes three or four days, but eventually, the uptrend is back in place and the pattern in Figure 9-23 turns out to be a winner.

Failure of the bullish side-by-side black lines pattern

For my example of a failing bullish side-by-side black lines pattern, I turn to Figure 9-24 and a chart of the drug company Bristol-Myers Squibb (BMY). This company is a very large drug corporation that develops new drugs and sells many high profile drugs already in existence. It's a great stock to trade because of the competitive nature and constant change in the pharmaceutical industry.

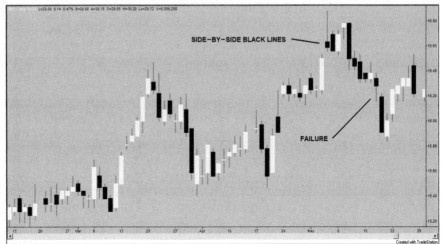

Figure 9-24:
The bullish
side-by-side
black lines
pattern fails
on a chart
of BMY.

The first day of the pattern featured in Figure 9-24 is a very bullish day, and it helps to continue a choppy uptrend. The second day has a gap opening, and the long wick at the top of the candle tells you that the day saw some pretty heavy buying. The second day does close lower, but a gap between the first and second day is established. Prices open higher on the third day, and more selling takes place during the day. Notice that the low of the second day isn't violated, and the gap remains in place.

This signal appears to have legs for the first few days, but prices soon start to roll over. After a couple of weeks, the low of the first day is eventually violated and the signal fails. In this instance, it's prudent to exit the trade even before the stop is hit. That's easy to say after the fact, of course, but the sheer amount of time that passes while the price action appears indecisive should be enough for a trader to call it quits on the trade.

The upside tasuki gap pattern

The three-stick trending pattern in this section can be considered a deviation of the patterns described in the preceding two sections. The upside tasuki gap can just as easily be called the upside white line beside black line pattern.

The name *tasuki* is a Japanese word for a sash that holds up a shirt sleeve. I've got to be honest: I'm not sure how that relates to the pattern, but it's fun to say, and the pattern can lead you to some great trades, so I won't question it.

Spotting the upside tasuki gap pattern

The upside tasuki gap starts with a white candle in an uptrend. The second day is much like the second day of the side-by-side white lines pattern that I explain earlier in this chapter. It gaps higher and closes higher for the day. The third day is much like the third day of a side-by-side black lines pattern (described in this chapter in the section "The bullish side-by-side black lines pattern"). There's an opening in the same range as the second day and then some lower trading, but the gap isn't completely filled in. Check out Figure 9-25 for a visual representation.

I like this pattern because it offers an attractive entry point, especially when compared to the side-by-side white lines pattern. Getting to buy on the low end of any candle when there's a bullish signal is fine with me.

Using the upside tasuki gap pattern for a successful trade

The chart in Figure 9-26 forms the basis for my explanation of how you can use the upside tasuki gap to make a profitable trade. The chart is for the stock of Illinois Tool Works (ITW). It's a great proxy on the overall economy because its interests are wide and varied. The company creates products that are used in just about every type of mechanical product you can imagine, from semiconductors to dishwashers.

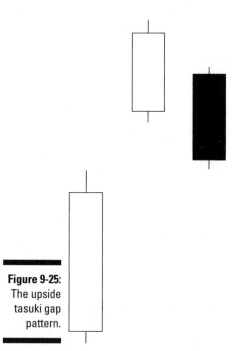

Figure 9-25:
The upside
tasuki gap
pattern.

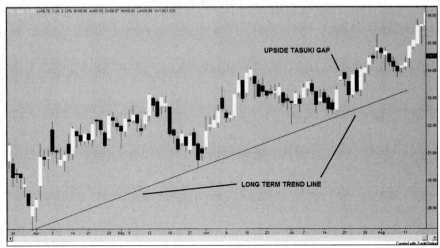

Figure 9-26:
An upside tasuki gap pattern that provides a useful signal on a chart of ITW.

The tasuki gap in Figure 9-26 just barely passed the rules for the pattern. The gap between the high of the first day and the range of the last day was so miniscule that I had to double-check the data to make sure it was valid. There's a gap there, but you have to get out the magnifying glass to see it!

I also chose to include more history on this chart than I do for the other examples in this chapter, to show that although the trend is sort of flat in the near term, there's a longer term uptrend in place, and that trend is actually tested with this pattern. I include a trendline on the chart to reinforce that point.

The nuts and bolts of the pattern are where they should be. The first day is a long white candle in the middle of an uptrend, and it's followed by a gap up and another up day. The third day encroaches the gap, but the gap is still intact at the end of the day, offering evidence that the trend should continue, as it does. If you spot this pattern and choose to take on a long position, you can ride the trend for a nice profit. You can also put on a long position knowing that you need to either get out of the trade on the appearance of a bearish reversal signal or some sort of trend break.

The tasuki gap fails to indicate more bullishness

I'm fond of the upside tasuki gap pattern, but it certainly does have, well, a downside. Have a look at Figure 9-27 for an example of what can happen when the upside tasuki gap turns out to be a dud.

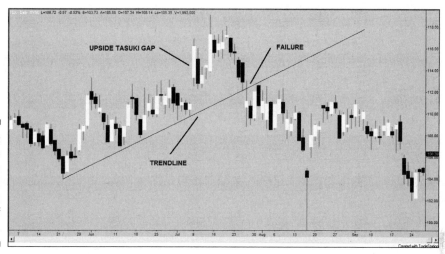

Figure 9-27:
The upside
tasuki gap
offers a bad
signal on a
chart of
FedEx stock.

The chart in Figure 9-27 is for the stock that represents ownership of FedEx Corporation (FDX). This is another stock that I love to trade, for a few reasons. First, on the business side, FedEx is exposed to the energy markets on the cost side of its business and the overall economy on the income side. As a result, it proves itself to be a very volatile (and fun to trade) stock. Second, the first industry for which I was ever given investment responsibility was transportation, and FedEx (Federal Express at the time) was an early company in my coverage. Finally, I grew up in Memphis (FedEx headquarters), where everyone knows someone at FedEx. Needless to say, the company is close to my heart.

On to the chart. During a well-defined uptrend, a long white candle appears on the chart, and that forms the pattern's first day. It's actually laying on a support line, which would be considered a bonus in this situation. I include a trendline on the chart. The second day is an up day, and a gap between the first and second day is created. Finally, the third day is a down day that encroaches but doesn't close the gap.

The pattern looks like a winner, and the failure takes a while to occur. But note that the low of the first day is violated — a sure sign of failure in this scenario. To introduce another possible level of failure, I also extended the trendline out to where the failure occurred. You can use this line as a stop that adjusts as time moves along. That's just another one of the countless ways you can exit a position when the theory behind the trade is no longer valid.

The upside gap filled pattern

The final bullish three-day pattern that I explore in this chapter is the upside gap filled pattern. It offers bullish trend confirmation, but it's particularly nice because the gap that's created gets filled without violating the prevailing uptrend. Sometimes gaps on charts are targets for either longs or shorts to push trading to fill the gaps. But with this gap filled, there isn't a gap present to encourage the shorts to take action.

Recognizing the upside gap filled pattern

The upside gap filled pattern is aptly named, as you can see in Figure 9-28. The first day is a white candle that occurs in an uptrend. The second day is bullish, with a gap opening and a closing that establish a gap. The third and final day is bearish, and it actually closes the gap, but it doesn't violate the low of the first day.

A low level for entry on the final day makes this pattern very attractive in my opinion. Also, as the low of the first day would be considered a stop level, losses are typically minimal when the pattern doesn't work as planned.

Making wise trades using the upside gap filled pattern

Examine the price action depicted in Figure 9-29 for a look at how you can profit from a trade by using the upside gap filled pattern. The stock charted is Edison International (EIX), a utility that deals primarily in southern California. This is actually the second time EIX has been used as an example in this chapter. (Have a look at Figure 9-15 for the first.) I guess utilities can be fun to trade!

The pattern in this chart emerges pretty early in an uptrend. The first day is an up day, and it's followed by a white candle for the second day, which gaps up. The third day is a down day that fills in the gap and closes in the range of the first day. The upside gap is filled!

The price action following the pattern is muted for a few days, and it even looks like the pattern will fail as prices come close to the low of the first day. But the bulls prevail, and the trend continues upward for some time.

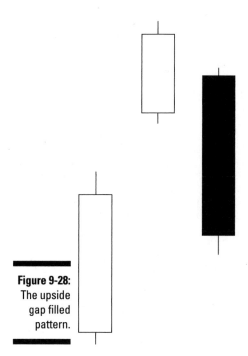

Figure 9-28:
The upside
gap filled
pattern.

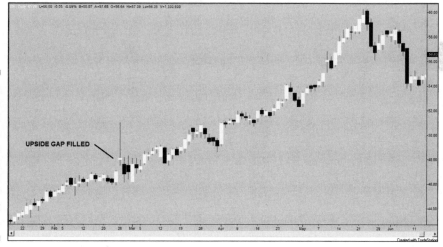

Figure 9-29:
The upside
gap filled
pattern
creates an
appealing
trading
opportunity
on a chart
of EIX.

The upside gap followed by lower prices

But the bulls don't always prevail, of course. The upside gap filled pattern can go wrong, and although it's ugly, you need to know what it looks like when it happens. Check out Figure 9-30. It shows a pattern failure on a chart for the stock of Comcast (CMCSA), which provides cable TV, Internet, and phone services to many Americans.

The pattern on the chart in Figure 9-30 occurs at what would've been the very beginning of an uptrend, *if* the pattern had worked out. There are a few up days that start to indicate that the trend is positive, and then the first day of the upside gap filled pattern appears as a very long white candle. It's followed by an upside gap that closes, leaving that gap in place. Finally, the third day is a down day that closes the gap and closes within the first day's range.

This pattern takes a while to fail, and like several of the other examples in this chapter, it may illustrate a situation where you'd be better served by bailing out of the trade because of time concerns than by exiting because of a clear price level violation. After all, you can probably do more with your money in another trade than you can with it tied up for what seems like forever in a questionable upside gap filled pattern trade.

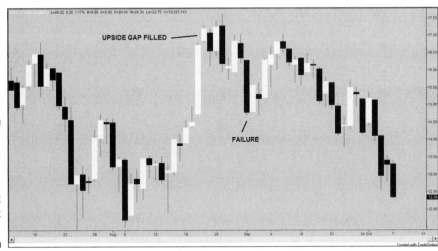

Figure 9-30:
The upside
gap filled
pattern
fizzles out
on a chart
of CMCSA.

Chapter 10

Trading with Bearish Three-Stick Patterns

In This Chapter

▶ Predicting a trend reversal with bearish three-stick patterns

▶ Working with bearish three-stick patterns that signal a downtrend continuation

*I*n this chapter, I focus on the biggest bearish formations included in this book: the three-stick bearish candlestick patterns. Throughout the next few pages I cover some of the most common bearish three-stick patterns that pop up on your charts.

If you flip back to Chapter 9, you can read about a variety of bullish three-stick patterns that can tell you when a downtrend is about to shift upward, as well as a few of those patterns that reveal when a downtrend continues. This chapter features the bearish counterparts of those patterns, and they can reveal when an uptrend is about to fall apart and head downward or when a downtrend is likely to continue. Use these patterns when you're looking to put on a short position or as sell signals if you've already established a long position.

Understanding Bearish Three-Stick Trend Reversal Patterns

Much like their bullish counterparts from Chapter 9, a host of three-day bullish patterns commonly indicate that a trend reversal is forthcoming. The patterns in this section tell you when an uptrend is nearing its end and when a downtrend is ready to begin. The bearish reversal patterns can be very useful for shorts, but keep in mind that shorting — especially with stocks — when the trend is up can be a difficult undertaking.

The three inside down pattern

The three inside down pattern is a handy reversal pattern that shows up fairly regularly. The indecision implied by the pattern's second day (an inside day) provides great insight into the action, telling you that the bears are starting to push against the trend.

Figuring out how to spot the three inside down pattern

The three inside down always occurs in an established uptrend:

1. **The first day of the pattern is an up day.**

   The bulls are in control on the first day of the three inside down.

2. **The second day is bearish, and it's also an inside day relative to the first day.**

   (The open is lower than the previous day's close, and the close is higher than the previous day's close.) The high and low of the second day also fall within the high/low range established on the first day of the pattern. The bears take over on the second and third days (see next bullet point).

3. **The pattern is completed on the third day with another down day that actually violates the low of the first day.**

As you may guess, this formation is usually a great sign that an uptrend is set to fizzle out. For an example, see Figure 10-1.

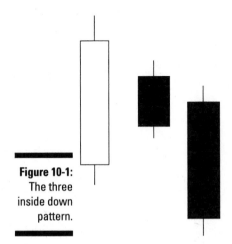

Figure 10-1:
The three
inside down
pattern.

Trading on the three inside down pattern

The preceding section shows how to identify the three inside down pattern, so now set your sights on Figure 10-2 for a real-world trading scenario where the pattern can potentially help you turn a profit. The chart in this figure is of Tribune Corporation (TRB), the owner of the *Chicago Tribune* newspaper, as well as the owner (as of this writing) of the Chicago Cubs. (The Cubs have been in what you could call a downtrend for the last 100 years, but that's a different story altogether.)

The three inside down pattern is the opposite of its bullish counterpart discussed in Chapter 9. It starts out with a bullish first day, but things start to turn bearish after that. Here's how the pattern unfolds:

1. **The first day is a long white candle that occurs in the midst of a pretty strong uptrend.**

2. **The following day, in textbook fashion, a down, inside day appears.**

   The open of the second day is lower than the close of the first, and the close of the second day is higher than the first. Both the wick and the body are "inside" the first day's price action.

3. **The third day reveals a takeover by the bears, and they begin to push prices down.**

   The stock opens lower and continues to trade down below the low of both the first and second days. The ensuing downtrend is strong, and it lasts for a few weeks.

If you watch this pattern develop and look to make a trade, you need to either be prepared to short near the close of the first day or pick an entry level to try to sell short on the second day.

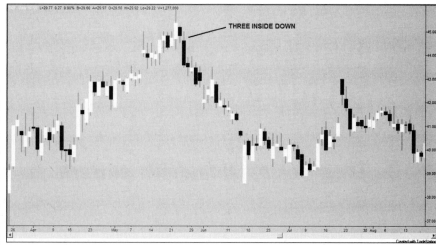

Figure 10-2:
The three inside down pattern precedes a trend reversal on a chart of TRB.

Failing to give a good bearish signal

If you've read through any of the preceding chapters, you already know that I never provide a winning pattern example without following it up with a similar pattern that fails. For my failure example of the three inside down pattern, I offer up the chart in Figure 10-3. This chart is for BEA Systems (BEAS), a provider of business-oriented software. As far as stock trading goes, software stocks offer as much volatility as any industry, and BEAS has been a great one to trade for years.

Figure 10-3 shows that the inside down day on BEAS occurs at the very beginning of an uptrend. It appears after some relatively strong days, so by trading it, you're either fighting a strong trend or catching the stock when it's due for a turnaround.

The first day in the three inside down pattern in Figure 10-3 is an up day, but it's nothing spectacular because of the recent bullishness. The second day is an inside day, and the third day reveals a rally by the bulls that falls short when the day closes down. The price action that plays out shortly after the pattern is pretty encouraging for the bears, but after a couple of weeks, the trend turns back up and the pattern clearly fails. The most liberal stop level for the three inside down is the pattern's high, but you can always go with a more conservative stop, such as the high of the last day.

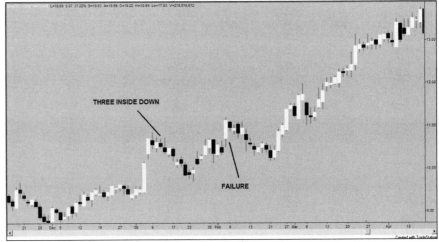

Figure 10-3: The three inside down pattern fails on a chart of BEAS.

The three outside down pattern

Like the closely related three inside down pattern from the preceding section, the three outside down pattern should show up pretty frequently on your charts. The pattern is a solid three-stick bearish trend reversal, and if you know how to correctly identify it, you can rely on it for some lucrative trades.

Spotting the three outside down pattern

This pattern shows up during an uptrend and commences with another up day in the bullish run. On the second day, the bulls get started again with a gap opening, but they don't control the price action for long. The bears find a selling point above the previous day's close and go to work driving down the price. This means that the second day has a close lower than the first day and a low that's lower that the first day. The second day is, therefore, an outside day relative to the first day.

On the third day of the three outside down pattern, the bears call the shots from open to close. The day produces a black candle with the open, high, low, and close all lower than the previous day's levels. The bears are now firmly in control. For an illustration, check out Figure 10-4.

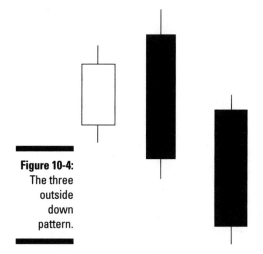

Figure 10-4:
The three
outside
down
pattern.

Making trades with the three outside down pattern

The three outside down pattern does an outstanding job of picking up a change in trend and offering a useful sell or short opportunity, and you can see it really sing in Figure 10-5. The chart in this figure is for Applebee's International (APPB). Applebee's operates in the restaurant industry, and stocks in that industry experience a lot of unpredictability. Restaurant stocks fluctuate with the economy, people's tastes, and even the weather. (Bad weather every weekend during a month can mean a bad month for a restaurant.)

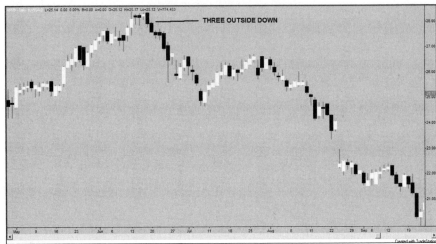

THREE OUTSIDE DOWN

Figure 10-5:
The three
outside
down
pattern
offers a
sound signal
on a chart of
APPB.

The first day of the pattern featured in Figure 10-5 is an up day, and although it's nothing to write home about, it's still an up day occurring in a prevailing uptrend. It's followed by an outside and down day. Both the body and wick of the second day are outside relative to the first day. Finally, on the third day of the pattern, the bears seize control and begin pushing prices down at the start of what becomes a sustained downtrend. In fact, it takes a couple of weeks before the bulls even attempt some sort of rally. The three outside down pattern predicted a trend reversal, and that's exactly what played out.

Offering a failing signal

But what happens when the three outside down pattern doesn't deliver on its suggestion that a downtrend is on the way? For an answer, take a look at Figure 10-6. The chart in Figure 10-6 displays price action for the stock of the biotech company Millennium Pharmaceuticals (MLNM). Biotech stocks can be wildly volatile and fun to trade. This chart is interesting because there's more there than just a failure of the three outside down pattern, and I explain the extra features in a moment.

The outside down pattern on this chart is a classic example of how the pattern appears as it gives a sell signal. The first day is bullish in a bullish trend, followed by a second day where the bulls push higher on the opening, but then the bears push back, creating a down day that's outside compared to the first day. Finally, the bears are in control on the final day as they push prices even lower.

After the pattern, a couple more bearish days exist, and then the trend takes a turn to the upside. As I said, biotech stocks can be highly unpredictable! The pattern fails and then something funny happens. Take a look. You may think I highlighted another instance of the bearish outside day pattern, but that's not the case.

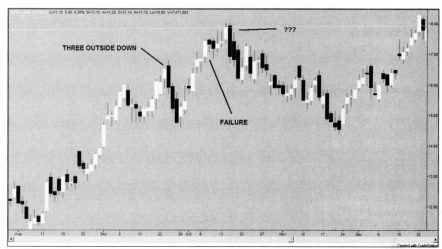

Figure 10-6:
The three outside down pattern offers a failing signal on a chart of MLNM.

It's a little difficult to tell, but the highs of the first and second days marked with *???* are equal. This disqualifies the pattern as an outside down pattern. So does a penny of price action on the second day really mean that there was a huge difference in the trading behind these three days? Apparently not. A new downtrend that lasts several weeks pops up right after the appearance of what you may call the "almost bearish outside pattern."

Splitting hairs on candlestick pattern formation can cost you a profitable trade. Just because there's a very small price difference that seems to disqualify a pattern, don't be too quick to disregard the formation altogether. The psychology behind the pattern that almost panned out is the same as what drives a by-the-book pattern, and you may be able to make a successful trade, if you aren't harshly strict with your pattern evaluations.

The three black crows pattern

The pattern featured in this section looks just plain ugly. The three black crows pattern certainly isn't much to look at, but it can benefit your trading activities if you can spot it and trade it wisely.

Identifying the three black crows pattern

If you're into the kind of bird watching that can lead to profits on the stock market, keep on the lookout for the three black crows. This pattern includes three down days in a row, and it must occur during an uptrend for it to be valid. Set your sights on Figure 10-7 for an example.

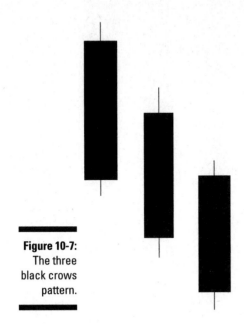

Figure 10-7:
The three
black crows
pattern.

The first day of the pattern may actually include a gap opening when compared to the previous day, but even if the bulls are in charge at the start of the day, it doesn't last long. The bears push prices lower, and the result is an obvious down day. The next two days see lower price levels across the board. Both the second and third days are black candles with lower opens, highs, lows, and closes. The bears have definitely taken over.

Making trades with the three black crows pattern

The example of a successful three black crows pattern that I provide is based on a chart of a stock that's closely tied to the stock market. TROW is the symbol for T. Rowe Price Group, which is an asset management firm that provides mutual fund investments for individuals and retirement plans. Its business is based on people's confidence in investing in the market. This confidence moves right along with trends in the stock market, so TROW and other asset management stocks are always good trading vehicles. Take a moment to review Figure 10-8 and allow me to explain how the three black crows can take flight for an attractive trade.

The three black crows show up shortly following a gap up in an uptrend. The black crows fill the gap up, which I consider to be a pretty encouraging sign. As you can see, each day of the pattern is a black candle, and each level is lower than the previous day's levels.

It's safe to say that this sign is pretty bearish. After all, sellers are putting pressure on a stock for three straight days. This also means that there's been a lot of downward price movement in a short period of time — an indication that there can be an opportunity to make a sale a little higher than the close of the pattern. That's the case with the pattern in Figure 10-8, and for the next few days, the pattern holds, despite a weak attempt by buyers to resume the uptrend. A patient trader that sold even the day after the pattern would be rewarded with a nice entry point.

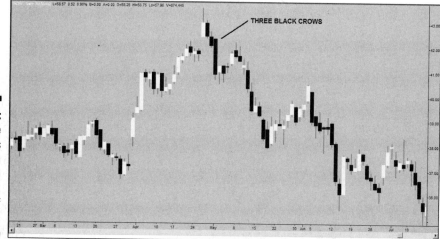

Figure 10-8: The three black crows predict a trend reversal on a chart of TROW.

Failing to signal lower prices ahead

If you're the kind of trader who insists that this pattern always works out when it appears, you may end up eating crow. The three black crows can fail, as you can plainly see in Figure 10-9.

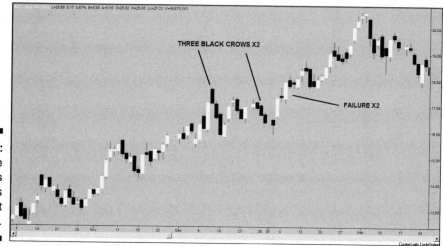

Figure 10-9: The three black crows pattern fails on a chart of INTC.

Figure 10-9 is a chart of Intel (INTC). Intel produces semiconductors, but you'd think they make birdfeeders with all the black crows flocking on this chart! Okay, maybe not. The chart is a little unusual because it includes two failures of the three black crows pattern:

✔ The first occurrence of the pattern appears in an uptrend that starts with a gap up on the first day, which brings in three solid days of selling. The bulls make a run, but the signal stays valid because, although there's a slight uptrend, no price action violates the levels set by the three black crows — for the time being, at least.

✔ The second occurrence of the three black crows comes in the continued uptrend, but it features slightly lower levels than the first pattern. A hopeful trader may be excited by the presence of two sets of the three black crows pattern, but his hopes will soon be dashed when the high of both patterns is violated.

The three black crows covers a lot of ground on the down side, and placing a stop at the high of the first day leaves you with a lot of room to accumulate losses before getting out of the position.

When working on a three black crows trade, try to pick a stop that achieves a middle ground between what you can tolerate in terms of losses and where you really believe the pattern will no longer be valid. You may first consider the midpoint of the pattern, which can be a prudent level depending on your ability to take a loss.

The evening star and bearish doji star patterns

You didn't think I could get through a chapter without discussing a doji pattern, did you? I confess my love for the doji several times in this book, and I'm happy to report that the two patterns described in this section make me grow only fonder of dojis and the trading opportunities they present.

The evening star and bearish doji star patterns are technically two different patterns, but they're so close and the trading psychology behind them so similar that I lump them together in this section.

Recognizing the evening star and bearish doji star

Both the evening star and bearish doji star patterns start with an up day, followed by a gap opening and then a doji for the second day (for the bearish doji star), or at least a day with very tight trading action in either direction (for the evening star). The gap between the first and second days attracts sellers, which keeps the stock from going much higher than the first day's open. The third and final day is down, and this final day closes the gap between the first and second days. After the struggle of the doji or near doji second day, the bears show their teeth on the third day, and the price action begins to trend downward. Take a gander at Figure 10-10 for an example of both the evening star and bearish doji star patterns.

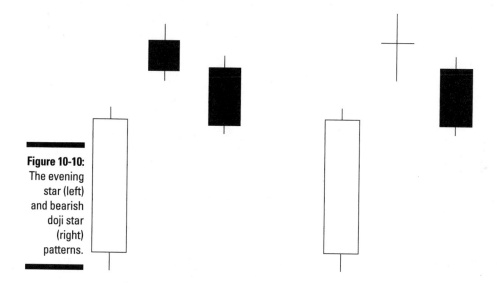

Figure 10-10:
The evening
star (left)
and bearish
doji star
(right)
patterns.

Using the evening star and bearish doji star patterns to make trades

For a sound example of the evening star pattern that pans out in a real-world trading environment, check out Figure 10-11. The chart in that figure is for a company called Archer Daniels Midland (ADM), a large distributor of corn.

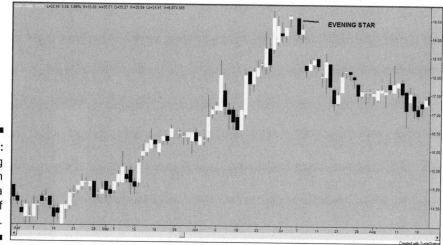

Figure 10-11:
The evening
star pattern
works on a
chart of
ADM.

As you look at the chart, notice the following:

✔ The first day is just another up day in a very long uptrend.

✔ The second day adheres to the price action that occurs on the second day of a doji or evening star pattern; there's a small gap up and a tight trading range between the open and close. It's not quite a doji, but it's certainly enough to qualify as the second day of an evening star pattern. (If it were a bona fide doji, then the pattern would be a bearish doji star pattern, but the price action and result would be basically the same.)

✔ Finally, the third day is a down day, and the pattern is complete.

I like the example in Figure 10-11 because it works quickly and includes a nice gap down that probably resulted from some negative news about the company. Without that news (and the corresponding gap down), the pattern wouldn't have formed correctly, and predicting the trend reversal would've been much more difficult.

Failing to indicate lower prices

You can find a case where the evening star pattern fails in Figure 10-12. It's a chart of Pep Boys (PBY), which is an auto parts retailer. (I've been analyzing and trading retail stocks for years, so forgive all the examples.) I believe retail is a good sector for novice traders to focus their efforts because the retail business is easy to understand, and plenty of public retailers exist for trading.

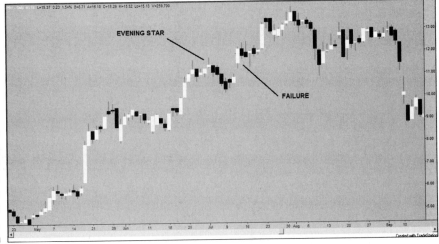

Figure 10-12:
The evening star pattern loses pep and offers a failed signal.

The evening star pattern in Figure 10-12 shows up during an uptrend, and it begins as it should, with an up day. The trend in question appears to be rolling over a bit — an encouraging signal. The second day is also up, with a small gap created between it and the first day. Note that the open and close of the second day are closer to the low than the high, which is also encouraging as the pattern develops. The third day is a down day, and it appears that a downtrend is commencing. Looking good!

But then disaster strikes. The downtrend is short lived, and anyone trying to short the signal is out of luck. Just a couple of days after the pattern emerges, the stock starts to trade higher again, and then with a gap opening and a strong bullish day, the pattern completely fails.

The bearish abandoned baby pattern

The bearish abandoned baby pattern is fairly rare, but when it pops up, it can be a very powerful indication that a quick trend change is in the works. In fact, the abandoned baby pattern examples in this book — both the bullish examples in Chapter 9 and the ones I present on the following pages — were some of the most difficult patterns for me to find when I was gathering chart examples. And it's worth noting that it was especially hard to find examples where the pattern failed.

Spotting the bearish abandoned baby pattern

A bearish abandoned baby pattern starts with an up day in an uptrend. That's followed by a day that sticks way out by itself on the chart, and that day is often a doji with a gap opening that isn't filled in. The third day is down and includes a gap down opening between the second and third days. You can see a bearish abandoned baby in Figure 10-13, but please don't call child services. It's only a candlestick, after all.

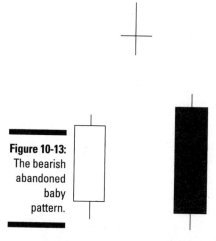

Figure 10-13:
The bearish abandoned baby pattern.

Trading on the bearish abandoned baby pattern

I'm fond of the bearish abandoned baby example on the chart in Figure 10-14 — a chart of the stock for eBay — because the trend is rolling over at the same time that the pattern shows up. The first day is clearly bullish, and the uptrend is in place, even though it looks to be rolling over. There's a gap between the first and second day, and the open and close of the second day are in a tight range. That range falls near the low end of the wick, which serves as a bearish indicator. The third day is up, but only after a very large gap down opening. Even though the bulls make a run on the third day, the close is pretty discouraging for them, because it falls near the low of the first day. After the final day, a sustained downtrend kicks in, and anyone who was working a clever short would be in for some profits.

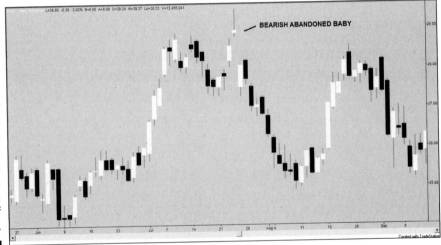

L=38.80 -0.36 -0.92% B=0.00 A=0.00 O=39.24 Hi=39.37 Lo=38.33 V=12,455,041

BEARISH ABANDONED BABY

Created with TradeStation

Figure 10-14:
The bearish abandoned baby pattern comes out a winner on a chart of eBay stock.

Failing to signal lower prices ahead

Now for a failing bearish abandoned baby. It's a rare occurrence, but it does happen. In this case it happens on a chart (in Figure 10-15) of Xilinx, Inc. (XLNX), a maker of basic semiconductors that go into just about any electronic product you can think of. XLNX has so many ups and downs that I honestly believe you can make a trading career trading only its stock. It's a wild ride.

The bearish abandoned baby appears in Figure 10-15 at the beginning of an uptrend. The pattern has an up first day, followed by a gap opening and a second day with a fairly narrow range. The third day kicks off with a gap down opening, and the gaps on either side of the second day mean that the pattern is in place.

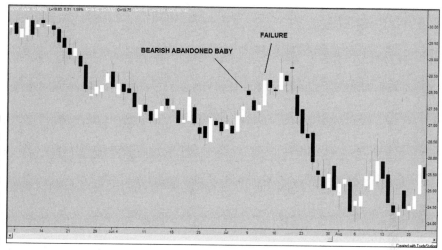

Figure 10-15: The bearish abandoned baby pattern fails on a chart of XLNX.

The signal doesn't hold up for very long. A long white candle occurs just two days after the pattern, invalidating the trend reversal signal. Shorts would be stopped out, and sellers would be disappointed because the price is headed higher in the short term.

The bearish squeeze alert pattern

Like its bullish counterpart from Chapter 9, I'm fond of the bearish squeeze alert. This signal either works or doesn't work quickly, and it appears frequently because the criteria for the pattern are relatively flexible.

Familiarizing yourself with the bearish squeeze alert pattern

The bearish squeeze alert pattern can take on a few different forms, and you can get a feel for one of them by reviewing Figure 10-16. The first day of the pattern has to be a down day, and the longer the better. The second and third days can be up or down, just as long as they're inside days relative to the previous day. That means that both days must have a high that's lower than the previous high and a low that's higher that the previous low. In other words, the body of each candle has to have a range that doesn't exceed the upper or lower ends of the body of the previous day's candlestick.

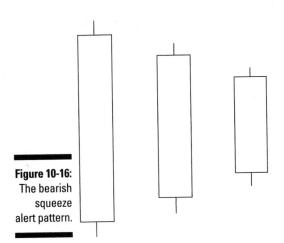

Figure 10-16:
The bearish squeeze alert pattern.

Using the bearish squeeze alert pattern in your trades

After you've figured out how to spot the various forms that the bearish squeeze alert can take, consider how to use it for trading. To get started, take a look at the chart in Figure 10-17. The chart shows the price action for the stock of the investment bank JP Morgan Chase (JPM). The stock has close ties to the market, and the company has operations in just about every facet of the financial world. JPM is also one of the oldest banks in America, dating back to 1823. That probably seems like a long time, but remember that candlestick charting was around several hundred years before J.P. Morgan hung out his shingle.

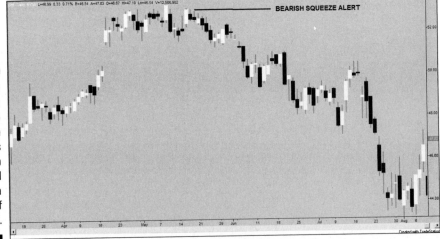

Figure 10-17:
The bearish squeeze alert pattern comes through with a useful signal on a chart of JPM.

The bearish squeeze alert in this chart occurs at the top of an uptrend that appears to be fading a little. The first day is an up day, but it doesn't quite make a new high for the recent uptrend. The second and third days are both inside days relative to the first day, and the bears would be happy to see that both days are also black candles.

When you see black candles for the second and third days of the bearish squeeze alert pattern, it's a good sign. The bears are controlling the price action and offer additional assurance that the prevailing uptrend is about to roll over.

The bears also appreciate the third day, where the body of the candlestick is low in the range of the day's trading action and near the low of the day. If you spot a similar pattern in a similar environment, get ready to short!

Falling short with the bearish squeeze alert pattern

Like the successful bearish squeeze alert pattern example in Figure 10-17 (see preceding section), the failure example in Figure 10-18 happens on the chart of an American icon: Coca-Cola (KO). As a steadily growing consumer company, Coca-Cola's shares usually aren't terribly volatile and, therefore, may not be the best trading stocks around.

There's a very solid uptrend in place before the pattern in Figure 10-18 emerges. A long white candle shows up on the first day, followed by two inside days, both of which are black candles. The pattern is completed, but the bears have only one day to feel good about their short position before the pattern is proved invalid. The day after the pattern is a bearish day, and it really does appear that the trend will turn, but then the bulls show up on the second day after the pattern and violate any level that can be considered resistance.

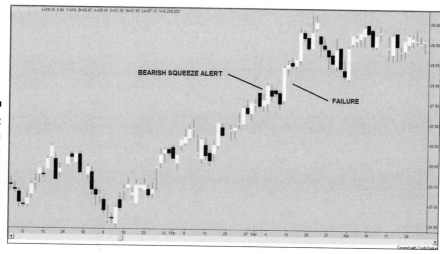

Figure 10-18: The bearish squeeze alert pattern doesn't work out too well on a chart of KO.

Forecasting Downtrend Continuations

Like the patterns described in the preceding pages of this chapter, the bearish three-stick patterns that foreshadow the continuation of a downtrend are mirror images of their bullish counterparts, which you can read about in Chapter 9. The patterns in this section are useful, but more so as confirmations for trades that are already on than as inspiration to initiate a new trading position.

You can initiate new positions by using bearish three-stick continuation patterns, but keep in mind that with trending signals there's already been some price movement in the direction you'll be trading (sometimes considerable price movement). Trends are your friends, but they don't last forever.

The bearish side-by-side black lines pattern

The first of the bearish three-stick trending patterns is the bearish side-by-side black lines. It's just plain ugly if you're a bull or an owner of the security with price action that produces the pattern on a chart. The pattern is extremely bearish, and if you see it as you're looking through your charts, you can feel pretty confident that the prevailing downtrend will keep on diving.

Identifying the bearish side-by-side black lines

The bearish side-by-side black lines pattern has a distinctive appearance, and you can see it firsthand in Figure 10-19.

The days play out like this:

- The first day is a down day that comes on the heels of a downtrend.

- The second day has a gap down and also trades bearishly. Note that the gap between the high of the second day and the low of the first day isn't filled.

- On the third and final day, the bears have their way again and, like the second day, there's a lasting gap. The bears are definitely in charge.

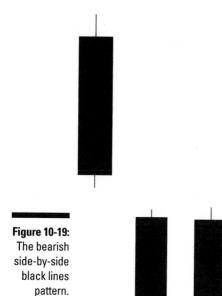

Figure 10-19:
The bearish
side-by-side
black lines
pattern.

Using the bearish side-by-side black lines pattern

You can harness the bearish power of the bearish side-by-side black lines to give yourself confidence that a downtrend will continue. For an example, see Figure 10-20, which includes a chart of one of my favorite companies. I'm a red-blooded American, and I love my Direct TV (DTV). Even though I love the company's products and service, if the right pattern shows up, I'm more than happy to short the stock and cheer for it to drop. Seems a little odd to be watching financial television stations on Direct TV and using the information to profit when the company's stock heads south, but such is the ironic life of the trader.

It's also worth noting that because of the competitive nature of its industry, DTV has been a great stock to trade for years.

As you can see in Figure 10-20, the stock is already in the early stages of a downtrend when the bearish side-by-side black lines start to develop. The first and second days are down, and there's a substantial gap between them. The third day is also a bearish day, and so the pattern is complete, and the downtrend continuation is verified.

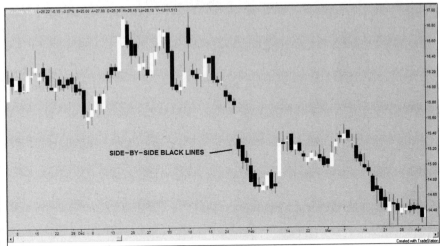

Figure 10-20:
The bearish
side-by-side
black lines
pattern
successfully
confirms a
downtrend
on a chart of
DTV.

(chart label) SIDE–BY–SIDE BLACK LINES

Failing to confirm a downtrend

Although normally there's some rebounding shortly after the appearance of a trending pattern like the side-by-side black lines, that's not the case with the pattern in Figure 10-21. You can spot a little bit of bullishness a few days after the pattern shows up, but there's no real move into the gap.

You may ask yourself if an ultra bearish pattern like the bearish side-by-side black lines can ever fail. The answer is a resounding *yes*. For an illustration, consider Figure 10-21, which features a chart of CenturyTel (CTL), a provider of telecommunication services in 25 states. Telecommunication companies have to deal with constant change and competition, and their stocks are very volatile and, therefore, great for trading.

The chart in Figure 10-21 is a fun one because two instances of the bearish side-by-side black lines pattern show up. One appears early in a downtrend, and the other one pops up a little later. The gaps are small on both patterns, so not a lot of distance is covered. And each pattern is followed by some buying, which gives patient traders a better entry level for a short than they would've found at the completion of the pattern. The entry opportunity is fine, but the pattern turns out to be a dud. Both patterns fail at the same time, and I indicate exactly where and when that failure occurs. The bearish side-by-side black lines pattern is rare, and when it appears, it's almost always legit, so don't expect to see too many examples similar to this one.

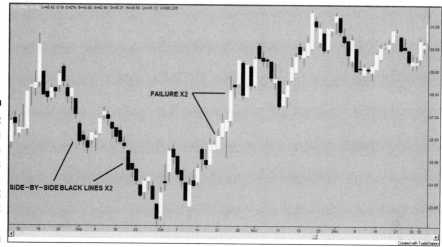

Figure 10-21:
The bearish side-by-side black lines pattern fizzles out on a chart of CTL.

The bearish side-by-side white lines pattern

The bearish side-by-side white lines pattern is similar to the pattern in the previous section, but its second and third days are white candles instead of black ones. It's still a bearish pattern, but not quite as bearish.

Spotting the bearish side-by-side white lines pattern

The first day of this pattern is a long black candle in a downtrending market or stock. The second day kicks off with a gap down opening, and throughout the course of the day, the bulls push prices higher. The bulls try hard, but they're unable to push prices over the low of the first day, and this failure results in a gap.

The final day of the pattern once again sees a lower opening and a push at higher prices, and once again, the first day's low isn't reached. After two days of effort from the bulls, a gap still remains on the chart. You can see what I mean in Figure 10-22.

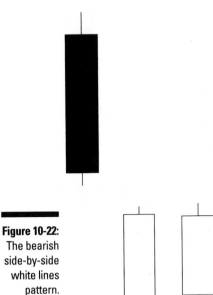

Figure 10-22:
The bearish
side-by-side
white lines
pattern.

Working with the bearish side-by-side white lines

Figure 10-23 offers a look at a successful occurrence of the bearish side-by-side white lines pattern. The figure is a chart of Monsanto (MON), which is a supplier of agricultural products to farmers in the United States and Germany. The stock's exposure to agricultural markets means that it's unpredictable and presents some nice trading opportunities as a result.

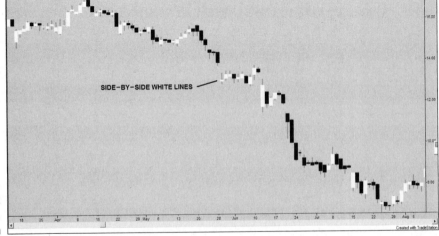

Figure 10-23:
The bearish
side-by-side
white lines
pattern
predicts a
downtrend
continuation
on a chart
of MON.

The bearish side-by-side white lines show up in Figure 10-23 in a downtrend, and the first day is a down day. The second day opens with a gap down, but the bulls go to work and the stock trades up a little. However, there's a fairly substantial gap left between the first and second day. The third day opens lower, and once again, the bulls give it a go, but they don't do much to move the price into the gap between the first and second days. The result? A bearish side-by-side white lines pattern. Then for the next few days the stock is basically trendless, but soon a patient short is rewarded as the downtrend starts up again.

Failing to predict a downtrend continuation

In a perfect world the bearish side-by-side white lines pattern would always provide a safe, comforting signal that a prevailing downtrend will continue for days, weeks, or even months to come. But this is the real world, and sometimes these things fail. For a look at how a failure can happen, refer to Figure 10-24, which represents ownership in Exxon Mobil (XOM). I'm using it for an example of a pattern with side-by-side white lines, but it's better known for a product that keeps automobiles everywhere running *between* the white lines.

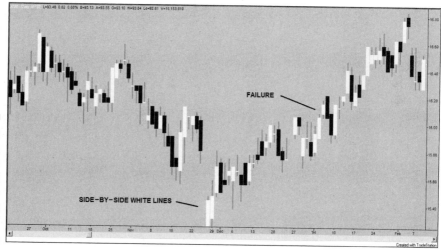

Figure 10-24: The bearish side-by-side white lines pattern fails on a chart of XOM.

As for the chart, the pattern appears with a downtrend in place. The first day is a long black candle, and it's followed by a big gap and a bullish second day. The gap begins to get filled during the bullish third day, and that upward momentum continues. If you wait for a rock solid failure level before exiting a short, you have to wait a few weeks, but you probably recognize the strong uptrend and exit before that painful level is reached.

The downside tasuki gap pattern

The downside tasuki gap pattern is the mirror image of a bullish version that you can read about in Chapter 9. Compared to the other bearish three-stick trending patterns in this chapter, this pattern is more useful for you if you're looking to put on a new trade. This is because of the higher closing price that occurs when the close of the third day moves into the gap between the first and second day.

Understanding how to identify the downside tasuki gap pattern

The downside tasuki gap begins with a black candle that appears during a downtrend. The second day sees a gap opening downward and bearish trading that result in a lower closing. When the third day rolls around, however, the bulls show up to push prices higher. They push enough to make the third day an up day with a closing price that's higher than the high of the second day. But don't count on the bullish behavior to continue. The bears are willing to sell within the gap between the first and second days, and they soon stop the bulls in their tracks. Want to see an example? Check out Figure 10-25.

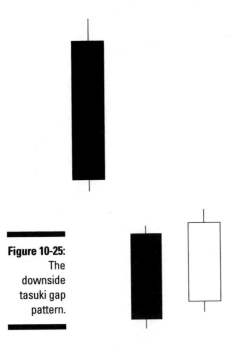

Figure 10-25:
The downside tasuki gap pattern.

Making a trade with the downside tasuki gap pattern

The downside tasuki gap is one of the bearish three-stick trending patterns that makes for a good candidate when you're looking to initiate a short position.

Figure 10-26 is a chart of International Paper (IP). The downside tasuki gap shows up in a downtrend, and coincidentally enough, the action that takes place before and including the first day of the downside tasuki gap is another pattern that I cover in this chapter: the three black crows (see the section, "The three black crows pattern" earlier in this chapter).

The second day of the downside tasuki gap pattern sees a gap down that isn't filled. The third day is an attempt by the bulls to move the price higher, and it stalls very low in the gap between the first and second day. The pattern is then followed by a pretty sustained downtrend.

Because the tasuki gap finishes close to the high of the pattern, you may want to enter on the close of the third day if you're looking to short. In this example, that strategy would've provided you with an excellent short entry before the continuation of the downtrend.

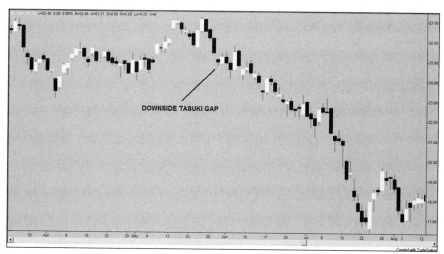

DOWNSIDE TASUKI GAP

Figure 10-26:
The downside tasuki gap pattern works on a chart of IP.

Catching the failing trend at the end of the pattern

For my failure example of the downside tasuki gap, I turn to a chart of Harrah's Entertainment (HET). Harrah's operates casinos throughout the United States, and just like gambling in their establishments, trading their stock can be quite exciting because it's an unstable security in an unpredictable industry. The chart appears in Figure 10-27.

Figure 10-27 is a fun example of the downside tasuki gap. If you've read through any of the other examples in this chapter, then you're probably expecting an outright pattern failure, but in this case an exit signal shows up before the pattern fizzles out. An astute user of candlestick patterns may have caught this signal before the trend changed and taken a profit instead of being stopped out for a loss.

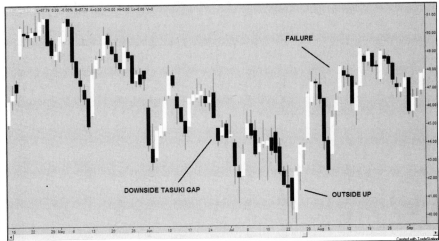

Figure 10-27:
The downside tasuki gap pattern (kind of) fails on a chart of HET.

The first day is a down day at the upper end of the downtrend. This day is followed by a gap down that isn't filled during the day and a down second day. Finally, on the third day of the pattern, a small rally occurs, and prices trade inside the gap, but the gap isn't filled.

Trading after the pattern in Figure 10-27 is interesting, with a few attempted rallies that get into the gap but don't trade over the high of the first day. There's also a drop to new lows, so the price action is really quite varied. Then, after the drop, a bullish reversal pattern shows up!

One more thing to look for in Figure 10-27: I highlight an outside up day — a bullish reversal pattern — that precedes a change to an uptrend. A wise candlestick pattern user would use that as an exit signal or even a chance to put on a long position. On the flip side, a short who isn't looking out for candlestick patterns wouldn't see the writing on the wall and would probably be stopped out in the next few days as prices exceed the pattern's highs.

The downside gap filled pattern

The downside gap filled pattern rounds out my discussion of the bearish three-stick trending patterns. It's the most tradeworthy of all the patterns in this section because its close is higher than the others. It also calls for some pretty tight stops, so you'll know quickly whether the pattern is going to succeed or fail.

Recognizing the downside gap filled pattern

As you can see in Figure 10-28, the downside gap filled pattern starts off with a down day in a downtrend. Like the other trending patterns in this chapter, the second day is a gap down, and it's bearish. At first the gap between the first and second day isn't filled and remains on the chart. On the third and final day there's a lower open, but then the bulls push the price higher over the course of the day. The gap between the first and second day is then filled. However, at some point the bears decide it's time to take over again and the rise in prices stops, usually in the lower half of the first day's trading range. The downtrend is still in place.

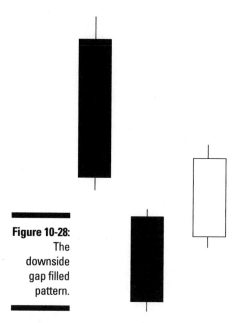

Figure 10-28:
The
downside
gap filled
pattern.

Trading the downside gap filled pattern

To give you an idea of how you can trade the downside gap filled pattern, I provide the example in Figure 10-29. It's a chart of Ingersoll Rand (IR), a manufacturer of various commercial and consumer machinery goods. The company is tied to the overall economy, so the stock can experience periods of volatility that present ample trading opportunities.

The downside gap filled pattern appears at the upper end of the downtrend, beginning with a black candle for the first day. There's a gap down opening for the second day, and the gap isn't filled as the day progresses bearishly. The third day completes the pattern with an up day that fills in the gap, and the downtrend continues after that.

If you shorted using this pattern, you'd be pleased to see some bearish action that continues for a while after the pattern is completed. However, after a few weeks, a bullish reversal pattern emerges. There's a doji followed by an up day in a downtrend, which is usually an indication that prices have reached a bottom. That would mean that it's time to exit your short position and walk away with your profits.

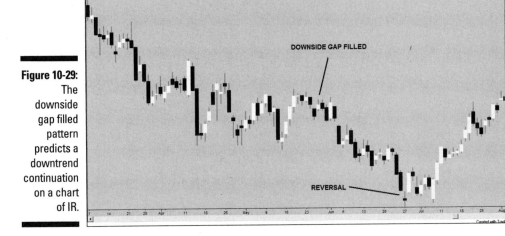

DOWNSIDE GAP FILLED

REVERSAL

Created with TradeStation

Figure 10-29:
The
downside
gap filled
pattern
predicts a
downtrend
continuation
on a chart
of IR.

Failing to signal a continuing downtrend

I hate to end the chapter on a down note, but I do feel obligated to present you with a failing example of the downside gap filled pattern. For that I turn to Figure 10-30, a chart of DuPont (DD).

The pattern emerges in a downtrend, with a black candle that's followed by a gap down, which is eventually filled on the third day. All is as it should be in terms of pattern formation, but if you look closely, you can see an indication that the pattern may not hold up for too long. The strength of the downtrend appears to be moderating, and because the trend has been in place for a long time, it may lead you to believe that a reversal is on deck. These indications prove to be true when the trend turns upward over the course of the next couple of weeks. The high of the pattern is violated, rendering it null, void, and more than a little annoying.

Figure 10-30:
The
downside
gap filled
pattern
provides a
dud signal
on a chart
of DD.

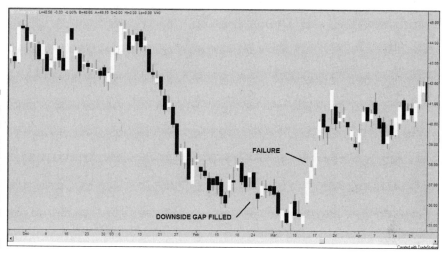

FAILURE

DOWNSIDE GAP FILLED

Part IV
Combining Patterns and Indicators

The 5th Wave

By Rich Tennant

"Right now I'm working with a combination of charting techniques. Japanese Candlesticks, some Elliot Waves, and a dash of Magic 8-Ball."

In this part . . .

Sometimes I get worried that my vocal cords are going to give out because I spend so much time singing the praises of candlestick charts. In Part IV, though, I sing a different tune. No, I don't discourage you from using candlestick charts — far from it — but I do show you how to combine candlestick charts with other types of technical indicators and encourage you to use those combinations in your trading strategy.

Chapter 11

Using Technical Indicators to Complement Your Candlestick Charts

*Y*ou can use nothing but candlestick patterns when trading, and some traders have proven that to be a profitable route. But that shouldn't make you think twice about combining candlesticks with other technical indicators. You can take advantage of a wide range of indicators to confirm the conclusions you draw from your candlestick charts, and your results are often more reliable and profitable. You may very well find that you can't live by candlesticks alone!

Many candlestick patterns — from single sticks to complex multiple-stick formations — depend on the market context in which they appear. For example, a bullish signal in a bearish market sparks skepticism and may even be ignored. But what constitutes a bull or bear market? (As I write this, I have a financial TV show on in the background and two market professionals are vigorously debating whether we're in a bull or bear market. If these market pros can't agree on the nature of the market, how are individuals supposed to figure it out?) It's simple: use technical analysis! More specifically, use indicators that attempt to define the market trend.

Traders use many different types of technical indicators to enhance and complement their trading styles. Traders are always trying to come up with the perfect combination of indicators and signals. (I confess to walking around with old business cards and a pen so I can jot down trading ideas when they pop in my head.) You never know when inspiration will strike! That brilliant new way to incorporate candlestick charting in a new trading scheme may reveal itself at any moment.

Technical indicators share one of a couple of goals. The first is to define the current trend, whether up, down, or even sideways (more on that later). To quote a popular trading saying, "The trend is your friend." The other indicators try to identify market extremes or reversals. That information allows a trader to "fade the market," or go against the trend in hopes that the trend will soon fade out and reverse. There are heated arguments over whether trading with the trend or trying to profit from reversals is the key to successful trading, and as long as traders are still making a living (and losing their shirts) using both styles, the debate will continue.

There are more complex indicators than you can shake a (candle)stick at. (In fact, *Technical Analysis For Dummies,* by Barbara Rockefeller [Wiley] covers them extensively.) In this chapter, I clue you in on a few tried-and-true indicators that you can use to determine the trend of the market and make your candlestick-based decisions even more reliable. These indicators include trendlines, moving averages, relative strength index (RSI), stochastics, and Bollinger bands.

Using Trendlines

Trendlines can be the most basic of all technical indicators. A trendline is exactly what it sounds like: a line on a chart that shows the general direction a stock is trending. If a stock is moving up in price, its trendline slopes upward from left to right. If a stock is trending down in price, its trendline slopes downward from left to right.

In this section, you discover how to draw a trendline on a chart. Also, some hints on how to determine the direction (up or down) are given. Finally there's a quick overview of how machines (a computer) can draw trendlines for you.

Drawing trendlines

Trendlines seem pretty straightforward, but drawing a trendline can be tricky. Based on how you think a stock is performing, you draw a line of support (in a bullish case) or a line of resistance (in a bearish case).

You can construct a trendline with nothing more than a printed out chart, a ruler, and a pencil. If you can't find a ruler, just close this book and use the spine. Anything that allows you to draw a straight line between two points will do. To draw a trendline, simply draw a line that connects two or more low price points (for an upward trending line) or two or more high price points (for a downward trending line). Figure 11-1 shows a prime example of a trendline.

Don't let the ease of trendline construction fool you into thinking that trend-lines are simple or cut-and-dried. In fact, it's difficult to refer to a trendline on a chart as a technical indicator because the drawing of the line is such a sub-jective task. Much like the market experts debating on TV, it's very likely that two traders can come up with completely different lines when asked to draw what they consider the most significant trendline on a chart. If a trader hap-pens to be biased against a certain stock for some reason, she may be more inclined to look at a chart and find a downtrend.

Despite all the subjectivity involved with drawling trendlines, some very suc-cessful traders rely heavily on them for their buy and sell decisions. When I began my career as a runner in the cattle trading pits 15 years ago, a very successful trader I knew based decisions on nothing more than daily charts and trendlines that he'd drawn during his train ride every morning. I've heard that he's still using the same method today.

Considering trendline direction

Although different trendlines drawn on the same chart may differ a bit, you'll usually find that at least the direction of the trendlines are the same. Trendlines can trend up, down, or not at all. For simplicity's sake, Figure 11-1 has an obvi-ous up (bullish) trend. (I say it's obvious, but I wonder how many of my col-leagues will insist I'm wrong!) After you determine that a trend is bullish, you may consider it with a bullish candlestick pattern and look to buy. On the other hand, if you witness a bearish candlestick pattern, you may be inclined to ignore it, or at least to take caution before implementing a sell signal.

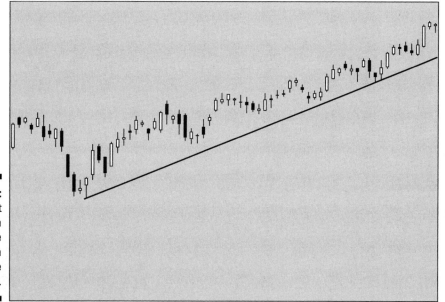

Figure 11-1:
A chart showing a trendline with a positive trend.

Taking trendline direction into consideration helps you determine the status of the market. Understanding the market helps you use the most appropriate candlestick pattern — one that makes your trading decisions more effective and profitable. Trendlines can be subjective, but there's no easier or quicker way to define a trend.

Taking advantage of automated trendlines

You can take some of the subjectivity out of trendline drawing by using a software package that constructs trendlines for you. All you have to do is choose your preferred time frame, and the software does the rest. Even Microsoft Excel includes this option in its charting function. (In Chapter 4, I explore how to use Excel for charting, but for now, I point out the way Excel determines a trendline for the data presented.)

Figure 11-2 displays the same data as Figure 11-1, but instead of the hand-drawn approach, this trendline was generated by Excel. The placement of the line is a bit different than in Figure 11-1, but the trend is still clearly positive.

Using software cuts down on the subjective nature of trendlines, but it doesn't completely remove subjectivity. There's still a subjective component to software-drawn trendlines. The user still determines the time frame for the trendline, which can have a definite impact on the type of line that's generated. As with any computer program that involves user input, the data you get out is only as good as what you put in.

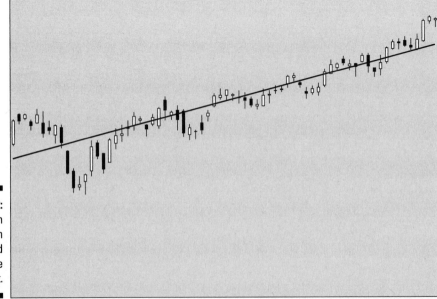

Figure 11-2:
A chart with an automated trendline placed on it.

Utilizing Moving Averages

When it comes to technical analysis, it doesn't get much easier than drawing a trendline. But what if you're in need of a slightly more complex indicator? The next step up from drawing trendlines is calculating moving averages. Put simply, a *moving average* is the average of the closing prices of a stock over a certain period of time. You can compare a closing price with a moving average to help you determine a trend.

Like most technical indicators, there are several different types of moving averages, and I explain a few in this section. First, though, it's important that you understand how to make good choices about the time frames you use when calculating your moving averages.

Selecting appropriate moving average periods

The time frames of your moving averages are determined by the number of closing prices you include. To decide on that number, consider the types of trading decisions you make based on your moving average. Pick a time frame that's appropriate for the amount of time you intend to have a trade on. For a trade that's to be held for only a day or two, a five- to ten-day moving average will suffice.

For instance, the five-day example in Figure 11-3 is very short-term and is most useful for traders who trade for a day or two, or even for less than a day. I trade a system based on a moving average that uses data from only the two previous days' closing prices. The holding period for this system is just half a day, so the short moving average makes perfect sense.

The range of moving averages I've seen used on charts varies from 2 days to 200. A 200-day moving average is very long-term, but in many circles it's considered very significant when determining a stock's long-term trend. In fact, the common definition of a long-term bull or bear market can be whether an index is trading above (bull) or below (bear) its 200-day moving average.

Using simple moving averages

The most basic type of moving average is the simple moving average. It's also the easiest to calculate and the most common — so common, in fact, that the word "simple" is often left off when a simple moving average is displayed on a chart. Look at Figure 11-4, where a five-day simple moving average is calcu-lated by using the closing prices from five previous days. It can't be much easier: The five closing prices are added up and divided by five. If you keep the number of closing prices in your simple moving averages low, you can easily work them out with a calculator.

The five-day simple moving average in Figure 11-4 comes out at 114.20, and the closing price on the fifth day is 113.87. Some technical analysts would say that indicates a downtrend, because the close on the final day is lower than the moving average. That can be very useful information if you're work-ing on a short-term trade.

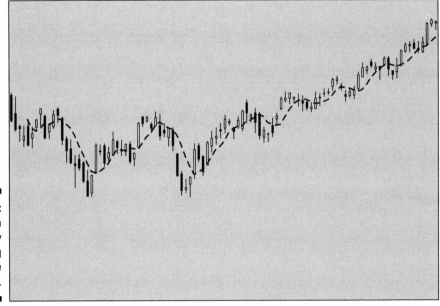

Figure 11-3:
A chart with a five-day moving average on it.

Day	Close
1	114.70
2	114.73
3	114.14
4	113.56
5	113.87
Total	571.00
Total / 5	114.20

Figure 11-4:
A quick calculation of a five-day moving average.

But if you've got a longer term trade in mind, it wouldn't make much sense to fret over the fact that a closing price dipped below a five-day moving average. There just aren't enough data points (closing prices, in this case) involved — a relatively minor change in a closing price can have a sizable impact on the average. A moving average calculated over a longer period of time (with many more closing prices) — say, 100 days or more — is less likely to reveal any closing prices that cross the average.

The longer your time horizon for a trade (or even an investment), the longer the moving average you need.

Figures 11-5a and 11-5b contain the same pricing data, but Figure 11-5a has a 5-day moving average, while Figure 11-5b uses a 20-day moving average. Notice the extreme differences in trends between the two charts.

Using other types of moving averages: What have you done for me lately?

Two fairly common deviations on the simple moving average are the *weighted* moving average and the *exponential* moving average. These types of moving averages are calculated in different ways, but they both have the same goal: to place more emphasis on recent prices.

Why would a trader want to explore more complex moving averages? Well, the major advantage one of these more complicated moving averages has over the simple moving average is that it's better at revealing a change in trend more quickly. Being able to detect trend changes faster helps to make you a more agile trader. Also, traders (especially short-term traders), have very short memories. Ask me what the market did yesterday, and I'm pretty sure I can give you a quick answer. Ask me what it did two Fridays ago, and I would be quickly pulling up a chart (a candlestick chart, of course!) to get you an answer. Because a short-term trader places more emphasis on more recent price action, using a charting method that does the same typically works better for shorter term styles of trading. Weighted and exponential moving averages both emphasize recent price action, and the only substantial difference between the two is the method of calculation.

If you were to rank the three most commonly used types of moving averages — simple, weighted, and exponential — according to their emphasis on recent price action, exponential moving averages, which place *a lot* of emphasis on recent prices, would top the list. Weighted moving averages would be a close second and simple moving averages a distant last.

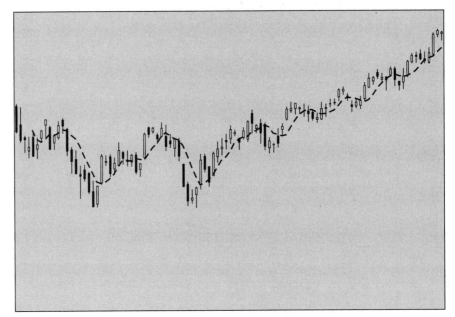

a

Figure 11-5:
A 5-day and
20-day
moving
average
compared
together.

b

Calculating a weighted moving average

To calculate a weighted moving average, multiply the most recent stock price by the total number of prices in your chosen time frame. Then multiply the second most recent stock price by the total number of prices *minus one,* and — using the same method — work your way back to the first price in your time frame.

For Figure 11-6, I've taken the same five-day data used for the simple moving average in Figure 11-4 and calculated a weighted moving average. ***Note:*** For Day 5, the weighted close is equal to 5×113.87 or 569.35, while the weighted close for Day 1 is simply the closing price $\times 1$ (114.70). To determine the weighted moving average, the weighted closing prices are added up and divided by the sum of the weights. In this case, that number is

$$[(1 \times \text{Day 1 closing price}) + (2 \times \text{Day 2 closing price}) + (3 \times \text{Day 3 closing price}) + (4 \times \text{Day 4 closing price}) + (5 \times \text{Day 5 closing price})] \div 15.$$

Day	Close	Weighted Close
1	114.70	114.70
2	114.73	229.46
3	114.14	342.42
4	113.56	454.24
5	113.87	569.35
15 Total		1710.17
Total / 15		114.01

Figure 11-6: A calculation of a 5-day weighted moving average.

Refer to Figure 11-4 and Figure 11-6 for the difference between the simple moving average and the weighted moving average. There's a pretty significant difference! The lower recent prices mean that the weighted moving average is quite a bit lower.

Calculating an exponential moving average

You can calculate an exponential moving average in a handful of different ways, and I suggest that you use . . . none of them. The math involved in the calculations is a bit complex, and for your purposes, I recommend leaving the hard work to a charting package. (See Chapter 4 for more info on popular charting software.)

Combining two moving averages

Comparing closing prices with moving averages is a great way to use moving averages to determine a trend, but it's not the only way. You can also combine and compare two moving averages to define the current trend. For example, you may calculate both a 5- and 20-day moving average for a stock, and then compare them to spot a trend. To do so, work your way though the following steps:

1. **Calculate the two moving averages, using the process described earlier in this chapter.**

2. **Determine which of your two moving averages is fast, and which is slow.**

   The fast moving average is always the one with the fewest number of data points (closing prices). It's labeled "fast" because its small number of data points makes it prone to change much more quickly (completely different than the reasons someone gets labeled "fast" in high school). The slow moving average is slower to change because of its heftier number of data points.

3. **Compare your moving averages to spot a trend.**

   If the fast moving average is higher than the slow moving average, that indicates an uptrend. The logic is exactly the same as comparing a closing price to a moving average to determine trend, but the fast moving average takes the place of the closing price.

   If you notice this type of trend, be more inclined to follow a bullish candlestick pattern and consider buying. If the fast moving average is lower than the slow moving average, that indicates a downtrend. If that's what you see, you should follow a bearish candlestick pattern and look to sell.

Take a look at Figure 11-7, which contains the same data as the previous charts in this chapter, but overlays both a 5- and 20-day moving average. The 5-day moving average is represented by the solid line, while a dashed line is used for the 20-day moving average. You can clearly see the higher volatility of the 5-day moving average compared to the 20-day. And you can also see that the chart indicates an uptrend!

Experts often use a combination of the 5- and 200-day moving averages to define a long-term bull or bear market. These choices may seem somewhat arbitrary, but they've been cemented as rules of thumb in the market.

Combining three moving averages

Two moving averages can be pretty useful company, but is three a crowd? Who really needs to use three moving averages? Believe it or not, some very successful longer term trading systems make comparisons using three moving averages. The technique is useful because it allows the market to be defined as having no trend, as opposed to either an up or downtrend.

You may be thinking, "No trend? The market and stock prices change daily! There has to be a trend!" But some markets (and individual stocks in particular) have long droughts without an up or downtrend. Identifying a market without a trend can be extremely helpful, as it's pretty difficult to make money trading when there isn't much price movement. With that in mind, taking a look at combining three moving averages is certainly worth the time.

Comparisons using three moving averages are made by identifying each average as either fast, medium, or slow. Just like comparisons with two moving averages, the one considered "fast" has the lowest number of data points. The slow moving average has the most data points, and the medium one is somewhere in the middle. To help you visualize, see Figure 11-8, which contains a 5- and 20-day moving average but also includes an additional 10-day moving average.

In Figure 11-8, the averages are represented by different lines:

- ✔ The 5-day moving average is represented by the solid line.
- ✔ The line with long dashes is the 10-day moving average.
- ✔ The 20-day moving average is the line with the short dashes.

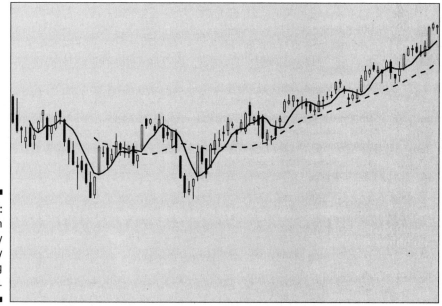

Figure 11-7:
A chart with both a 5-day and 20-day moving average.

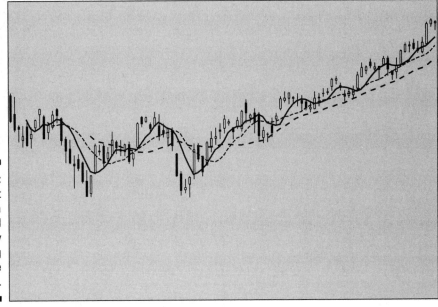

Figure 11-8:
A chart
showing a
5-, 10-, and
20-day
moving
average
combined.

With any chart containing three moving averages, you can pick out an uptrend when the fast moving average is higher than the medium one, and the medium one is higher than the slow one. You can see an uptrend on the right side of this chart, where all three moving averages are in order and trending together.

You can identify a downtrend when the fast moving average is lower than the medium one, and the medium one is lower than the slow one. If the fast-, medium-, and slow-moving averages aren't lined up either fast to slow or vice versa, you can safely say that the market has no trend.

Knowing the type of market you're dealing with is key to using many candle-stick patterns correctly, so you may need to use three moving averages. That's especially true for longer term trading. The more certain you can be about a trend, the more likely you are to properly identify and trade effectively on a bullish or bearish candlestick pattern.

Examining the Relative Strength Index

My personal favorite indicator is the relative strength index (RSI). The RSI compares the strength of a stock's up days against the strength of its down days, and RSI proponents believe that as a result, the RSI can cut through erratic changes and really confirm price movement. This index is considered a leading indicator because you can usually count on the direction of a security's RSI to change ahead of its price action.

The origin of overbought and oversold levels

You may be wondering how the overbought and oversold levels were established. Those benchmarks came from the mind of renowned technical analyst J. Welles Wilder, who introduced the RSI in his 1978 book *New Concepts in Technical Trading Systems*. In the book, Wilder recommends using 30 as an oversold level (an attractive area to buy) and 70 as an overbought level (an area to exit or sell short). Look at Figure 11-9. The oversold level of 30 and overbought level of 70 are indicated with lines along the bottom of the chart to allow you to see when the level penetrates either of these significant levels. He also suggests using 14 as the standard number of price periods for calculating RSIs, which is the input used for the chart in Figure 11-9.

The RSI is classified as a *momentum oscillator*. The "momentum" in that term comes from the fact that as a security is in an up or downtrend, the RSI's trend should correspond. And it's an "oscillator" because RSIs fluctuate between 0 and 100 percent.

Another attractive feature of RSIs is they include levels that indicate when a security is considered overbought or oversold. When the security reaches one of these levels, a savvy trader should be on his toes, waiting for a corresponding change in the trend of the RSI, or even better, some sort of revealing bullish or bearish candlestick pattern that lets him know it's time to buy or sell.

Calculating the RSI

Calculating an RSI is fairly complex, even when using a spreadsheet. Instead of spending several pages going through the steps for calculating an RSI, I give you a brief overview of the formulas that drive it:

1. **Add up the price change on up days and the price change on down days for the number of periods (usually 14) in your look-back range.**

2. **Take those individual sums and divide them by 14.**

3. **Then calculate the relative strength (not the relative strength index) by dividing the up day average by the down day average.**

   RS = Average up days ÷ Average down days

The RSI takes the up and down days and plugs that data into a fairly complex formula, resulting in a reading between 0 and 100. The following equation explains the math behind the RSI:

RSI = 100 − (100 ÷ Relative Strength)

Reading an RSI chart

As with many technical indicators, RSIs are much easier to digest in chart form. In Figure 11-9, the lower chart is a daily six-month long chart on Intel, (symbol INTC). The top section of the chart is a basic candlestick chart depicting the price action in Intel stock from July to December 2007. Numerous bullish and bearish candlestick formations are charted on this chart, but for now, just focus on the RSI component.

In the bottom quarter of the chart in Figure 11-9, there's a slow-moving line that depicts the RSI. This line is normally how an oscillator is depicted on a chart. Unlike a moving average, which is imposed on top of a chart's price component, the RSI (or any other similar indicator) appears *below* the price component. Note how the RSI seems to flow along and mirror the movements of the closing prices. However, at times the RSI either flattens while the price continues to move or even moves in the opposite direction. This change is called a divergence.

Divergences are the key to using the RSI, and a divergence combined with a corresponding candlestick pattern that matches the direction of the divergence can provide you with a profitable trade signal.

But the RSI's usefulness doesn't end with its role as a momentum indicator. RSIs may also be used as signals that reveal when the price of a security has reached a level that's too high or too low for the near term, or a level where a reversal of trend is more likely.

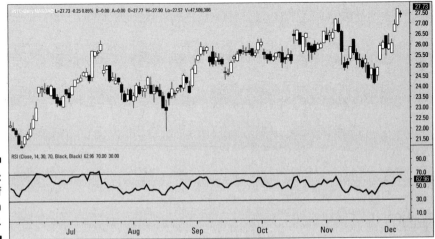

Figure 11-9:
A chart of
INTC with
the RSI on it.

The simplicity may sound too good to be true, and of course, it is. Using the RSI by strictly buying when it hits 30 or selling when it hits 70 is a disastrous strategy. It does make for a good rule of thumb, however, when you consider it alongside a signal from a candlestick pattern or a divergent move in the RSI relative to the price chart.

Combining a divergent RSI with a candlestick pattern is a smart move, and adding the overbought or oversold levels into the equation is even smarter, and can provide you with much more reliable buy and sell signals. The strength of the RSI as both a momentum and oscillating signal is why it's one of my personal favorite indicators.

Cashing In on Stochastics

Another useful indicator with an extremely clumsy name is the *stochastic oscillator*. This momentum indicator considers the current closing price of a security in relation to a high-low range of prices over a set number of look-back periods. This oscillator can be very useful when used in tandem with your candlestick charts. And in addition to its usefulness as an indicator of momentum, the stochastic oscillator may also be used as an overbought or oversold indicator when readings are at extreme levels: 30 percent for oversold and 70 percent for overbought (see the section on RSI earlier in this chapter).

Grasping the math behind the stochastic oscillator

George Lane developed the stochastic oscillator in the late 1950s. The math behind it is pretty remarkable for an indicator some 50 years old. There are actually two readings for a stochastic oscillator that are combined on a chart. They're referred to as the slow (%D) and the fast (%K) stochastics. The slow one is generally a moving average of the fast one.

The formulas for the slow and fast stochastic oscillators are as follows:

- **Fast Stochastic:**

    %K = 100 × (Recent Close – Lowest Low(n) ÷ Highest High(n) – Lowest Low(n))

    N = number of periods used in calculation

- **Slow Stochastic:**

    %D = 3-period moving average of %K

Interpreting the stochastic oscillator

Luckily, most (if not all) charting software calculates the stochastic oscillator for you, so you don't need to memorize or even fully understand the formulas behind it (whew!). You really just need to know how to interpret the lines on a chart. For a depiction of how the stochastic oscillator shows up on a chart, refer to Figure 11-10. This is a chart of the same INTC data in Figure 11-9, but the RSI has been removed, and a stochastic indicator has been inserted.

When interpreting the stochastic oscillator, you use methods similar to those used in interpreting the RSI and moving averages (see respective sections earlier in this chapter).

Using stochastic oscillators as you would two moving averages

Knowing how to use two moving averages is helpful when interpreting stochastic oscillators. For defining a trend, if both the fast (%K) and slow (%D) stochastics are trending higher, and the fast line is higher than the slow line, you're looking at an uptrend. It's like when you're using two moving averages, and the moving average with the shorter look-back period is up above the moving average with the longer look-back period: The trend is considered up.

Another parallel to using two moving averages is that a change in trend may be signaled when the fast stochastic changes from being over or under the slower stochastic. Keep an eye out for those important changes.

The rule on this is if the fast stochastic is above the slow one, an uptrend is in place; if the fast one is under the slow one, a downtrend is in place. When they cross, there's a trend change! When they are in overbought territory and the fast one crosses under the slow one, that may be considered a good selling opportunity. Conversely, when they are in oversold territory and the fast one crosses over the slow one, it's a good buying opportunity.

Using stochastic oscillators as you would the RSI

You can use the stochastic oscillator as an overbought or oversold indicator, just as you use the RSI (covered in the section, "Examining the Relative Strength Index"). Like the RSI, both the fast and slow stochastic levels oscillate between 0 and 100 percent. Below 30 is considered oversold (a buying level), and above 70 is considered overbought (sell level).

The benefit of having a slow and fast stochastic is that when the overbought or oversold levels are reached and a corresponding crossover of the fast and slow stochastic occurs, you can enjoy a much more reliable signal. For example, if both of the stochastics are in overbought territory, and you see the slow stochastic move from over to under the fast one, that's considered a sell signal. The reverse is also true: If both stochastics are oversold, and the slow one moves from under to over the fast one, that makes for a nice buy signal.

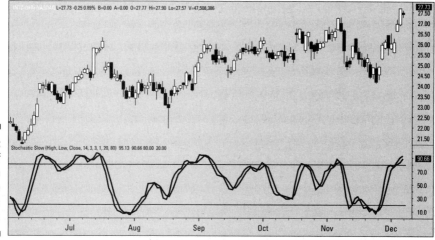

Figure 11-10:
A chart of
INTC with
the
stochastic
oscillator.

Buddying up with Bollinger Bands

The idea behind Bollinger bands is that when a price for a security gets too high above or below a moving average, that security may be considered overbought or oversold. Bollinger bands look just like moving averages on a price chart (see "Utilizing Moving Averages," earlier in the chapter), but they're positioned a certain distance above and below the real moving average on a chart. The bands mark the areas where a security may be considered overbought or oversold.

Bollinger bands received their name from the renowned technical analyst John Bollinger.

Creating Bollinger bands

You may do well to leave the necessary calculations of Bollinger bands to a charting package, but it starts out simple enough with the calculation of a simple moving average of a price series. (Find that process in this chapter's "Using simple moving averages" section.) Bollinger suggests a 20-day moving average, and many charting software programs use that as the default, so that's always a good place to start.

After calculating the 20-day moving average, things get a bit trickier. The bands that run above and below the moving average are based on a statistical measure known as *standard deviation*. The bands are placed a certain number of standard deviations higher and lower than the moving average.

Without getting into too much detail, the distance of the bands from the moving average is determined by the amount of volatility in the market. The more the market is moving around, the wider the bands are spread.

As the standard deviation rises and falls with the level of market volatility, the overbought and oversold levels tend to adjust for the market environment. An excellent example of a Bollinger band chart can be seen in Figure 11-11. This is the same data used in the previous two figures, but now the only indicators on the chart are the Bollinger bands.

Using the bands

Bollinger bands make for great overbought or oversold indicators. Broadly speaking, when the price of a security is higher than the upper Bollinger band on a chart, you're in a sell area, and when the price is lower than the lower Bollinger band, you're in buy territory. As you can see in Figure 11-11, there are plenty of buy and sell opportunities using these bands. But not every one of those opportunities is worth acting on immediately, so combining them with your handy candlestick charts can be an ideal way to minimize risk and separate the great signals from the mediocre ones.

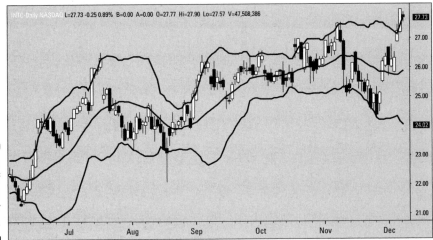

Figure 11-11: A chart of INTC with Bollinger bands.

Chapter 12

Buy Indicators and Bullish Reversal Candlestick Patterns

. . . .

In This Chapter

▶ Making successful long trades by combining the relative strength index and candlesticks

▶ Using stochastic indicators and candlestick patterns for profitable long trading

. . . .

*T*his chapter clues you in on the ways in which you can begin combining your trading tools to make your trades even more efficient and profitable. More specifically, the strategies I describe in the next few pages help you understand how you can use two buy indicators (the relative strength index — RSI — and stochastics) in tandem with bullish trend reversal candlestick patterns to pick the best times and situations for entering and exiting long trades.

I've found the two technical indicators I discuss in this chapter to be reliable and relatively easy to combine with candlestick patterns. However, please don't think for a second that the RSI and stochastic indicators are the only ones that work well with candlesticks. There are several others, and I strongly encourage you to research those indicators and find some that work best with your personal trading style.

Buying with the RSI and Bullish Reversal Candlestick Patterns

The *relative strength index* (RSI) is a fairly reliable indicator that can tell you whether a stock or market is overbought or oversold. The RSI fluctuates between 0 and 100, although it hardly ever reaches either of those levels. You can choose the levels between 0 and 100 that you think indicate that a stock is overbought or oversold, but for the sake of analysis in this chapter, I use 30 as my oversold level and 70 as my overbought level. Therefore, RSI readings under 30 tell you that a bottom could be coming soon and that you should be ready to buy, and readings over 70 should lead you to consider putting on a short or selling a long. (For more of the nitty gritty details of the RSI, check out Chapter 11.)

The RSI has two potential uses when you're working on candlestick analysis:

✔ You can combine the information from an RSI with reversal patterns to further confirm that a reversal is imminent, and it's time to take a long position.

✔ You can also use the RSI to help you select your exit levels, whether they are stops to prevent losses or exits that allow you to walk away with a tidy profit.

Using the RSI to help pick a long entry point

In this section, Figure 12-1 provides a solid example of the type of situation that calls for using the RSI in combination with a bullish reversal pattern. This chart is from Applied Materials (AMAT), which is a very large technology company that creates machinery used to manufacture semiconductors. The free-wheeling, rock 'n' rollin', throw-caution-to-the-wind experts in this industry refer to it as the semiconductor equipment industry.

A three inside up reversal pattern appears after a couple of bearish days, during a short-lived downtrend. (Check out Chapter 9 for more on the three inside up pattern.) The RSI helps confirm that the candlestick pattern is sound because the RSI closes under 30 on the pattern's first day. That means that the stock is oversold if the standard oversold level 30 is being used, and bullish buyers will soon be on the scene to drive up the price of the stock.

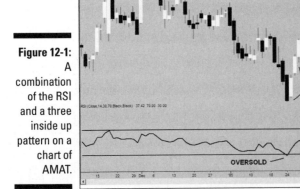

Figure 12-1: A combination of the RSI and a three inside up pattern on a chart of AMAT.

INSIDE UP REVERSAL PATTERN

OVERSOLD

The last two days of a three inside up pattern are bullish days. Bullish behavior generally means that the RSI is moving out of the oversold level. Consider RSI levels over the course of a pattern, not just on one of the pattern's days.

Bullish reversal patterns like the three inside up usually end with bullish moves, so it would be pretty rare to find an RSI reading under 30 (or whatever level you consider oversold), at the end of a pattern.

It's also worth mentioning that some traders use the RSI to buy when it goes below the oversold level and then moves back above this level. That move is more important to them than the simple act of the RSI dipping below the oversold level, and they use it as confirmation that the trend has reversed.

On the AMAT chart in Figure 12-1, the trend definitely reverses on the three inside up pattern combined with an RSI reading under 30. The result is an uptrend that lasts for a few weeks but never quite reaches the overbought level. If you watch a stock and see a bullish trend reversal candlestick pattern that coincides with an oversold reading on the stock's RSI, buy and look for an uptrend to dominate the chart soon.

I offer one more example of how you can use the RSI in combination with a bullish reversal pattern in Figure 12-2. This figure features a chart of the stock for Amazon (AMZN). The RSI on the chart in Figure 12-2 spends some time trading around the oversold level of 30, dipping below and then rising above that level on two different occasions. What's the difference between these two instances? The second (and successful) move was accompanied by a bullish reversal pattern.

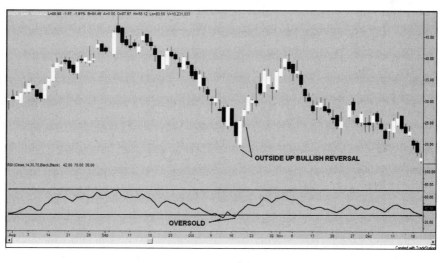

Figure 12-2:
An RSI and trend reversal pattern indicate where to buy on a chart of AMZN.

A bullish three outside up pattern (refer to Chapter 9 for details) appears on this chart at a time when the RSI closes under 30 and then rises over the oversold level. The resulting move is an uptrend that lasts a couple of weeks and then rolls over. If you spot those developments and quickly establish a long position, ride the uptrend for a while and then trade out when things start heading south. The result is a nice quick profit. In fact, from the bottom of the pattern to the spot where the stock rolls over is a move of 100 percent, or a double-your-money move from below 20 to just about 40. All that in about four weeks! You can see how combining candlestick patterns with RSI signals can tip you off to the best spots to enter a long position.

Using the RSI to help pick long exits

An additional benefit to using technical indicators for determining entry points is that they may also help you figure out when it's time to exit a position. When used properly for entries, an indicator tells you when to buy an oversold security or sell short when a security's price reaches an overbought level. You can take advantage of that same concept when deciding when to exit trades.

For example, suppose you took a long position on a stock when you saw that its RSI was oversold, and as a result you're sitting on what could turn out to be a handsome profit. But then the RSI changes course, and soon it's into the overbought level. What should you do? You may have a trading rule in place that tells you that it's time to exit the trade without considering other options. But you may also take a slightly more liberal tack and simply keep a close eye out for trend breaks or reversal patterns. You can play out the situation in several ways, and if you can combine the technical indicator with your knowledge of candlestick patterns, you stand a much better chance of exiting the trade at the most opportune moment.

For short-term long trades involving the RSI, I begin to look for an exit point when the RSI trades over 50. Until that level is reached, I stick to the stop level prescribed by the candlestick pattern I used to enter the trade. After the RSI reaches 50, I start to watch for a reversal or trend break. You may think that I'm potentially leaving too much profit on the table, but just because a stock has traded higher and the RSI is above 50 doesn't mean I'm out. It just means I'm more cautious if I think things are going to turn. Consider a similar strategy for yourself.

For an idea of how you can combine candlestick patterns with the RSI to figure out when to enter and exit a trade, look at Figure 12-3 — a chart of the oil and gas exploration company Devon Energy (DVN). As you can see, the stock trades off pretty hard, and the RSI is well under 30. Then around the time that the RSI trades back up to about 50, a bullish reversal pattern appears. It's the three outside up pattern, and you can read all about it in Chapter 9.

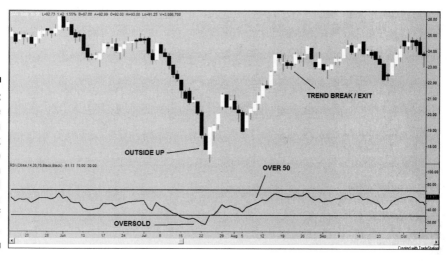

Figure 12-3:
Using the
RSI and a
candlestick
pattern to
select an
entry and
exit on a
chart of
DVN.

If I were trading the scenario you see in Figure 12-3, I'd place a stop loss order based on the low of the candlestick pattern and keep that stop in place until the RSI crosses above 50. That way I'd still be in the trade even if a small pullback occurred. After the RSI reached 50, I'd simply keep an eye on the trend. The trend eventually heads higher with a clearly defined trend break, and when that trend break occurs, I'd execute a sell order and pocket a nice profit. I know that it looks quite easy in hindsight, but it really is a prime example of how you can use the RSI in conjunction with candlestick patterns, particularly bullish reversal patterns.

Still not convinced? I offer another example in Figure 12-4. That figure features a chart of Texas Instruments, which is a technology and semiconductor company that trades under the symbol TXN. You can see that the ideal entry point is when the RSI has been under 30, and then a three outside up pattern appears which indicates that the trend is headed upward, and you need to buy and take on a long position.

After a promising start, the stock stalls out and things look a bit disappointing. The trading is essentially trendless for a couple of weeks. The support level isn't broken, and an uptrend doesn't develop. If you stay patient, though, eventually you see the stock make a small run. The RSI gets back up to 50, and then on the following day, a hanging man pattern appears. (Flip back to Chapter 6 for more on the hanging man.) That's a reversal signal, which indicates that the trend is heading southward, and the time has come to sell the stock, enjoy a small profit, and move on to the next trade.

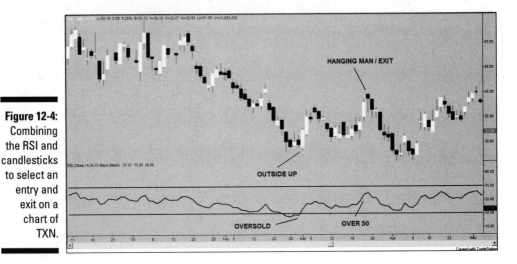

Figure 12-4:
Combining
the RSI and
candlesticks
to select an
entry and
exit on a
chart of
TXN.

Buying with the Stochastic Indicator and a Bullish Reversal Candlestick Pattern

The stochastic indicator is another very useful indicator for detecting over-bought or oversold security conditions. It has two components: the slow and the fast stochastic. When the fast is under the slow, there's a downtrend in place, and when the fast is higher than the slow, there's an uptrend. The slow and fast stochastic indicators oscillate between 0 and 100 and have fairly complex look back periods, much like the RSI. (See "Buying with the RSI and Bullish Reversal Candlestick Patterns" earlier in this chapter for more info on RSI.)

For simplicity's sake I use the 14-period look back, which is a standard level in charting packages. The standard oversold level for a stochastic indicator is 20, and the standard overbought level is 80. For a detailed explanation of the nuts and bolts of the stochastic indicator, flip back to Chapter 11.

You can use the trend reversal signals that stochastic indicators provide in combination with candlestick patterns to pick outstanding entry points for your trades. And you can also utilize stochastic indicators to select exit points — just keep an eye out for when the slow and fast stochastics cross. Allow me to elaborate in the following sections.

Using the stochastic indicator to help pick a long entry point

You can use the stochastic indicator to determine a good time to buy a stock if you watch for instances where the slow and fast levels both trade below the oversold level of 20, and then the fast stochastic crosses over or goes higher than the slow stochastic. I've always felt confident in the stochastic indicator because of that feature; even though the levels are technically oversold, it's not truly a buy signal until the trend starts to move just a little bit higher. And it's even more comforting when you combine it with a bullish reversal candlestick pattern. You can see what I mean in Figure 12-5.

Figure 12-5 is a chart of Johnson Controls (JCI), a manufacturer of large systems and parts for cars and buildings. The company is very much tied to the overall economy, and I like trading it for that reason.

The chart begins with a downtrend. The slow and fast stochastic levels trade below the oversold level of 20. Then a three outside up reversal pattern appears on the chart, when the stochastic levels are still well under the 20 level. But the second two days of this pattern are very bullish, and the slow and fast stochastic readings start to move higher. The icing on the cake is a cross of the fast stochastic over the slow. The stochastic indicator is indicating an uptrend, the stock has been oversold, and a bullish reversal pattern has developed on the chart. It's the perfect time to put on a long position!

Figure 12-5:
The stochastic indicator and a bullish reversal candlestick pattern signaling a buy on a chart of JCI.

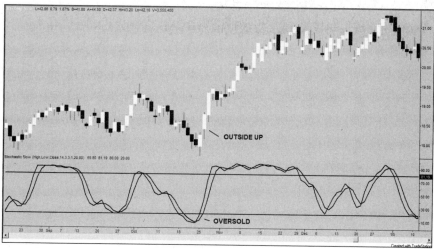

The trend that follows the sequence of events in Figure 12-5 is pretty impressive. It's so strong that the stochastic indicator stays in an overbought state for several weeks.

You can see another example of how you can combine the stochastic indicator with a bullish reversal pattern in Figure 12-6. The chart in this figure is of the stock TXU, a Texas utility that was taken private while I was in the process of writing this book.

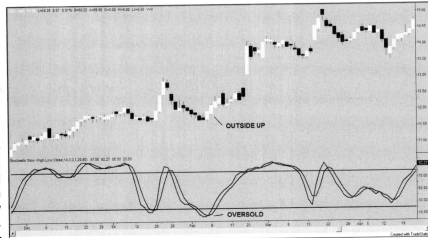

Figure 12-6: The stochastic indicator and a bullish reversal pattern signal a buy on TXU.

The stock has clearly been in a downtrend. (Note that the downtrend occurred after a bearish pattern appeared on the chart a few weeks prior — aren't candlesticks great?) The stochastic readings reach the oversold level, and a three outside up pattern develops. At just about the same time, the fast stochastic moves above the slow one, signaling a change in trend from down to up. It's time to buy, buy, buy! The uptrend continues for several weeks, and a savvy trader who identifies the combination of the stochastic indicator and the bullish reversal pattern will have her profits piling up.

Using the stochastic indicator to help pick long exits

You can also use the stochastic indicator to help you determine when it's time to exit a long trade. For instance, if you're in a long position and the fast stochastic moves below the slow stochastic, that can tip you off that the uptrend may be changing to a downtrend, and the time for getting out of your long is probably drawing near.

Stochastic indicators can signal a trend change even when the stochastic readings haven't yet reached an overbought or oversold level. For an example, check out Figure 12-7 — a chart of the 30-year U.S. Treasury bond futures. I highlight a case where an uptrend changes to a downtrend outside of a stochastic indicator's overbought level. Notice, too, that some other mid-level trend changes appear earlier on the chart.

Just keep in mind that with your exits, you may need to act and get out of a trade when the fast and slow stochastics cross, regardless of whether they're in overbought or oversold territory.

I provide an excellent example of how you can combine the stochastic indicator with a candlestick pattern to identify a successful entry point and profitable exit in Figure 12-8. This chart of Plumb Creek Timber (PCL) shows the company's timber lands throughout the United States.

You can see that the entry point shows itself after a downtrend, when the stochastic levels make an upward break after spending some time under the 20 buy level. The break coincides with a three outside up bullish reversal pattern, and that combination of factors is a crystal clear indication that it's a good time to get in on a long trade. The uptrend gets going quickly after that.

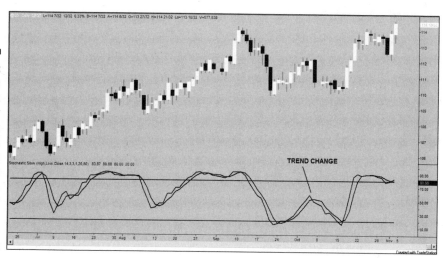

Figure 12-7: The stochastic indicator signaling a trend change on a chart of the 30-year U.S. Treasury bond futures.

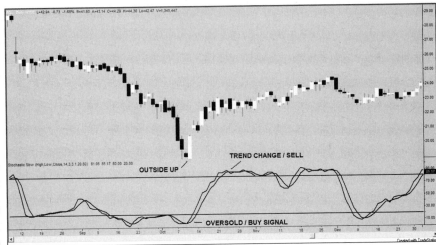

The stock trades higher, and both the slow and fast stochastic readings move up with it. They both reach an overbought level, and then as the trend dwindles, the fast stochastic crosses under the slow one. That's a good indication that the uptrend is on its last legs, and it's especially true in this case because the crossover occurs with both stochastics above the overbought level of 80. The stock does continue to grind higher but not for long.

The final example to close out the section is a bit different from the other examples in this chapter because it's a relatively lousy trade (albeit one with a small profit) and it includes a doji (dojis are covered in Chapter 5). It's all included in Figure 12-9, which features a chart of Apple Inc. (AAPL).

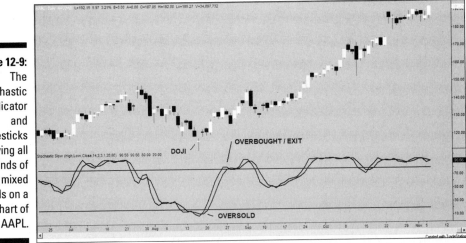

The chart shows that the stochastic levels are under 20 after a short-lived downtrend. The levels then cross, forecasting the emergence of an uptrend. There's also a doji hanging out all by itself — another indication that the trend direction is about to change. The stochastic levels get over 80 pretty quickly, and the early stages of an uptrend begin to appear. It looks like it's time to buy.

But wait. Although the stochastic levels run to 80, they then cross again, indicating that the uptrend may not be around much longer. A nimble trader can recognize this sign as the time to exit and be happy with a profit, no matter how small. An even nimbler trader notices that just after the crossover to a downtrend, a bearish reversal candlestick pattern emerges.

I didn't highlight it, but if you look closely, you can see a three inside down candlestick pattern. You can also see that the stochastic readings indicate a forthcoming shift to a downtrend. Many traders see that and think that an opportunity to make some money on a short is on the way. They're wrong. The stock climbs much higher and stays overbought for some time. If a trader initiated a short position, hopefully he included a solid protective stop.

Chapter 13

Sell Indicators and Bearish Reversal Candlestick Patterns

In This Chapter

▶ Using the relative strength index and candlestick patterns for your short trades

▶ Shorting with combinations of the stochastic indicator and bearish candlestick patterns

*T*echnical indicators are useful in many trading situations, and as I describe in the other chapters in Part IV, you can use them in tandem with candlestick patterns to conduct some outstanding trades. In this chapter, I fill you in on how to combine a couple of common technical indicators with bearish candlestick patterns to help you make wise decisions about short trades.

I focus much more on the prospects for shorting than the opportunities to use candlesticks and indicators to tell you when to exit a long trade, because realizing when to exit a long is relatively easy: If it looks like a trend is ready to tank, sell and get out!

I know some people are resistant to short selling, but it's part of the game, and not using the short side of trading puts you at a disadvantage. Risks are involved, but if you employ the methods I describe in this chapter, you can minimize those risks. With any luck, after reading my Chapter 13, you won't have to file Chapter 13!

Shorting with the RSI and Bearish Candlestick Patterns

The *relative strength index* (RSI) is an indicator that can reveal an oversold or overbought security. The RSI typically appears in an area below a chart, and visually, it's represented by a line that moves up and down between 0 and 100. It's really up to you to choose which levels in that range will be considered overbought and oversold, but in this chapter, I use 30 as my oversold level and 70 as my overbought level. That means that an RSI reading under 30 tells you that a bottom is forthcoming. Be ready to buy when that situation presents itself. Using 70 as an overbought level means that an RSI over 70 should alert you to either put on a short or sell a long position, because the trend is about to head south. You can read all about the nuts and bolts of the RSI in Chapter 11.

When combined with candlestick patterns, the RSI can provide an even stronger indication of when the situation is ripe for executing short trades or selling on long positions. In this section, I discuss the ways in which you can combine your candlestick charts with the RSI to make some clever, profitable trades.

Picking short entry points with the RSI and candlesticks

When using the RSI combined with a candlestick pattern to pick a good time to enter a short position, you want to see an RSI reading over 70 (or your personal overbought level) that coincides with the formation of a bearish candlestick pattern. If you have your eye on a chart and you see those two things come together, get your short pants on! (That's just a figure of speech, of course — I encourage everyone to wear pants of an appropriate length while trading.)

What better way to master these scenarios than to see them on a chart, so please take a gander at Figure 13-1. This example is a situation when you can combine the RSI with a bearish reversal candlestick pattern to figure out when to put on a short. The chart in Figure 13-1 is of the stock for Masco (MAS), a manufacturer and distributor of home improvement and building products. With fundamental exposure like that, it's an excellent stock to trade when the economic outlook is in question.

The RSI in Figure 13-1 goes into the overbought range early in November, and when you see that happen, start looking for bearish reversal candlestick patterns. In this example, the pattern comes in the form of a gravestone doji. (Check out Chapter 5 for the gravestone doji details.) The gravestone doji can indicate a reversal in either direction, but in this case there's an established uptrend, and the RSI reading has been overbought for some time, so it's very safe to say that this particular gravestone doji is signaling a bearish reversal.

Figure 13-1:
An overbought RSI reading and a doji reversal pattern signal when to initiate a short on a chart of MAS.

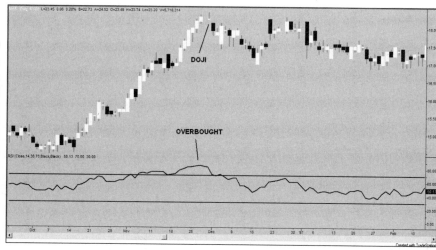

If you keep an eye on this overbought RSI and you spot the gravestone doji, you'd put on a short position, because the gravestone doji really shows that the bears are taking control of the price action after a run by the bulls. The pattern is followed by a small downtrend that lasts just a couple of weeks. You wouldn't be able to go out and start shopping for yachts if you trade this pattern successfully, but it's certainly worth studying, because it's a fairly reliable indication of bearishness.

Perhaps it's most important to note that this example shows you how the RSI (or other technical indicators, for that matter) can be very useful when you spot a reversal signal that doesn't tell you definitively which way the trend will go. You've got to really be sure of the market environment in those cases, and the RSI can tell you what you need to know.

Good things do come in pairs, so I provide another example of how you can combine the RSI with a bearish candlestick pattern in Figure 13-2. This figure features a chart of the futures contracts that trade based on the level of U.S. Treasury bonds.

You can see in Figure 13-2 that the price action produces a three inside down pattern, which is a pretty reliable bearish reversal pattern that I describe in detail in Chapter 10. The pattern's first day is a white candle that occurs in an uptrend. More importantly, this first day combined with the price action leading up to it causes the RSI reading to close over 70, which tells you that you're looking at an overbought situation. The pattern is complete with a bearish second day that's inside the first day, and a down final day.

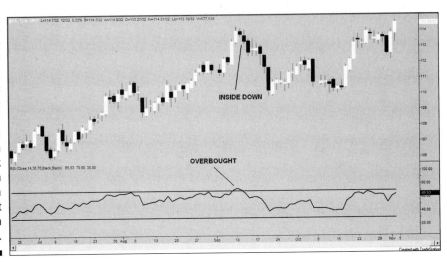

Figure 13-2:
A chart of
the U.S.
Treasury
bond futures
with the RSI
and a
bearish
candlestick
pattern
signaling a
useful short
position
entry.

If you want to capitalize on a situation like this, enter a short sale near the completion of the pattern or be prepared to put on a short on any small rebound during the next couple of days. The combination of the candlestick pattern and the overbought level of the RSI turns out to be a solid sell signal. The price action following the end of the pattern results in a quick drop of over three points in the Treasury bond futures. Although three points may not sound like a lot, consider that a point move in a single contract is worth $1,000 (when you're on the right side).

Using the RSI to help pick short entry and exit points

You can combine the RSI with your candlestick patterns to pick wise entry points for a short trade. But that's not the whole story. You can also use that same combination of trading tools to indicate when you should exit a short.

Figure 13-3 presents a situation in which a combination of the RSI and a bearish candlestick pattern can show you when to get in *and* out of a short position. The chart is for Peabody Energy (BTU), a mining company that focuses on coal production.

Peabody Energy's symbol may seem a little odd at first, but BTU stands for British Thermal Unit, which is a measure of the heat value of various fuels. Makes sense for a coal producer, right?

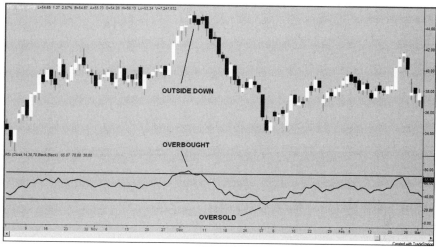

Figure 13-3:
A chart
of BTU
where a
combination
of the
RSI and
candlesticks
indicate a
short entry
and exit
point.

The bearish candlestick pattern in Figure 13-3 starts to develop after several up days in a row. Along with this strength in the stock's price, the RSI rises to a level over 70 (overbought). The three outside down pattern then appears, with a black candle on the second day that's an outside day relative to the first day. The pattern is completed with a down day on the third day. (To understand the inner workings of the three outside down pattern, check out Chapter 10.) The uptrend is reversing to a downtrend, so the time is right for entering a short.

There's another element to the chart in Figure 13-3 that's worth highlighting. The three outside down pattern is completed when the RSI level is just a hair over 70. Seeing the RSI in an overbought range when a reversal pattern is completed is pretty rare, because a reversal pattern normally occurs when a trend changes direction, and when that happens, the RSI usually ends up in the middle range between overbought and oversold.

The exit level for this short isn't set in stone, but it should definitely yield a profit on the trade. The RSI moves down below 50 fairly quickly with the downtrend, and that should serve as a signal to start keeping an eye out for some sort of exit pattern or reversal in the downtrend. Unfortunately, another reversal pattern doesn't come along to tell you when to exit the short. But that doesn't mean that you have to just take a stab in the dark to figure out when to get out. There's a period of four days where the downtrend appears to be in trouble; the trend flattens and a couple of bullish days pop up. You can decide at that point that the trend has run its course, and it's time to get out and take a profit. You can enjoy even larger profits if you hold on just a little while longer, because the downtrend kicks back in and the stock trades lower still. But you have to exit the position sometime, and a good opportunity for that comes when the RSI pushes below the oversold level. Even without a pattern to confirm it, that should serve as a pretty solid sign that it's time to exit and book your profits.

I provide one more example of how you can use the RSI in tandem with bearish candlestick patterns to flesh out short entries and exits for short trades in Figure 13-4. This chart is of Radio Shack (RSH), which is an electronics retailer that covers the U.S. with more than 1,000 stores.

The RSH stock in Figure 13-4 is in a well-defined uptrend with the RSI reaching just a tad over 70. The day that the RSI reaches 70 is also the first day of a three outside down pattern (see Chapter 10 for details), and that serves as a signal for you to enter into a short trade.

If you short after seeing this combination of an overbought RSI and a bearish reversal candlestick pattern, you're quickly rewarded with a gap down on the opening of the day after the pattern is completed. You may shudder a bit two days later when there's a gap up and the high of the pattern (a resistance level) is approached, but that level isn't violated and the signal remains valid. The stock continues to trade off, and during this downtrend the RSI works its way down to below 50. Here is where you should start watching out for an exit point.

The exit signal in Figure 13-4 comes quickly, with a one-day reversal pattern. With the downtrend in place and the RSI in the bottom half of its range, a hammer day appears. (You can read all about the hammer pattern in Chapter 6.) The signal is a reversal pattern, and determining the trend that follows the pattern generally depends on the market context in which the pattern appears. The prevailing trend is clearly down in this situation, so you can bet that the hammer indicates that a switch to an uptrend is in the works. That turns out to be just the case, and the stock starts trading higher.

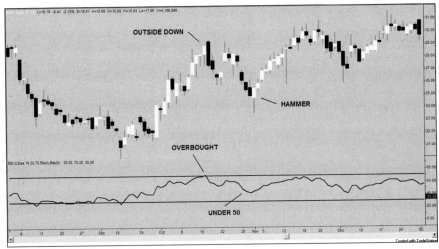

Figure 13-4:
A chart of RSH where the RSI and two bearish candlestick patterns tip you off on the best entry and exit points for shorting.

The hammer pattern serves as a useful short exit signal in Figure 13-4, but the profits on the trade weren't exorbitant. However, you still earned some revenue, and by using the candlestick pattern for an exit signal you avoided seeing your earnings winnowed down (or even turned into losses) as the trend heads upward for a stretch.

Using the Stochastic Indicator and Bearish Candlestick Patterns for Shorting

If you're interested in another reliable technical indicator that you can combine with bearish candlestick patterns to help you in your short trades, look no farther than the stochastic indicator. The *stochastic indicator* can be a very useful trading tool when you're trying to determine when a security is overbought or oversold. You can read all about the stochastic indicator in Chapter 11, but for this discussion just keep in mind the following points:

✔ The stochastic indicator includes two components: the fast and slow stochastic.

✔ The fast and slow stochastics oscillate between 0 and 100.

✔ When the fast stochastic is under the slow stochastic, there's a downtrend in place.

✔ When the fast stochastic is above the slow stochastic, there's an uptrend in place.

✔ The stochastic indicator can be based on a variety of look back periods. In this chapter my examples have a 14-period look back, which you'll find is a standard level in charting packages.

✔ Overbought and oversold levels on the stochastic indicator can vary, but in this chapter I use the standard levels of 20 for oversold and 80 for overbought. Keep in mind that this is slightly different than the standard oversold and overbought levels used for the RSI.

This section focuses on how to use the stochastic indicator alongside your candlesticks in shorting situations. Keep in mind, though, that you can use the same information to help you figure out when to get out of a long position. The rule is fairly simple. If you have a long position and the trend looks like it's going to head downward, exit and book your profit!

Picking short entry points

Picking the best entry point for a short can be a difficult undertaking, but using the stochastic indicator as a supplement to your candlestick patterns can make the task much easier. For a prime example of how the stochastic indicator can be used with a bearish candlestick pattern to pick a short entry, take a look at Figure 13-5.

In the figure, you see a chart of Convergys Corporation (CVG), a provider of specialized software solutions for business customers. Its headquarters is in Cincinnati, Ohio, and Cincinnati's airport code is CVG. Coincidence? Nah, probably not. As you can see, the stock's price action is pretty bullish for a few days, and the result is a stochastic indicator reading over 80. The three inside down candlestick pattern forms shortly after the indicators reach this overbought level. Feel free to flip back to Chapter 10 for more information on the three inside down candlestick pattern.

The situation is ripe for a short entry, and the short entry situation gets even better when the fast stochastic crosses under the slow stochastic while both are still in overbought territory. If you see that combination of factors come together, you should be quick to enter a short position, because all signs point to a forthcoming downtrend.

For a second example, see the chart of Xerox (XRX) stock in Figure 13-6. Xerox has become synonymous with document solutions for all businesses great and small.

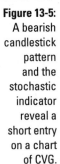

Figure 13-5:
A bearish candlestick pattern and the stochastic indicator reveal a short entry on a chart of CVG.

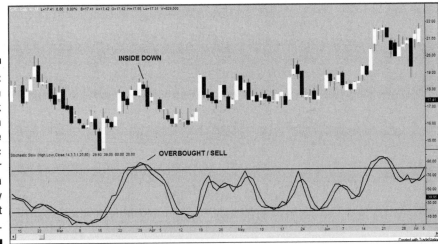

Figure 13-6:
Short entry
points are
signaled by
bearish
candlestick
patterns
and the
stochastic
indicator on
a chart
of XRX.

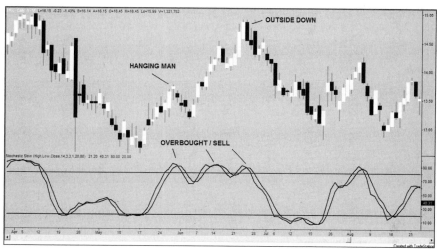

In the middle of the chart in Figure 13-6, I highlight three points where the stochastic reading is overbought. Two of those points are accompanied by bearish candlestick patterns, and one isn't. Guess which ones provide the best entry point signals? I explain each scenario:

✔ The first of the three points at which the stochastic indicates that the stock is overbought occurs as the stochastic indicator comes to the end of an uptrend that was in place for a few weeks. The overbought level is reached just when a hanging man (a bearish reversal signal covered in Chapter 6) appears on the chart. On the very next day, the fast stochastic crosses under the slow stochastic, which signals a short entry point and a confirmation of the hammer pattern as a reversal signal.

Initiating a trade on this day, can prove profitable. Bearish activity prevails for a few days after the signal, but it's not the significant downtrend a short seller would hope for. Still, though, it can result in a profitable trade.

✔ The second of the three points comes when the stochastic indicator rebounds into overbought territory. The indicator almost provides some signals, but nothing really comes of it for a few days. Finally, the indicator appears to signal a short entry opportunity, but as you can see, there isn't a corresponding bearish candlestick pattern.

If you rely solely on the stochastic indicator in this situation and initiate a short position, you'll be sorry. The downtrend promised by the stochastic indicator doesn't appear, and the stock continues to trade higher. Ouch!

✔ The last and best of the three signals occurs after the trend has contin-ued upward and the stochastic readings have reached an overbought level yet again. This time, though, the three outside down pattern (see Chapter 10 for more details) emerges, and during the pattern's formation the fast stochastic crosses under the slow one. A downtrend is probably on the way, and entering into a short position is smart at this time. Then you'd be rewarded handsomely, because the stock trades off heavily for quite some time and the potential profit is quite attractive.

Deciding when to get in and out of shorts

Knowing when to exit a trade can be as important as knowing when to make an entry, and luckily the stochastic indicator — when used in combination with bearish candlestick patterns — can provide you with guidance for cov-ering a short. Truth be told, the stochastic indicator actually does an okay job on its own, but when you use this indicator correctly with candlesticks, the odds of success are in your favor. To close out this chapter, I present a couple of examples of how you can use the stochastic indicator with bearish candlestick patterns to determine when to get in *and* out of a short.

The first example comes in the form of Figure 13-7 and a chart of First Horizon National (FHN), which is the parent company of First Tennessee Bank and some other financial subsidiaries. Also, for the sake of full disclo-sure, I used to work for this company, and their stock is the first I ever owned. But I'm talking about Wall Street, here, not Memory Lane, so let me get on with it.

Figure 13-7:
The stochastic indicator and bearish candlestick patterns signal entry and exit points on a chart of FHN.

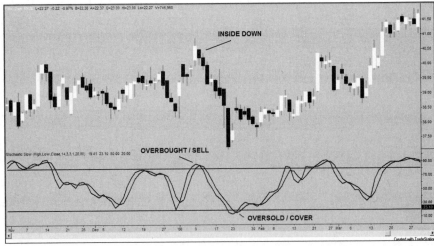

The stochastic readings in Figure 13-7 are in overbought territory when the first day of a three inside down candlestick pattern emerges. Coincidentally, the fast stochastic crosses under the slow stochastic as the pattern comes together, and the result is a full-blown short-sell signal.

The resulting downtrend stays in place for a couple of weeks, and the stochastic levels finally reach an oversold level after a long black candle pushes prices down. The following day sees a small rebound, and more importantly, a cross of the fast stochastic over the slow one. That's your exit signal.

Keep in mind that generally speaking, you can forego a revealing candlestick pattern and rely on another technical indicator when picking a spot to exit a trade. Exits are usually a little less precise, and often one technical indicator is enough to go on. It's better to have a candlestick pattern for confirmation, but it isn't absolutely necessary.

You'd need to get out of the short in Figure 13-7 quickly, because the next day gaps higher and the gap isn't filled. Prices just keep moving up, which is pretty scary for a short in this position. Not exiting quickly when a stop loss signal is hit can result in worse losses. Figure 13-7 is a prime example.

Figure 13-8 is a real beaut. This chart is of Vornado Realty Trust (VNO), a real estate investment trust that owns office buildings in the New York City area.

Figure 13-8: Bearish candlestick patterns and the stochastic indicator provide entry and exit signals on a chart of VNO.

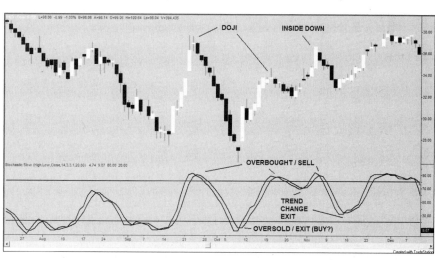

This chart is another good example because there are three potential action-able signals in a row, each with its own unique characteristics. Working from left to right:

✔ The first highlighted candlestick reversal pattern is a doji that occurs after several very strong days in a row that have pushed the fast and slow stochastic readings into the overbought range. The fast stochastic crosses under the slow stochastic on the day after the doji, and that cross confirms the doji and offers a short entry point. The resulting bearish price action is pure happiness for shorts: ten bearish days in a row after the confirmation day. It culminates with both stochastic read-ings reaching the oversold level.

Then, on the tenth down day, another reversal signal appears! It's a hammer pattern, and given the market environment, it's pretty clear that this hammer indicates that the trend will be heading upward soon. It's time for the shorts to cover and walk away with an appealing profit.

Before I move on to the second sell signal on this chart (the next bullet point), note that the hammer pattern isn't just an exit signal. It can also be used as a buy signal for a long trade! There's nothing wrong with making money on the same stock being both long and short. From personal ex-perience I can tell you it's actually a lot of fun, and can be quite profitable!

✔ The second sell signal on the chart in Figure 13-8 is a gravestone doji, and it appears because the stochastic levels are both in overbought territory (details of the gravestone doji in Chapter 5). Much like the first signal, it's followed by a down day that results in a crossing of the fast stochastic under the slow one. That's confirmation that the gravestone doji indeed signaled a trend reversal, and it presents a short entry opportunity.

The second trade doesn't work out quite as well as the first, but if you trade nimbly you may break even at the very worst, and you more than likely will book a small profit if you follow the rules. The entry day is fol-lowed by a little bearishness, but the bulls come in and cause the sto-chastic indicator to show a change in trend to the upside. A quick exit of the short would be in order.

✔ The third sell signal has a pattern that's a little more elaborate and is a three inside down reversal pattern (covered in Chapter 10). Like the previous two reversal signals (previous two bullets), it occurs with the stochastic indicator in the overbought range, and during the pattern formation the stochastic indicator signals a change in trend to the downside. You guessed it: That serves as a short entry signal.

The exit on this last trade is pretty quick and not terribly profitable. Once again the stochastic indicator changes trend just a few days after the short entry point. Luckily, if followed correctly, a small profit would've been booked.

Chapter 14

Using Technical Indicators Alongside Bullish-Trending Candlestick Patterns

*Y*ou can combine candlestick patterns effectively with a variety of technical indicators to produce information that helps you decide when to put on and get out of trades. Like candlestick patterns, many technical indicators tell you when a trend is about to reverse, but several others can let you know that a prevailing trend continues. These indicators are powerful weapons that can add to the versatility of your trading arsenal.

If you understand how to use technical indicators in tandem with bullish-trending candlestick patterns, it's easier for you to spot situations where buying to enter a long position is a wise move. And you can also use technical indicators to confirm market or individual security predictions that you've made based on candlestick patterns.

I cover all that and more in this chapter, and I focus my discussion on two of the most common technical indicators: trendlines and moving averages. If you need a refresher on those two indicators, flip back to Chapter 11. If you have a basic understanding of how they're created and how they work, read on and get trading!

Using Trendlines and Bullish-Trending Candlestick Patterns for Buying and Confirmation

The trendline is one of the oldest and easiest to understand of all the technical indicators. You'd be hard pressed to find any current charting software that won't draw a trendline automatically for you, but you can also hark back to the good ol' days and draw a trendline yourself with nothing more than a chart, a ruler, and a pencil. If you need to get familiar with trendlines or brush up on what you already know, flip back to Chapter 11.

Trendlines have a positive slope during an uptrend or a negative slope during a downtrend, and those simple signals can be very useful when you're trying to confirm your opinion of the market trend.

In this section, I show you how to use the trend confirmation that trendlines provide in combination with bullish-trending candlestick patterns, which signal that a trend in place will continue. You can use the combinations to decide when it's time to buy to enter a long position or when you should stick with a trade to realize additional profits.

Using trendlines and bullish-trending candlestick patterns to pick long entry points and confirm trends

Because trendlines are so useful for trend confirmation, you can trade with confidence when you combine bullish trendlines with bullish candlestick patterns. That tandem can help you decide when to stick with a position or initiate a new one.

It's pretty obvious where a trendline should be drawn on a chart, but sometimes you may question its placement. Don't stress about it too much, because as a trend goes along and changes, you can always alter the trendline accordingly. I present a couple of examples of how you can combine a positive trendline and bullish-trending candlestick patterns in this section.

The trendline and bullish pattern on a chart

Figure 14-1 is a chart of Apple Inc. (AAPL), the computer company turned consumer electronics company that's scored big with iPods and iPhones.

Figure 14-1:
A chart
of AAPL
with
a couple
of bullish-
trending
candlestick
patterns and
a positive
trendline.

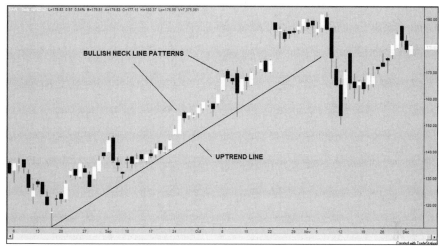

Both of the patterns on this chart are bullish neck line patterns, where a bull-ish day is followed by a gap opening. (You can read all about the bullish neck line pattern in Chapter 7.) That attracts some bears, and they push the clos-ing price down near the point where the bulls raised the price the previous day. If you spot these patterns while reviewing charts, you can feel quite con-fident that an uptrend is indeed in place, and you'd be wise to anticipate higher prices and a buying opportunity.

The first of the two bullish neck line patterns occurs after the uptrend has been in place for only a few days. After recognizing that pattern, you should draw a trendline to better define the uptrend and buy to enter a long posi-tion. The trendline makes it easier to see the strength of the uptrend, and it provides a support level for several days to come.

In the midst of the established uptrend, another bullish neck line pattern appears. It's a bit above the trendline, and it shows up after the trend has been in place for quite awhile, so buying to get into a long position may not be the best move. It's like a stale green traffic light: You know it's going to turn soon. On the other hand, it's still a bullish-trending candlestick pattern, so if you saw it and were already in a long position, you can be confident that the uptrend carries on at least a little farther.

Another example of a trendline working with a bullish pattern

My second example of bullish candlestick patterns and trendlines working together is present in Figure 14-2. In that figure, you see the exchange-traded fund (ETF) based on the 100 biggest stocks trading on the NASDAQ exchange. The symbol for this ETF is QQQQ. Hopefully, I can provide some A's for all those Q's.

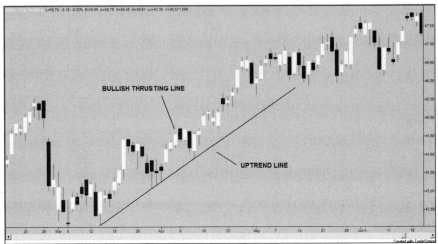

Figure 14-2:
A chart of
QQQQ with
a bullish
trendline
and a bullish
thrusting
line pattern.

On the chart in Figure 14-2 a bullish thrusting line pattern emerges as QQQQ is just a few days into an uptrend. This pattern is one of my favorites because the close is an attractive entry point due to a bit of retracing of the price into the range of the pattern's first day. Buying low while in an uptrend is the best of both worlds!

This bullish thrusting line pattern shows up several days into a bullish trend. If you see it on a chart, you may want to draw a trendline to further define the uptrend and give yourself a support level. If that level is violated, you know it's time to sell and exit the trade.

Picking long exits and determining stop levels with trendlines and bullish-trending candlestick patterns

In addition to confirming trends and letting you know when to get in on a long trade, trendlines can also help with your decisions on when to exit a trade. Put simply, a bullish trendline may serve as an exit point when it occurs in a bullish trend. It's not always easy, because trendlines are constantly changing, but that can also be a plus because the trendline is moving in the same direction of your position (higher). Sound confusing? Let me clear things up with a couple of examples in the next sections.

Trendline and patterns for entries and exits

Figure 14-3 is the same chart I use in Figure 14-2, but the trendline has been expanded a bit to include a level where you exit a long trade if you use the trendline to define the prevailing uptrend.

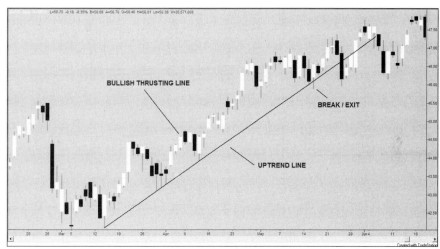

Figure 14-3: A chart of QQQQ where a bullish-trending candlestick pattern and a bullish trendline indicate an entry and exit point.

Once again, the pattern is a bullish thrusting line pattern that pops up in an uptrend, and the trendline, which offers a support level for the uptrend, is established. In a nutshell, if the stock continues to trade above this line, it's still in an uptrend. And as long as it's in an uptrend, you want to be on board with a long position!

You can clearly see the exit level in Figure 14-3. The stock has a day where it drops below the trendline, and that's where you want to get out. In fact, placing a stop order on the level of that trendline would be a good idea, so that any dip below it would result in an exit. You may be a bit dismayed shortly after because the stock quickly recovers and the trend resumes for a few more days. There was still a little more money to be made, but you can take comfort in the fact that you followed the rules and exited the trade when it was prudent. Hindsight is 20/20, of course, and in the long run you come out ahead if you stick with your rules.

Another entry and exit with a trendline and bullish pattern

I provide one more example of how you can use a trendline alongside a bullish candlestick pattern to pick an exit level in Figure 14-4. The chart in this figure is for the stock of General Electric (GE). At this point it's pretty difficult to get away from GE if you're living in the developed part of the world.

Exiting with a trendline

You may be wondering how it's possible to use a trendline as an exit stop level because it moves every day. That's a valid concern! Unlike the set points associated with candlestick patterns, a trendline's level on a chart changes daily. You can deal with that challenge in one of two ways:

✔ The first is to determine the level of the support trendline each and every day, and place an appropriate stop order that's good only for that day. That strategy works well because the line moves with the trend and your exit point moves accordingly daily. On the downside, you do have to commit to making the change every single day, which can be tough for some busy amateur traders.

✔ Second, you can choose to exit the trade only if the closing price is lower than the trendline. Going with that strategy keeps you from having to place trades everyday, but it does require you to check your chart toward the close of each day. It's attractive because it can keep you from getting stopped out of a potentially valid trade if the price happens to take a slight dive. On the flip side, though, the price can fall dramatically under the trendline during the day and close at a low level as well, meaning that your exit would be far lower than if you went with the first stop level strategy.

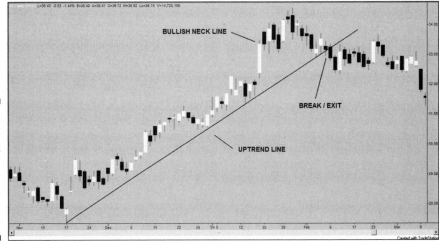

Figure 14-4: A bullish candlestick pattern and a trendline point to an exit on a chart of GE.

The chart in Figure 14-4 is interesting because the bullish neck lines pattern appears and there's an uptrend in place, but what to do in terms of trading action is a little blurry. The prevailing trend is a long one, and the pattern occurs with quite a lot of price difference between its close and the trendline that would be drawn at that time. (The trendline on the chart would be old news by then.)

Even though the trend is your friend, sometimes stocks get so far ahead of the trend that holding out for a better entry price — on both the long and short side — or possibly just skipping the trade altogether is wise. The example chart in Figure 14-4 proves prudent to pass on the trade, because if a long position is initiated, then its exit level comes up rather quickly and the trade appears to be a small loser.

Combining Moving Averages and Bullish-Trending Candlestick Patterns

The moving average is a technical indicator that is reliable and easy to understand, at least as far as technical indicators go. See Chapter 11 for more info on moving averages.

In basic terms, a moving average is the average of the closing prices of a security over a certain period of time. Moving averages can be helpful when you're looking to confirm a trend, so you can rely on them to boost your confidence in the trading decisions you make based on bullish-trending candlestick patterns.

Using moving averages with bullish-trending candlestick patterns to confirm trends

If you haven't yet made your way through my discussion of technical indicators in Chapter 11 or you need a refresher, the first rule of thumb with using moving averages as trend indicators is if a security's price is above the moving average, an uptrend is in place. With that in mind, take a gander at my first example of combining moving averages with bullish-trending candlestick patterns.

Charting the moving average and a bullish-trending pattern

Figure 14-5 is a chart of the stock for Yum! Brands (YUM). When you realize that Yum! Brands operates various fast food restaurants, including KFC, Taco Bell, and Pizza Hut, you can understand where it got its company's name and stock symbol.

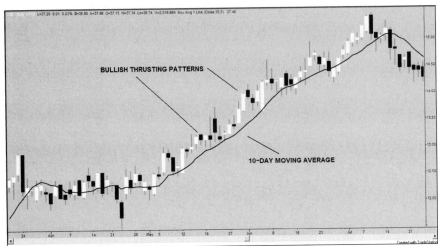

Figure 14-5:
A chart of YUM featuring a couple of bullish-trending candlestick patterns and ten-day moving average that confirm an uptrend.

In Figure 14-5, YUM is trading over its ten-day moving average for several weeks. In the middle of that sustained uptrend, two bullish thrusting line patterns appear. The patterns appear about two weeks apart, and after both occurrences, the stock continues to trade higher. These patterns and the ten-day moving average certainly confirm each other on this chart. The moving average is tested several times, but the price holds for quite awhile until it starts to top out on the right side of the chart. If you monitor this situation on a chart, you'd initiate a long position after spotting one of the two patterns, and ride it until you stopped out or noticed a trend reversal signal of some sort.

The trend reversal signal shows up rather quickly, and before I move on to the next example, I want to point out just where the uptrend in Figure 14-5 starts reversing. I didn't highlight it on the chart, but if you look closely, you can spy a bearish reversal candlestick pattern at the top of the uptrend. It's a three outside down pattern, and it's another case of how getting very familiar with the appearance of candlestick patterns can pay off when trading.

The example in Figure 14-5 uses only one moving average, but don't feel like you have to stick to using just one. You may very well want to add more moving averages to your charts, and using two or more can be revealing if you can keep up with them all.

Using a couple of moving averages and a bullish-trending pattern

When you use two moving averages on a candlestick chart, the trend is defined by the location of one moving average relative to the other moving average. When the moving average with the lower number of days is trading higher than the one with more days, the trend is positive. For the examples in this chapter that include two moving averages, I use 10- and 20-day moving averages. So when the 10-day moving average is higher than the 20-day moving average, the trend is positive. Sound simple enough? I'll dive right in with an example.

Sticking with the fast food theme, Figure 14-6 is a chart of McDonald's (MCD). It's an Illinois-based chain of hamburger restaurants that often uses a clown in its ads — maybe you've heard of it? This chart includes both a 10-day and a 20-day moving average, and for much of the chart the former is higher than the latter, which means that an uptrend is in place, and after looking at the chart it's hard to argue.

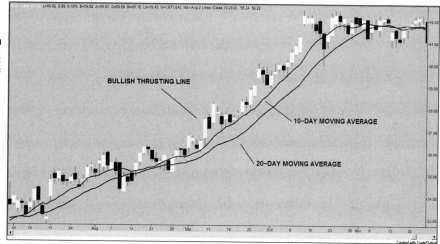

Figure 14-6: A chart of MCD with a 10- and 20-day moving average and a bullish-trending candlestick pattern that confirm an uptrend.

As if the evidence provided by the moving averages weren't enough, further assurance of the bullish trend comes in the form of a bullish thrusting line pattern. It turns up just a few days after the 10-day moving average has cleared the 20-day moving average. Looks like an uptrend is on the way! And nothing makes traders hungrier than a strong bullish candlestick pattern appearing early in an uptrend.

Using the moving average and bullish-trending candlestick patterns to pick long exits and determine stop levels

Making a wise decision when it comes time to pick an exit point or stop level for a long trade can be the difference between booking a tidy profit and suffering a frustrating loss.

In the preceding section, I explain how you can use moving averages when you're deciding when to get in on a long trade, but you can just as easily use them when you're trying to figure out when to exit a trade. If you're in a long position and a moving average reading tells you that the trend is headed for a reversal, be prepared to sell and get out. Allow me to elaborate with a couple of examples.

An entry and exit with a single moving average and bullish pattern

Figure 14-7 is a chart of the oil giant Exxon Mobil (XOM). Over the course of several days, the stock on this chart establishes an uptrend and it's solidly over the ten-day moving average. Although quite a bit of ground has been covered, the bullish thrusting line pattern shows up, and the conditions are ripe for a buy signal.

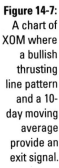

Figure 14-7:
A chart of XOM where a bullish thrusting line pattern and a 10-day moving average provide an exit signal.

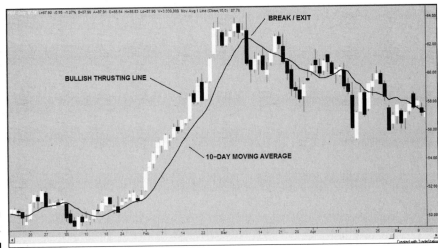

After the buy signal, the stock continues to work its way higher until there's a break of the ten-day moving average. That break signals the potential end of the uptrend, and it means that if you entered a long position after spotting the bullish thrusting line pattern, you need to exit. The price at the exit is high above the level of the pattern, so you walk away with a tidy profit. Not bad!

Setting stops is trickier with moving averages than it is with trendlines. You can anticipate the level of a trendline because it's simply the slope of the line moving forward by a day (or other time period). However, the moving average level changes more erratically, depending on the price action.

If you can't constantly monitor your trading positions, use the previous day's moving average as a stop. If a security dips below the prior day's moving average, initiate a sell.

In the case of the XOM trade in Figure 14-7, a stop should've been in place because the price continued to fall and settled well under the moving average on the day it broke this support level.

An entry and exit with two moving averages and a bullish pattern

Another example of how to combine moving averages with bullish candlestick patterns comes in the form of Figure 14-8, a chart of the futures contract that trades based on the level of the United States ten-year Treasury notes. This chart has a great uptrend that can lead to a very appealing entry and exit if a trader makes the right moves.

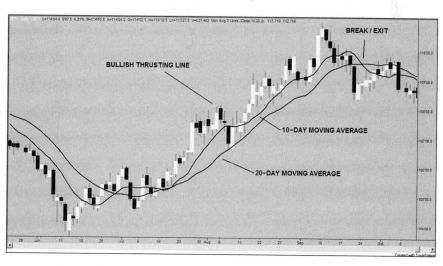

Figure 14-8:
An entry and exit with two moving averages and a bullish pattern.

The bullish thrusting line pattern appears several days into the uptrend, but it's so close to the ten-day moving average that it's hard to think that the contracts have gotten too far ahead of themselves. Looks like a pretty reasonable level to enter a long trending trade.

After the entry has been executed, things continue to go swimmingly with the 10-day moving average staying above the 20-day moving average. The 10-day and even the 20-day moving averages are violated by the absolute price of the contracts, but that's not an exit signal because the trend changes when the 10-day moving average moves under the 20-day. In this case, keeping that in mind keeps you from getting out of the trade too early and missing profits or even taking a loss.

The added check offered by the combination of two moving averages is one of the primary reasons I use more than one moving average with my candlestick charts whenever possible.

The downside to using two moving averages is that you have a tougher time figuring out just where to set your stop orders. If you want to use a moving average crossover as an exit signal, you may find it very hard to do so if you have a job or another reason that you can't check in on your trades throughout the course of the day. Some commercial software packages send you an e-mail when a crossover is imminent, but if you can't access your e-mail all day, that's not much help.

My advice is that if you want to use a moving average crossover as your stop level, don't worry about a crossover that may occur during the day until the moving averages get close to each other. After you see that happen, you can start to estimate where an appropriate stop should be placed. And you can always just wait until the crossover has occurred and exit on the following day, if you can deal with the occasional slight erosion of your profits on a trade.

Chapter 15

Combining Technical Indicators and Bearish-Trending Candlestick Patterns

*I*n this chapter, I explore the ways you can use trendlines and moving averages with bearish-trending candlestick patterns to uncover promising trading opportunities. Those two versatile types of technical analysis methods are great for detecting downtrends, and when you pair them with bearish-trending candlestick patterns, it can be much easier for you to pick the best spots for entering short selling trades. And as if that weren't enough, you can also use that potent combination to determine when it's time to cover your short position and (hopefully) pocket a profit.

Putting Trendlines Together with Bearish-Trending Candlestick Patterns for Selling and Confirmation

Trendlines are one of the most straightforward technical indicators. If an uptrend is in place, a trendline has a positive slope. If a downtrend is the order of the day (or week or month), a trendline has a negative slope. This concept sounds simplistic, but it can be hugely helpful when you're trying to determine a market's trend. If that trend turns out to be down, you can use a downward-sloping trendline alongside bearish-trending candlestick patterns to inform your short trading decisions.

If you're blanking on trendlines, make a quick flip to Chapter 11, where I discuss them in detail.

Short trades and trend confirmation with trendlines and bearish patterns

Selecting the most appropriate time to get into a short trade can be a trying task. Timing is critical, and any decision-making help can be a real blessing. Luckily for you, considering trendlines and bearish-trending candlestick patterns together can provide just that type of help. I show you what I mean in this section with a couple of real-world examples.

A short trade example with a bearish trendline and candlestick pattern

You can find the first example in Figure 15-1, which features a chart of Altera Corp. (ALTR), a maker of semiconductors that go into a variety of electronic and industrial products.

Figure 15-1: An ALTR chart where a few bearish-trending candlestick patterns and a very long bearish trendline reveal a short trade entry.

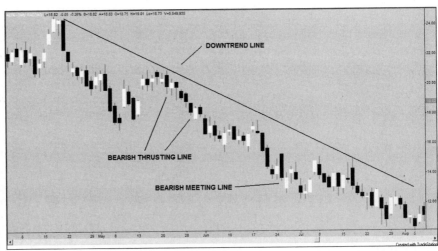

The downtrend in the chart in Figure 15-1 is about as convincing as you can find. The stock just keeps grinding lower. Short sellers would be pinching themselves with each passing day! The downtrend is so pronounced, in fact, that I run out of room for it on the right side of the chart.

The first bearish pattern that pops up on the chart is the bearish-thrusting line pattern (see Chapter 8 for details), and its bearish prediction should be just what you need to initiate a short position. This pattern's appearance helps to establish a bearish trendline, which just keeps on extending until the chart runs out of room.

The second pattern is another bearish-thrusting line pattern, and it signals that the price will continue to drop. It also makes for a nice second chance for any traders who didn't get on board with a short position after the first pattern, because the downtrend looks to still be in its early stages.

This trend stays in place for a fairly long time, and then a new bearish-trending pattern appears. This time it's a bearish neck line pattern (also described in Chapter 8), which predicts a continuation of the downtrend; at this point, however, the downtrend has been in place for quite a while, and it's probably too long to initiate a new short position. However, if you're already in a short, it's very comforting to see some assurance that even lower prices may be on the horizon in the immediate future. If that's the case, hang on and ride the downtrend just a bit lower to maximize your profit!

Another bearish trendline and bearish pattern leading to a short trade

One more example of how you can combine a bearish trendline and a bearish-trending candlestick pattern is on display in Figure 15-2. This diagram is a chart of Motorola Inc. (MOT). Originally a maker of radios and an innovator in the creation of the car radio, it's now known mostly for its cell phones.

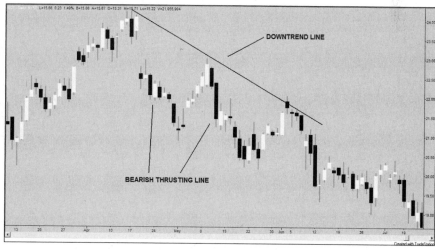

Figure 15-2: A chart of MOT where a bearish-trending candlestick pattern and a bearish trendline signal a short trade entry point.

As you can see, a downtrend is in place when the bearish-thrusting line pattern appears not once but twice. (The bearish-thrusting line pattern appears *many* times in Chapter 8, where I discuss it extensively.) When the first pattern appears, the stock has moved so much in such a short period of time that it's tough to place a trendline based on recent activity. More aggressive traders initiate a short sell after seeing this first pattern, even though a definable downtrend isn't really in place. Then after the appearance of the second pattern, you have a good opportunity to draw a downtrend line by using the high of the rally between the two patterns.

The second pattern presents another possible entry point, and some may think it's more reassuring than the first pattern because of the downtrend line. The trend points down and the pattern pops up, but there's a lot of room between the end of the pattern and the trendline, so the risk level is relatively high. It's a pretty perilous short trade to enter at this point.

Bearish trendlines and candlestick patterns leading to short entries and exits

Trendlines are useful not only for determining the ideal time to get into a short trade but also for figuring out when to exit. This section focuses on the ways you can evaluate trendlines alongside bearish-trending candlestick patterns to pick the best time to cover a short.

Shorting and covering using a trendline combined with a candlestick pattern

Figure 15-3 features a chart of the stock for one of The Big Three — Ford Motor Company (F).

The candlestick pattern highlighted on the chart in Figure 15-3 is the bearish-thrusting line pattern, and it pops up in the midst of a pretty significant downtrend. The trendline is established based on the peak of the last bullish trend and the high a few days later. If you're looking for an illustration of the nature of the downtrend, this trendline fits the bill, and the stock price stays under this trendline for some time.

You can see that midway between the pattern and where the trendline is broken, the high comes perilously close to pushing above the trendline at one point. That event offers a trendline validation of sorts. Then a few weeks later, the trend flattens out, and the trendline is broken. If you short this stock, that's when you want to get out of the trade.

Determining trading levels with trendlines

Trendlines are great indicators for a lot of reasons, but one slightly tricky feature of trendlines is figuring out how to use them as exit stop levels. This judgment is difficult because they move every day. How can you deal with that? You have a couple of choices:

✔ First, you can draw a new trendline every day, to keep up with the changing price action. This method works because your line moves consistently with the trend, and you can place corresponding stop orders that are good for that day only. But that method can also be taxing, because you have to commit to changing the trendline every single day.

✔ The other option is to set up a stop that gets you out of the trade only if the close for a day is above your trendline. That strategy eliminates the need for a daily trendline change, but it does require that you check your chart toward the close of each day.

Some traders also like the second option because it keeps them from getting stopped out of a trade if the price makes a little run above the trendline, but other traders contend that the price can rise dramatically (and close quite a bit higher) and erase profits or even cause losses before the stop took effect. It's up to you to decide which method works best with your trading strategy and style.

Figure 15-3:
A chart of F with a downtrend line and bearish-thrusting line pattern revealing a short exit.

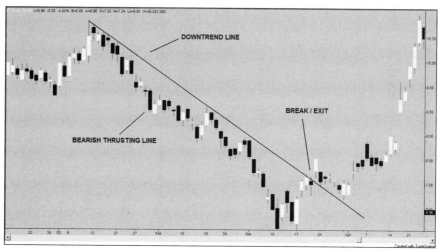

One final note on the chart in Figure 15-3 before I move on. Astute chart observers will notice a bullish reversal pattern at the bottom of the downtrend; did you catch it? It's the *bullish three outside up* pattern, and it signals that the downtrend is about to change directions and head up. You can always use a reversal pattern as an exit when it shows up on a chart, and in this case it helps you lock in just a little more profit on the short trade. Also, if you're so inclined, you may use this bullish pattern to establish a long position.

Exiting one trade doesn't mean that you have to stop working with a particular security for any period of time. If you're in a trade and riding a prevailing trend, and you spot a trend reversal candlestick pattern, don't rule out the possibility of exiting the current trade and jumping right back in with another trade that rides the trend in the opposite direction!

Shorting and covering with a downtrend line and bearish pattern

I'll offer one more example before I wrap up this explanation. Figure 15-4 is a chart of the futures contracts that trade based on the Swiss franc level versus the U.S. dollar.

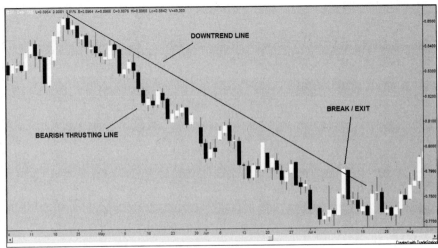

Figure 15-4:
A bearish-trending candlestick pattern and a downtrend line reveal a short exit on a chart of the Swiss franc futures.

The contracts are in a downtrend when the bearish-thrusting line pattern shows up. The trendline I drew on this chart leaves a lot of room for retracing to a stop, but if you see this signal and decide to take the risk, your reward can be pretty amazing.

Soon after the exit, this chart becomes a little heartbreaking for the shorts because the stock moves even lower and it's clear the shorts could've made additional profits. It's frustrating, but you have to make sure that you don't let situations like this get you down. As I say time and time again, it's better to stick with trading rules and exit when it's prudent than to break rules, take risks, and lose your shirt in the long run.

Combining Moving Averages and Bearish-Trending Patterns for Short Situations

The moving average is another technical indicator you can combine with bearish-trending candlestick patterns to help figure out when to enter and exit your short trades. You can read all about moving averages (and several other technical indicators) in Chapter 11, but, broadly speaking, a *moving average* is the average of the closing prices of a security over a certain period of time.

Moving averages are very useful in confirming trends, and that functionality makes them good bearish-trending candlestick pattern partners. Read on to find out more.

Pinning down short entry points and confirming trends

You can use one or multiple moving averages to determine trends on a chart, and in this section I work with real-world examples of both.

A short trade using a signal moving average and bearish pattern

Figure 15-5 is a chart of Merck & Co, Inc. (MRK) — one of the world's largest pharmaceutical companies. I like this example because you can clearly see how the moving average defines the trend and how that trend is enthusiastically confirmed by a bearish-trending candlestick pattern (or two).

It's hard to argue that the stock is in a downtrend when the first bearish-trending candlestick pattern appears. That pattern is followed quickly by a bearish-thrusting line pattern. All this bearish signaling occurs over the course of just four trading days and with the stock well under the ten-day moving average.

This chart makes a very good case for the use of moving averages over trend-lines because when the first candlestick pattern appears, it's very difficult to draw a line that corresponds with the recent price action. But moving averages avoid this problem by relying on mathematically defined levels that don't have to be shaped to fit recent prices, and in this case a ten-day moving average is appropriate.

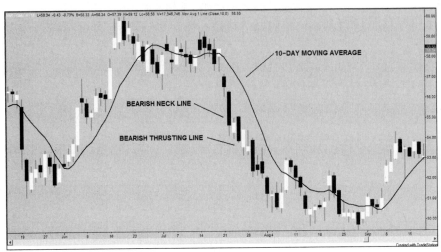

Figure 15-5:
A chart of
MRK with
two bearish-
trending
candlestick
patterns
and a ten-
day moving
average that
signal a
short trade
entry.

If one moving average is good, are two moving averages great? That's often the case, because you can compare the two moving averages to glean even more information about the nature of the price action and the prevailing trend.

When using two moving averages on a chart, you can detect a bearish trend when the moving average with fewer days looking back, or the one that uses a fewer number of days in the calculation (the fast one), is below the moving average with more days looking back (the slow one).

Two moving averages and a bearish pattern giving a short signal

You can see a great example of how it's possible to combine two moving averages with bearish-trending candlestick patterns in Figure 15-6, which is a chart of American Express (AXP), a company best known for its credit card business. This chart is dominated by a bearish trend, revealed by a 10-day moving average that stays mostly below the 20-day moving average.

Two different candlestick patterns show up on the chart in Figure 15-6. The first pattern is a straightforward bearish neck lines pattern that pops up while trading is going on well below both moving averages. A signal like that is enough to justify an entry point in most similar situations.

The second pattern is a bearish-thrusting line pattern, and it appears while the downtrend is still in place. Note that part of the first day of the pattern trades over the moving averages, and a few of the days before the pattern show trading over the moving averages as well. But the trend remains bearish, and the 10-day moving average stays below the 20-day moving average. That means the downtrend is still intact, and you want to hang on to your short position for the immediate future.

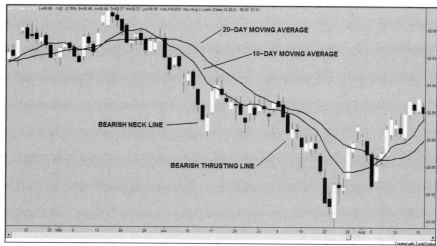

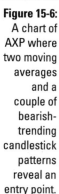

Figure 15-6:
A chart of
AXP where
two moving
averages
and a
couple of
bearish-
trending
candlestick
patterns
reveal an
entry point.

Using moving averages and bearish-trending candlestick patterns to pick short exits and select stop levels

Moving averages can be a huge help when you combine them with bearish-trending candlestick patterns to pick short trade entry points, but you can also use that dynamic duo to help you determine stop levels and exit points. I wrap up this chapter with a couple of examples that show you how to do just that.

A single moving average and bearish pattern for a short trade and trade exit signal

Figure 15-7 features a chart of the stock for the media conglomerate Time Warner (TWX). This chart has a single ten-day moving average, and the bearish trend is in place when the stock price is lower than that moving average.

The stock is trading under the ten-day moving average when a bearish-thrusting line pattern appears. If you watch this chart and wait to initiate a short position, that's the wisest place to do it. At that point the price has been under the moving average for only a couple of days, but it appears that a downtrend has been in place for some time. The price works lower, but enough volatility exists to cause the stock to trade over and under the ten-day moving average fairly frequently.

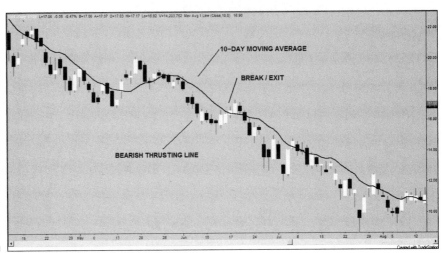

Figure 15-7:
A ten-day
moving
average and
a bearish-
thrusting
line pattern
on a chart
of TWX
reveal a
short trade
exit point.

This frequent volatility ends up really frustrating a short seller on this trade. Even though the trend continues lower for some time, a short seller with a stop that kicks in when the price moves or closes over the ten-day moving average — both logical stops — would be stopped out of position fairly quickly. But the downtrend continues, and more profits can be made. This *whipsawing* (quick moving around) of the price action makes a good argument for using two moving averages, and you can see an example of that strategy in the next section.

In cases where there's such volatility, it may be best to leave trading in this stock to the more seasoned traders or possibly just trade fewer shares of this stock than you normally would until you become more familiar with this type of action.

Two moving averages along with a bearish pattern for a short sale and exit trade

Figure 15-8 is a chart of Citigroup Inc., (C), and it includes both a 10- and 20-day moving average. For the majority of the time covered on this chart, the 10-day moving average is under the 20-day moving average, indicating that a downtrend is in place.

A bearish-thrusting line pattern shows up on this chart during the prevailing downtrend, providing a potential entry point for a short trade. It turns out to be an attractive entry point, because the 10-day moving average doesn't cross over the 20-day moving average for several potentially profit-producing days.

Figure 15-8:
A chart of C
where 10-
and 20-day
moving
averages
combine
with a
bearish-
thrusting
pattern to
reveal a
short trade
exit.

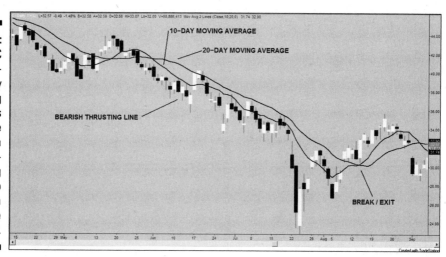

Picking stop levels and exit points can be difficult when you're working with more than one moving average on a short trade, so consider taking an easy route and setting a stop level that gets you out of a short on a close after the moving averages have crossed.

It's also worth noting in Figure 15-8 that the price trades above the 10-day moving average several times, and even over the 20-day moving average on a few occasions. This occurs even though the downtrend stays in place and the 10-day stays below the 20-day. Using these two moving averages together keeps you in the trade longer, making for a much more profitable trade.

Part V
The Part of Tens

The 5th Wave — By Rich Tennant

"I read about investing in a company called Unihandle Ohio, but I'm uneasy about a stock that's listed on the NASDAQ as UhOh."

In this part . . .

If you're looking for some easy-to-digest general information about candlestick charting, look no further than Part V. This part is the Part of Tens, where you find two helpful chapters on the myths of charting, trading, and candlesticks, and then ten things to remember about technical analysis.

Chapter 16

Ten Myths about Charting, Trading, and Candlesticks

*T*hroughout this book I reveal how charting techniques — especially candlestick charts — are a path to making money in the markets. But my views on the subject aren't unanimous among those interested in the markets. Many folks are critical of technical analysis in general. Also, some say there's no benefit in keeping an eye out for candlestick patterns. (I know, unthinkable!) Many of you who've attended business school have heard the arguments from professors (not professional investors or traders) that the markets are efficient and nothing can be done long term to out-perform this efficiency. But rest assured that the reverse is true. I've worked with some very smart people who've done just what these professors say can't be done, and they've done it well.

In this chapter, I dispel ten common myths and misconceptions about trading and candlestick charts to set your mind at ease and help keep you confident in your trading pursuits.

There's No Difference between Candlesticks and Bar Charts

If you've already read some of the material in this book, hopefully, you roll your eyes when you see this myth. Candlestick charts are far superior to ordinary bar charts, for a whole host of reasons:

✔ Candlestick charts are aesthetically appealing.

✔ They also feature patterns that can be easily discerned and used as the basis for profitable trading decisions.

✔ Although the exact same price action shows up on bar charts, the dull presentation makes it difficult for you to pick up on the intricacies of the price movement.

✔ There aren't any exotic names for bar chart patterns. After you're used to *marubozus* and *dojis* and *haramis,* how can you go back?

Market Efficiency Makes It Impossible to Beat the Market over the Long Run

They drilled this into my head in college and did it again in graduate school. Why, oh why was I trying to get a degree in finance to get into the investment field if it was impossible for me to make any money at it? Why were all these classes full of people wanting to move on to careers picking stocks, making investments, or trading securities? Because some people do make good money as investors and traders. And because everyone believes that America is the land of opportunity, and with hard work, you can achieve some level of success.

Market efficiency is the belief that all investors have access to the same information and are making informed investing decisions. Some say that because these decisions are well informed and rational, current market prices reflect the proper value of a stock or commodity. But that simply isn't true. Traders make impulse purchases, and prices are always moving. Prices do get out of line, and it's possible to profit from the results.

Only a Full-time Professional Can Make Money in the Markets

Plenty of professionals make money as traders or full-time investors. If this game is truly made up of winners taking money from losers, how can a part-time amateur with a small account and limited time for analysis be expected to profit? It's easy: focus.

One of the most successful traders I know is a person in the state of Arkansas who does nothing but focus on trading stocks in a specific retail stock. I won't say which one, but it's very, very large. He knows the company inside and out, and trades nothing but options and stock on this particular big box store, where you can get anything and everything. He's been doing this for years and doing well at it. As a side note, he doesn't work for the company — he just happens to live where it's based, and he's watched it emerge as one of the largest companies in the world.

If you work in a particular industry, focus on the stocks in that industry. You already have a leg up on the competition because you have a fundamental knowledge of the industry through experience, which is something that many traders will never gain. For instance, if you work for a regional bank, find a handful of similar banks to focus on, or if you work for a construction company, focus on the companies that supply to builders. By narrowing your focus, you may just find a small niche where you can profit while professionals are spreading themselves too thin looking at multiple stocks and industries.

Technical Analysis Is Nothing More Than Reading Tea Leaves

This one gets me every time, probably because I just love it when charting is compared to psychic or supernatural activities. It's ludicrous! There's quite a bit of upper level math that goes into various methods of charting and trading. Also, when back testing is conducted on technical trading methods, the statistical measures used are similar to those used to check for errors in other hard sciences.

Not convinced of the seriousness of technical analysis? Tell that to the members of the Market Technicians Association (MTA). The MTA is a professional society with a professional designation called a Chartered Market Technician (CMT) that requires hours of study and the successful completion of three levels of tests to obtain. There are loads of extremely smart people that make a living using technical analysis who belong to this organization, and they all argue vehemently against the idea that technical analysis isn't a hard science. And you'd be hard pressed to find a tarot card or crystal ball owner anywhere in the group. For more information on the organization and the designation, you can visit its Web site at www.mta.org.

Charting Is for Short-Term Traders Only

Charts are wonderful for short-term trading. They depict the emotion behind what the market is doing and allow more rational traders to pick points to buy and sell. I can't imagine trading over the short term without them. However, long-term charts are also very useful, despite what you may hear from naysayers.

Those of you with full-time jobs outside of trading probably don't have the time to trade full time. If you still want to get involved with trading, one solution would be to trade by using longer holding periods. You simply need to work with longer time periods on your charts (use weekly instead of daily charts, for instance) and just plan on holding your trades for a bit longer.

One of the more successful technical traders is William O'Neil, the publisher of *Investor's Business Daily*. O'Neil has a longer term charting methodology that he highlights in his newspaper and through his charting service. If you're interested in longer term trading, seek more info on his strategies at www.investors.com.

You Must Be Rich to Start Trading

Don't get me wrong: No one should be speculating with money he or she can't afford to lose. If you're interested in day trading stocks, you must open an account with at least $25,000, which is more than most people can lose without suffering major repercussions. You shouldn't take out a second mortgage or bet the kids' college fund on a trading strategy, regardless of how confident you are in your abilities. Trading is stressful enough without worrying about the potentially devastating impacts of losing money if you don't have the appropriate means.

That said, you can also open a small account with a discount broker by using just a few thousand dollars, and trade lower priced stocks or futures contracts. In order to trade futures with a small account, you should concentrate on futures contracts that aren't terribly volatile or use some sort of strategy that employs stops to limit losses. You can get started with a small account, but you should be prepared to either expect limited returns or use very tight stops.

Trading Is an Easy Way to Get Rich Quick

Trading isn't easy. I can't emphasize that enough. Imagine working on something for a while, and then instead of reaping monetary rewards for your hard work, you end up losing money. If trading was easy, we'd all do it for an hour a day and live a life of luxury. Becoming consistently profitable requires quite a bit of hard work.

It took me a few years of working on systems (and losing some money) before I became consistently profitable trading for myself. My beautiful wife will attest to the amount of work I have and continue to put into my personal trading endeavor, which is almost like a second full-time job. However, I've noticed a direct correlation between how much time I devote to trading preparations and how well I'm doing. Hard work does pay off in trading, but don't expect to strike it rich with a half-hearted or lackadaisical effort.

Candlestick Charts Require More Data and Are More Difficult to Create

Okay, if you're drawing your charts by hand then yes, candlesticks are tougher to create. But with very few exceptions, candlestick charts are widely available and can be created by using the same information that's used to make bar charts. For more info on all the electronic resources you can tap into to view and build candlestick charts, flip back to Chapter 4.

The Trading Game Is Stacked against the Small Trader

This myth may have been true years ago, when almost all trading went through a trading pit or floor specialist. Now that the Internet has transformed trading into a mostly electronic medium, there aren't professionals standing between you and the execution of a trade. Technology has leveled the playing field.

Also, professionals used to pay much lower commissions than individual traders, but this too is in the past. There are several discount brokers that charge individuals the same low rates that institutions and large traders pay to trade. Small traders now have many versatile tools at their disposal and can more than fend for themselves in most markets.

Selling Short Is for Professional Traders Only

Selling short can be a difficult and nerve-racking business, especially when working with stocks. There may be extra fees involved, and if your broker is unable to borrow a particular stock, you may not even be able to put on the desired short position. And keep in mind that the overall long-term trend of the stock market is for prices to move higher, so you're always trying to buck the long-term trend when selling a stock short. Finally, in theory, the potential loss on a short is unlimited, while buying a stock limits your losses to the sum of your initial investment.

Despite all the downsides associated with shorting, I can honestly say that it's silly to assert that selling short is for professionals only. Not many individuals consider shorting, so there's ample opportunity to make money at it.

If you're interested in trying your hand at shorting, consider selling futures contracts short as an initial effort. The barriers for shorting futures contracts aren't quite as high as those involved with shorting stocks. Plus there's never a futures contract that needs to be borrowed — you just short and wait for a price drop to buy back.

Chapter 17

Ten Tips to Remember about Technical Analysis

In This Chapter

▶ Getting some sound advice on technical analysis

▶ Finding the right balance in your data

▶ Remembering to always back up your data

A debate continues to rage about the validity and usefulness of technical analysis in security trading. I'm a firm believer that, when used correctly, technical analysis is an outstanding trading and investing tool. There are also other methods of investing and trading, but for my purposes, technical analysis combined with candlestick charting has worked quite well. As you begin or continue your trading efforts, you almost certainly encounter differing opinions on technical analysis, and I use this chapter to set out ten points on the topic that you should remember as you cut through all the discussions and get down to the business of trading.

Charts Can Give False Signals

I am the first to admit that sometimes — in some cases up to 50 percent of the time — signals can be wrong. If all signals were reliable, then you could just see A and do B time after time, and you (and all your trading peers) would rake in the profits.

But the reality is that charts do give false signals, and it's up to you to use proper money management to limit the losses that can occur when good signals go bad. Always use wise stops when you put on a trade, and remember that when a signal fails, you must get out and move on.

People Will Give You a Hard Time

Some people regard charting and trading as nothing more than glorified gambling or guessing at the future. Let them talk. Just smile and bite your tongue, and think about the profit you just earned after closing out a winning position. Remember, people tend to make fun of things they don't understand.

Plenty of successful traders make a comfortable living using technical analysis as a primary trading tool. One of them even owns a professional baseball team. Who's gonna try to ridicule you when you're buying a sports franchise? Okay, your trading goals may not be that lofty, but you see my point.

There's No Definite Right or Wrong Opinion of a Chart

Because charting combines many factors and approaches, two traders or analysts can view a chart and have two completely different opinions about whether the chart is bullish or bearish. The reason for the differing points of view may be as simple as the time frame that each trader has in mind for a trade, or it can be something as unusual as one of the traders holding a bias about a particular stock or market depicted on a chart. Regardless of the reasons, both opinions have some measure of validity. Also, keep in mind it takes a buyer and seller to make a market, so when you make a trade, the other side of that trade has a differing opinion than you.

Try to remember that wrong opinions don't exist, just those that don't pan out in a specific scenario. You want people to at least be open-minded about your use of charts for trading and investing, right? So, you should offer others the same level of respect and consideration. After all, differing opinions are a crucial component of an active market!

A Single Chart Doesn't Tell a Whole Story

Multiple factors affect the prices of securities, from the health of the overall economy to industry-specific concerns to individual company events. And a multitude of individuals trade specific stocks daily, all with a variety of goals and time frames.

One solitary chart can't provide insight into what all the various players and influences are hoping to accomplish as they buy and trade a security over a period of time. Keep this in mind as you develop your trading strategy, and be sure to look at charts with time frames that don't necessarily match up exactly with the time line you use for your trades.

For example, you may be looking for a trade that lasts two or three days — a pretty short time frame. It certainly doesn't hurt to look at charts with a longer time frame as you search for a good environment for your trade. It may be a little confidence booster if you believe some traders with a longer time horizon are going to be on the same side as you! It's well worth the small amount of extra time and effort you spend to retrieve and study the additional chart.

Charting Is Part Science, Part Art

Although higher math is crucial for technical analysis, there's also what I like to refer to as the art component. Some people seem to have a knack for looking at charts and getting an instant (and profitable) feel for how the future trading action will develop with a stock or market. I think these few talented individuals just have a sixth sense, much like traditional artists have natural talents. These abilities are rare, but I've seen them in action. Unfortunately, it wasn't when I was looking in the mirror.

That said, I have been able to take the natural talents I do have for analyzing charts and enhance them with study and practice. You can do the same! Keep reading up on your patterns and maintain a watchful eye on your charts, and you can develop the ability to analyze and trade quickly and efficiently, too.

You Can Overdo It

I stated earlier in this chapter that you should consider varying time frames when putting together your trading ideas, but make sure you don't overdo it!

How can you overdo it? You can look at so many time frames and indicators that you end up seeing both bullish and bearish features on every security you analyze. You can end up with so much information influencing your opinion in both directions that you develop analysis paralysis, and you can't make a decision.

Don't overcomplicate your trades. Look at a few charts, draw your conclusions, and make a reasonable move. And don't forget to place your stops wisely! (For more information on stops, see the chapters with examples of trades starting with Chapter 7 and running through Chapter 15.)

Develop a Backup System

Whatever system you choose for your charting and data needs — whether it's a high-end system that charges hundreds of dollars a month or a free Web site — make sure to have a backup plan. No matter how costly or clever, systems do go down, and problems usually strike just when you need the systems the most. Make sure that you have a backup that you can rely on when you're faced with a system failure.

You should also have a backup system that you can use for confirmation when something just doesn't look right on a particular chart, or when it looks too good to be true. Data errors are a part of the game, and using a backup system for checking on what seems like a sure thing can save you some heartache and losses.

For more information on how to choose a primary and backup system for your data and trading needs, flip back to Chapter 4.

Error-Free Data Doesn't Exist

I can't emphasize the fact enough that error-free data isn't possible. If you start to back test your trading theories with historical data, keep in mind that there are errors in almost all data. Personally, I use two sources of data and compare them before performing tests, but I have the luxury of some programming knowledge and access to several data sources.

If you're on a limited budget, compare charts from two sources or use free data from two sources and make sure everything matches up. If you spot discrepancies, find a third data source and see which of your first two is correct!

No System Is Silly As Long As It Works

The world is filled with outrageous money-making theories, and the markets are no exception. However, if you have an idea of what works in the market, and you can properly test it and execute it to make consistent profits, your idea is worth incorporating in your strategy. I don't care if you say, "When it rains on Wall Street on a Friday it's time to short the DIA ETF" — if it works consistently, don't discount it, no matter how ridiculous it may seem. If something works historically for you in real money situations, keep an open mind when you're considering whether to keep doing it.

Past Results Don't Always Predict Future Performance

Sometimes the best laid trading plans just don't work. You can come up with a logical plan that's worked in the past and execute it while following all the right rules, and you can still fail to make money (or even lose it).

The market environment can change in erratic ways, and predicting what your trading peers will do all the time is very difficult. If you trade long enough, you're bound to get knocked down in situations where you expected to leap ahead. What's the best thing to do when that happens? Dust yourself off, chalk it up to experience, and begin looking for your next promising trade.

Index

• F •

• G •

reversal *(continued)*
  bearish *(continued)*
    inverted hammer, 164–167
    meeting line, 168–172
    piercing line, 172–174
    squeeze alert, 231–233
    technical indicators, 279–290
    three black crows, 223–226
    three inside down, 218–220
    three outside down, 220–223
    three-stick patterns, 217–233
  bullish
    doji, 137–139
    double-stick patterns, 124–145
    engulfing patterns, 124–128
    harami, 128–130
    harami cross, 130–134
    inverted hammer, 134–137
    meeting line, 140–142
    piercing line, 142–144
    squeeze alert, 201–204
    stochastics, 272–277
    technical indicators, 267–277
    three inside up, 188–190, 268–270
    three outside up, 191–193
    three-stick patterns, 187–204
    three white soldiers, 193–196
    thrusting lines, 145–147
  double-stick patterns
    bearish, 155–174
    bullish, 124–145
  fading or moderating trend, 159, 189
  single-stick patterns
    belt holds, 112, 113
    doji, 98, 104
    hanging man, 121
    open interest on candlestick charts, 42
    spinning top, 109–110
  stochastics, 272–277
  technical indicators
    bearish, 279–290
    bullish, 267–277
  three-stick patterns
    bearish, 217–233
    bullish, 187–204
risks of candlestick charting, 25–26
Rockefeller, Barbara
  Technical Analysis For Dummies, 14, 248
rolling over, 102

RSI (relative strength index)
  bearish, 279–290
  bullish, 268–272
  calculating, 261
  on candlestick charts, 43, 44
  defined, 43, 267–268
  entry
    long trading, 268–270
    short trading, 280–285
  exit
    long trading, 270–272
    short trading, 282–285
  long trading
    entry, 268–270
    exit, 270–272
  short trading
    entry, 280–285
    exit, 282–285
  stochastic oscillators, compared to, 264
  as technical indicator
    bearish, 279–285
    bullish, 267–272
    overview, 260–263
rules for trading, 15–16, 164

• S •

• U •

SINESS, CAREERS & PERSONAL FINANCE

0-7645-9847-3

0-7645-2431-3

Also available:
- Business Plans Kit For Dummies
  0-7645-9794-9
- Economics For Dummies
  0-7645-5726-2
- Grant Writing For Dummies
  0-7645-8416-2
- Home Buying For Dummies
  0-7645-5331-3
- Managing For Dummies
  0-7645-1771-6
- Marketing For Dummies
  0-7645-5600-2

- Personal Finance For Dummies
  0-7645-2590-5*
- Resumes For Dummies
  0-7645-5471-9
- Selling For Dummies
  0-7645-5363-1
- Six Sigma For Dummies
  0-7645-6798-5
- Small Business Kit For Dummies
  0-7645-5984-2
- Starting an eBay Business For Dummies
  0-7645-6924-4
- Your Dream Career For Dummies
  0-7645-9795-7

ME & BUSINESS COMPUTER BASICS

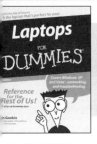

0-470-05432-8

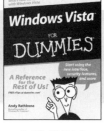

0-471-75421-8

Also available:
- Cleaning Windows Vista For Dummies
  0-471-78293-9
- Excel 2007 For Dummies
  0-470-03737-7
- Mac OS X Tiger For Dummies
  0-7645-7675-5
- MacBook For Dummies
  0-470-04859-X
- Macs For Dummies
  0-470-04849-2
- Office 2007 For Dummies
  0-470-00923-3

- Outlook 2007 For Dummies
  0-470-03830-6
- PCs For Dummies
  0-7645-8958-X
- Salesforce.com For Dummies
  0-470-04893-X
- Upgrading & Fixing Laptops For Dummies
  0-7645-8959-8
- Word 2007 For Dummies
  0-470-03658-3
- Quicken 2007 For Dummies
  0-470-04600-7

OD, HOME, GARDEN, HOBBIES, MUSIC & PETS

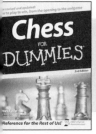

0-7645-8404-9

0-7645-9904-6

Also available:
- Candy Making For Dummies
  0-7645-9734-5
- Card Games For Dummies
  0-7645-9910-0
- Crocheting For Dummies
  0-7645-4151-X
- Dog Training For Dummies
  0-7645-8418-9
- Healthy Carb Cookbook For Dummies
  0-7645-8476-6
- Home Maintenance For Dummies
  0-7645-5215-5

- Horses For Dummies
  0-7645-9797-3
- Jewelry Making & Beading For Dummies
  0-7645-2571-9
- Orchids For Dummies
  0-7645-6759-4
- Puppies For Dummies
  0-7645-5255-4
- Rock Guitar For Dummies
  0-7645-5356-9
- Sewing For Dummies
  0-7645-6847-7
- Singing For Dummies
  0-7645-2475-5

TERNET & DIGITAL MEDIA

0-470-04529-9

0-470-04894-8

Also available:
- Blogging For Dummies
  0-471-77084-1
- Digital Photography For Dummies
  0-7645-9802-3
- Digital Photography All-in-One Desk Reference For Dummies
  0-470-03743-1
- Digital SLR Cameras and Photography For Dummies
  0-7645-9803-1
- eBay Business All-in-One Desk Reference For Dummies
  0-7645-8438-3
- HDTV For Dummies
  0-470-09673-X

- Home Entertainment PCs For Dummies
  0-470-05523-5
- MySpace For Dummies
  0-470-09529-6
- Search Engine Optimization For Dummies
  0-471-97998-8
- Skype For Dummies
  0-470-04891-3
- The Internet For Dummies
  0-7645-8996-2
- Wiring Your Digital Home For Dummies
  0-471-91830-X

parate Canadian edition also available
parate U.K. edition also available

able wherever books are sold. For more information or to order direct: U.S. customers visit www.dummies.com or call 1-877-762-2974.
ustomers visit www.wileyeurope.com or call 0800 243407. Canadian customers visit www.wiley.ca or call 1-800-567-4797.

SPORTS, FITNESS, PARENTING, RELIGION & SPIRITUALITY

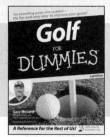

0-471-76871-5

0-7645-7841-3

Also available:

- Catholicism For Dummies
  0-7645-5391-7
- Exercise Balls For Dummies
  0-7645-5623-1
- Fitness For Dummies
  0-7645-7851-0
- Football For Dummies
  0-7645-3936-1
- Judaism For Dummies
  0-7645-5299-6
- Potty Training For Dummies
  0-7645-5417-4
- Buddhism For Dummies
  0-7645-5359-3

- Pregnancy For Dummies
  0-7645-4483-7 †
- Ten Minute Tone-Ups For Dummies
  0-7645-7207-5
- NASCAR For Dummies
  0-7645-7681-X
- Religion For Dummies
  0-7645-5264-3
- Soccer For Dummies
  0-7645-5229-5
- Women in the Bible For Dummies
  0-7645-8475-8

TRAVEL

0-7645-7749-2

0-7645-6945-7

Also available:

- Alaska For Dummies
  0-7645-7746-8
- Cruise Vacations For Dummies
  0-7645-6941-4
- England For Dummies
  0-7645-4276-1
- Europe For Dummies
  0-7645-7529-5
- Germany For Dummies
  0-7645-7823-5
- Hawaii For Dummies
  0-7645-7402-7

- Italy For Dummies
  0-7645-7386-1
- Las Vegas For Dummies
  0-7645-7382-9
- London For Dummies
  0-7645-4277-X
- Paris For Dummies
  0-7645-7630-5
- RV Vacations For Dummies
  0-7645-4442-X
- Walt Disney World & Orlando
  For Dummies
  0-7645-9660-8

GRAPHICS, DESIGN & WEB DEVELOPMENT

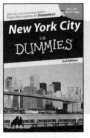

0-7645-8815-X

0-7645-9571-7

Also available:

- 3D Game Animation For Dummies
  0-7645-8789-7
- AutoCAD 2006 For Dummies
  0-7645-8925-3
- Building a Web Site For Dummies
  0-7645-7144-3
- Creating Web Pages For Dummies
  0-470-08030-2
- Creating Web Pages All-in-One Desk
  Reference For Dummies
  0-7645-4345-8
- Dreamweaver 8 For Dummies
  0-7645-9649-7

- InDesign CS2 For Dummies
  0-7645-9572-5
- Macromedia Flash 8 For Dummies
  0-7645-9691-8
- Photoshop CS2 and Digital
  Photography For Dummies
  0-7645-9580-6
- Photoshop Elements 4 For Dummies
  0-471-77483-9
- Syndicating Web Sites with RSS Feed
  For Dummies
  0-7645-8848-6
- Yahoo! SiteBuilder For Dummies
  0-7645-9800-7

NETWORKING, SECURITY, PROGRAMMING & DATABASES

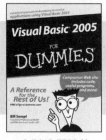

0-7645-7728-X

0-471-74940-0

Also available:

- Access 2007 For Dummies
  0-470-04612-0
- ASP.NET 2 For Dummies
  0-7645-7907-X
- C# 2005 For Dummies
  0-7645-9704-3
- Hacking For Dummies
  0-470-05235-X
- Hacking Wireless Networks
  For Dummies
  0-7645-9730-2
- Java For Dummies
  0-470-08716-1

- Microsoft SQL Server 2005 For Dummie
  0-7645-7755-7
- Networking All-in-One Desk Referenc
  For Dummies
  0-7645-9939-9
- Preventing Identity Theft For Dummies
  0-7645-7336-5
- Telecom For Dummies
  0-471-77085-X
- Visual Studio 2005 All-in-One Desk
  Reference For Dummies
  0-7645-9775-2
- XML For Dummies
  0-7645-8845-1